58847

DS
272
.I73
1979b

Irving, Clive.

Crossroads of
civilization

CROSSROADS
OF CIVILIZATION
3000 YEARS OF
PERSIAN HISTORY

The exquisite decorations in one of the upper chambers of the Ali Qapu, the gatehouse of the Safavid royal palace complex in Isfahan, include fretworked recesses which may have been acoustical, for the playing of music.
Ungainly from the outside, the Ali Qapu is full of surprises on the inside.
Its verandah overlooks the great *maidan*.

Clive Irving

CROSSROADS OF CIVILIZATION

3000 YEARS OF PERSIAN HISTORY

BOOKS
10 East 53d St., New York 10022
(a division of Harper & Row Publishers, Inc.)

ISBN 0-06-493238-9
LC 79:53052

Published in the U.S.A. 1979 by
Harper & Row Publishers, Inc.
Barnes & Noble Import Division

Printed in Great Britain

CONTENTS

Illustrations

All the photographs, with the exception of the illustrations on page 33
(*below*) and page 195 (*below*), were taken by Peter Carapetian

Maps

FOREWORD
by David Frost

There is an invisible, and flexible line on the world map which divides east from west. It has always been there; a division of experience, outlook and cultures. Our own history, and our own sense of history, has traditionally been shaped from our side of that line. As Professor Richard Frye says, ours is a linear view of history from ancient Greece to western Europe – the rest of the world was 'outside the theatre'. At the same time we have the irony that when we look at the history of the ancient near east virtually all the sources are 'western' – Greek, Roman and Biblical And in the nineteenth century it was western archaeologists who began to reclaim the factual base of our ancient past.

This book is the product of a unique alliance of eastern and western researches, undertaken to produce *The Crossroads of Civilization* television series. So that, in a real sense, it bridges the two worlds at a moment when each is trying to understand more of the other. Of our historical advisers, ten joined me on an odyssey through 3000 years of history and numerous others have brought to bear their scholarship during filming and throughout Clive Irving's researches for this book. They come from America, Europe and Asia.

The scope of this work, covering many thousands of miles and reaching into remote, almost inaccessible sites was possible only because of the help given by the Ministry of Culture and Arts in Tehran. And the collaboration of nationalities and cultures was made all the richer by the hospitality of the people of Iran, wherever we were. In the history of this land many came to claim it – among them, Alexander, the Arabs, Chingis Khan and Timur. But in the end, it claimed them. The same spell has worked on us.

DAVID FROST

PREFACE

Within the tradition of an author's acknowledgements to his sources, I have a special debt. Without the resources assembled to make the films from which this book is derived it would have been impossible to experience an extra dimension in academic advice: travelling to each of the major sites of Persian history with an historian whose work was centred there. Seeing at first hand every location one writes about is valuable enough; being able, at the same time, to explore it with an enthusiastic expert is luxury indeed. I have tried to do justice to this privilege. The historians have been extraordinarily generous with their time and with information which has often taken them years to verify. In archaeology, as I have seen, one missing piece of a fragmentary historical mosaic can be the fruit of seasons of labour, but that one piece can also turn history on its head. Working from both the traditional sources and the latest research, I have seen ancient theories collapse in the breath of modern scholarship. This is an exciting prospect; even a marginal revision from new evidence shows how alive history really is, and how the road pioneered so diligently by Herodotus really has no end.

As well as those historians who joined our inquiry *in situ*, many others have guided me in London. None of them, of course, can be responsible for my viewpoint; I have tried to pass their wisdom and their enthusiasms through my text and to communicate my own experiences. In so wide an arena there are, inevitably, conflicting views. Where these are crucial, rather than conceal the argument I have exposed it. These arguments may never be resolved; the vitality of history gains from them. In addition to the historians acknowledged on page 211, I am indebted to Sarah Hobson who, as the Head of Research, not only tracked down the academics for me, but travelled with us on many of the more demanding expeditions into the hinterland. I also owe a great debt to the example of the photographer, Peter Carapetian, whose persistence in reaching difficult sites has been rewarded, I think, by a unique pictorial record.

From the beginning, there has been one potential confusion over a name. In 1935 Persia officially became Iran. Both names are still in common use; officially either is permissible. Technically, 'Iran' has always been topographically correct for the Iranian plateau itself. Persia, which I find more evocative, stems (through Greek transmission) from the original heartland of Fars, or Pars. I have used 'Persia' generally until 1935, which is near the end of the period covered in this book, and 'Iran' where its topographical sense is material. This apart, western histories of the east are bedevilled by the confluence of Greek, Arab and Persian versions of names for people and sites. I have chosen the commonest usage, and avoided extremes of western classicism. Consistency is, in itself, the safest refuge.

CLIVE IRVING

1

Father of the Empire

3000-530BC

In 1821 a young Englishman, following a passion for unearthing the lost world of the ancient east, came upon a peculiar monument in the heart of the Iranian plateau. He noted in his diary:

> The very venerable appearance of this ruin instantly awed me. I found I had no right conception of it. I sat for near an hour on the steps contemplating it until the moon rose on it, and I began to think that this, in reality, must be the tomb of the best, the most illustrious, and the most interesting of Oriental sovereigns.

This was Claudius James Rich, who worked for the English East India Company. Rich had already made useful discoveries at the sites of legendary cities in Babylonia. Now, on the plateau, he was after one of the most persistently elusive landmarks of early civilization, the tomb of Cyrus, founder of the Persian empire. Since the fifteenth century, European travellers, using classical sources, had followed the same trail. But instead of the tomb of Cyrus, they found the 'Mashad–i Madar–i Suleiman' – the tomb of the mother of Solomon. The learned authorities concluded that this site was, after all, a red herring, and that the authentic tomb was at Fasa a hundred miles or more farther to the south.

One distinguished traveller to be misled by this southern theory was James Morier, author of the classic Oriental fable *The Adventures of Hajji Baba of Isfahan*. In 1809 Morier made a fine drawing of the tomb of 'Solomon's mother' and noted its striking affinity with the classical accounts; Arrian, the Roman biographer of Alexander, cited the eyewitness Aristobulus: 'The base of the monument was rectangular, built of stone slabs cut square, and on top was a roofed chamber, also built of stone, with access through a door so narrow that only one man at a time – and a little one at that – could manage painfully to squeeze through.' But Morier, having come so close, was not convinced: if it had only been where he thought it belonged, farther south, 'I should have been tempted to assign to the present building so illustrious an origin'.

Twelve years later, Rich decided that the error lay in the geography and in the name, *not* in the site. But before he could confirm it, Rich was dead, from cholera. It was another British traveller, Sir Robert Kerr Porter, who showed conclusively that Cyrus, not Solomon's ubiquitous mother, had rested in the gabled chamber on the stone plinth. Porter confirmed that the site was ancient Pasargadae, first capital of the Persian empire.

And so a remote legend became a little more tangible. The few sources on Cyrus portrayed not just the empire builder, but a man of rare qualities. In the Bible, the Book of Ezra tells of him liberating the Jews of Babylon and restoring their temple in Jerusalem. Herodotus gives a blend of legend and the sweep of Cyrus's military and political achievement. For more than two thousand years the knowledge of Cyrus rested on the classical accounts, not one of them Persian, most of them partial and all of them far from complete. Even with the discovery of Pasargadae the picture did not greatly clarify. Only in the last few decades has archaeology retrieved a new body of evidence. Even then, we gain a compelling knowledge of what Cyrus did, but recognize even more our agonizing ignorance of what made him tick. Stone there is aplenty; but the only confirmed representation of him is a relief at Pasargadae, and the top half of that is missing.

Pasargadae stands on the Dasht–i–Morghab (the Plain of the Water Bird), 6200 feet above sea level in the province of Fars – a word derived from 'Pars', a Greek variant for Persia. Fars is the heartland of ancient

Persia and is still, indelibly, Persian in the purest sense. To the west of the plain, high limestone ridges rise gradually to form the Zagros mountain range, one of the barriers of the Iranian plateau. These ridges, sculpted by seismic upheaval, seem to have a chemical reaction to light: they change colour according to the time of day – grey/purple at dawn, honey under direct sunlight and then, at sunset, a brief burst of opalescent orange. For most of the year the sun is relentless, but the highland plains are frequently relieved by swathes of green. Rivers come down through the Zagros, and over several millennia they have been cleverly tapped for irrigation.

One of these highland rivers, the Pulvar, runs the length of the Plain of the Water Bird and alongside Pasargadae. Beyond the tomb of Cyrus it turns into a gorge to run south into a tight valley, the Tang–i–Bulaghi. The river is followed on one bank by a dirt road; sometimes small herds of camel meander along the road, stripping the shrubbery of leaves. High on the limestone cliffs above, an occasional pair of gazelle dash through the sparse scrub oak. Once in this valley, there is a feeling that little has changed in thousands of years, and that here is the very essence of ancient Persia, a land alternately hard and rich, suited to a man and his horse. The thought is not fanciful. For the dirt road in the valley was once part of a royal road linking the capitals of the Persian empire and Asia to Europe. It stretched nearly two thousand miles, from Fars to the city of Sardis, near the shores of the Aegean.

The first sign of Pasargadae for a horseman coming from the gorge is the tomb, a plinth of six receding tiers of masonry, with the gabled tomb-chamber on top, more than thirty-six feet high. Like the mountains from which its stones were cut, the tomb changes colour with the light. It is striking, but not epic; four-square, solid and quite singular. There is an affinity of the place and the structure; they are at one, in balance. Not desolate but bare, the plain is made eloquent and slightly mysterious by this simple mark. The tomb is a statement, as effective today as when it was built.

In 550 BC, somewhere near the site of the tomb, Cyrus led the Persians into battle against the tribe who ruled over them, the Medes. There had been earlier battles in the uprising. This was the decisive one. Many of the Medes defected to Cyrus, apparently seeing more of a future with him than with their own ageing king, Astyages. The outcome was not only victory for the Persians; it led to the unification of the Persians and the Medes, and the creation of a force which went on to prevail over some of the most developed kingdoms and armies of the ancient world. In the end, it led to the first world empire. Cyrus never lost his attachment to the site of Pasargadae. Before he built his tomb there, he created a spacious royal park. The sensibility revealed in the building of Pasargadae remains one of our best clues to the nature of the man.

The Medes and the Persians were both tribes who moved into the Iranian plateau from Central Asia. The Medes came first, around the ninth century BC. Migrations of this kind, from the steppes, were led by mounted fighting men of the nomadic style, followed by their people, with their possessions in ox-drawn carts, and their herds of sheep and goats. Until about 750 BC the Medes were probably no more than a loose confederation of tribes. Gradually they then began to establish a kingdom, Media, in the north-west of the plateau, centred on the city of Ecbatana (modern Hamadan). A local chieftain named by Herodotus as Deioces is said to have founded Ecbatana as a circular, walled city.

The Persians followed the Medes on to the plateau around the eighth century BC. Their migration route would have been influenced by the already settled powers: west of the plateau, the Assyrian empire was dominant and western Iran was under an alert Assyrian regime. The Medes, as yet insecure in the shadow of the Assyrians, were in the Zagros. The Persians, in avoiding competition for land, moved south on a narrow route between the mountains and the desert until they reached the highland plains of Fars. To the south-west of them were a people and a kingdom of material importance both to the evolution of urban life in the ancient east, and to the future Persian empire – the Elamites.

Early civilization grew up in the lands encompassing Babylon, on the Euphrates, and Susa, the Elamite capital on the river Kerkha – the lands of the Fertile Crescent which followed the Tigris and Euphrates north from the Persian Gulf. The ancient states of Sumer and Elam initiated urban life around 3400 BC; between 3000 and 2800 BC the first script, proto-Elamite, appeared. When nineteenth-century archaeologists began tracing these ancient societies, the two most significant Elamite sites were close to each other in the lowland delta of the Fertile Crescent: Susa, and Choga Zanbil, a 'ziggurat' or sacred city built by the Elamite king Untash–Gal around 1250 BC. How far the

A view that symbolizes the emergence of an obscure tribe, the Persians, into a world power. This valley, the Tang-i-Bulaghi, was the route from the Persian heartland of Fars, to the north, ultimately to the shores of the Mediterranean. Through here ran the great Royal Road from Persepolis – and immediately beyond the valley is Pasargadae and the tomb of Cyrus.

Elamites penetrated the Iranian plateau long remained uncertain; until recently it seemed that they might have been confined to the lowland.

Another legendary Elamite city was known only from frequent archaic references: Anshan. Finding Anshan was crucial to understanding where and when the Elamites and Persians encountered each other. It was thought that Anshan would be on the western fringe of the plateau. Then, in 1971, a site later proved to be ancient Anshan was found, remarkably, two hundred miles farther east, right at the epicentre of the old Persian lands in highland Fars, adjacent both to Pasargadae and to its successor as a Persian capital, Persepolis. Like Choga Zanbil, Anshan has been dated in part as 'Middle Elamite', between 1300 BC and 1100 BC.

Anshan appears to have been the largest city of its time on the whole Iranian plateau. The implications of this discovery are profound. It means that the advanced urban and literate civilizations of Sumer and Elam were not restricted to the Fertile Crescent: their level of culture had extended well into the Iranian heartland. This, in turn, means that when the Persian tribes finally settled in Fars, around 700 BC, they did so alongside a people who were far more advanced than themselves in the art of government and organized warfare.

The hold of any society in the ancient world was tenuous; the security needed to develop both urban settlement and agriculture was seldom lasting. In the Fertile Crescent, so congenial to early civilizations, competition for territory was intense. The Middle Elamite civilization had a golden age around 1180 BC; Elam defeated Babylon and was enriched with immense booty, but then suddenly collapsed and disappeared completely from the historical records for three centuries. The Assyrians dominated the area, over-shadowing both the Babylonians and the nascent Medes.

But between 720 BC and 640 BC there was an Elamite renaissance, the neo-Elamite period, in the old empire's delta lands of Khuzistan, on the south-western fringe of the Iranian plateau. Anshan's role in this period is as yet unknown; it is possible that because of its position on the plateau it escaped the blow which ended the Elamite empire's resilient career: the destruction of Susa by the Assyrians in 640 BC. It is also possible that by this time the Elamites of Anshan were already in pacific union with their new neighbours on the plateau, the Persians. Anshan might have become a strongly independent wing of Elam. What was finally to matter was that Elamite knowledge, skills and

Early settlements excavated in Iran often reveal one layer of civilization building on top of another. The mound of Godin Tepe (RIGHT) in north-western Iran has successive developments going back at least to 5500 BC. In the lowland delta at the head of the Persian Gulf the Elamite king Untash-Gal built the great 'ziggurat' of Choga Zanbil (BELOW) around 1250 BC. It was dedicated to the god Inshushinak, who ascended to a temple on the top.

culture proved indispensable in the development of Persian power. The nomadic *hubris* of the Persians, fused with the refinements of Elam, was a formula for an historical sea change.

But there were also the Medes. They were forged into a nation by Cyaxeres, grandson of the Deioces who founded Ecbatana. Herodotus credits Cyaxeres with having created the Median army on formal lines which followed the Assyrian model: spearmen, archers and cavalry. Previously, says Herodotus, they were 'mingled in one mass'. The Medes then begin permanently to mark the map. Cyaxeres, says Herodotus, 'united all Asia beyond the Halys under his rule'. The Medes were the agents of an event fateful to the future of the ancient east, the fall of the Assyrian empire. In alliance with Nabopolassar, the founder of the neo-Babylonian empire, Cyaxeres set out to destroy the two centres of Assyrian power, Nineveh and Nimrud. By 612 BC, Assyrian power was broken for ever.

The removal of so oppressive a force left a power vacuum which none of the contemporary states was able to exploit. Of the three major powers of the time, two can be said to have been 'eastern' – Media and Babylonia – and one 'western' – Lydia. Of the two eastern states, Media was by far the least-known quantity. Babylon had, after all, been an urban centre as old as any, and the root of the Sumerian culture. And Babylon was an essentially Mesopotamian culture, whereas Media was something new: an aggressive expression of the tribal culture of the Iranian plateau, imbued with nomadic vigour and with only a few centuries of marginal settlement behind it. So the social, political and especially religious traditions of the two eastern powers were as different as their environments.

The neo-Babylonians worshipped Bel, whose eight-towered temple, rich in gold ornament, was the great shrine of Babylon. The nomadic background of the Medes, on the other hand, meant that their beliefs were still framed by the basic elements of the wandering life: they venerated the sky above and the earth below. They had a vocational priesthood; one of their six tribes supplied the priests for the rest. The Greek name for this tribe was Magioi, the origin of the 'Magi' who were to play a vital part in the religion of the plateau.

In contrast, the Lydians of western Anatolia had developed a Mediterranean culture. Theirs was an affluent and materialistic society, enriched by the ample deposits of gold available to them. The Lydians invented coinage, and minted a gold currency. They were virile aesthetes, with a libidinous reputation, and their empathy with Greece is acknowledged by Herodotus: 'The Lydian way of life is not unlike our own.' But despite these marked differences of style and taste between the three powers, it would be imposing a modern hindsight to see 'eastern' and 'western' mentalities already in opposition. It is a threshold in the organization of societies, each in its way seeking security and prosperity and to come to terms with the severe trials of life; aggression is still less an acquisitive urge and more a policy for security.

There is a search for organization and for order; the decisive element in bringing order was usually the quality of individual leadership. Loose confederations could be held together and directed only by the appearance of an outstanding personality: this had been the value of Cyaxeres to the Medes. Leadership had to be sustained by military success. After the fall of Assyria, Cyaxeres had to spend nearly two decades consolidating his dominion, but then he resumed an expansionist policy, aimed this time against Lydia. Five years of futile skirmishing followed. Finally, a truce was agreed with the river Halys as the boundary between the Lydians and the Medes. Marriages united the two royal families.

Disturbed by these arrangements, and especially by the growing ambitions of the Medes, the Babylonians built a massive defensive wall between the Tigris and the Euphrates – the Median Wall – to the north of Babylon. With the pact between Lydia and Media, power in the ancient east was, in effect, stalemated.

It was into this world of fragile alliances and latent ambitions that Cyrus was born. Astyages, whom he would eventually defeat at Pasargadae, inherited the Median throne. According to classical sources, he was Cyrus's grandfather for as part of another marriage of political convenience, Cyrus's father, Cambyses, is said to have married a Mede, Mandana, the daughter of Astyages. It is likely that by this time, around 600 BC, the Persians had become a force to be reckoned with. Astyages, worried about his southern flank, would have judged it prudent to marry a daughter into the ruling family of the restive Persians; a family with the dynastic name of the Achaemenians, after their first king, Achaemenes.

The presence already of a Persian royal line might give a misleading impression of settlement and court life. In fact, the Achaemenians were still essentially a tribal monarchy, and it is unlikely that there was any significant settled population in Fars at the time of the rise of Cyrus. Just as it still is today, the land was ideal for pastoral nomadism. The 'court', such as it was, would have been highly mobile. Even later, when the Achaemenians had great imperial palaces, their courts were constantly on the move, and Cyrus himself, throughout his life, was more often in the saddle than not. City life did not attract him.

A substantial clue to early Achaemenian power and its base comes from ancient Assyrian records. When the Assyrians destroyed Elamite Susa in 640 BC, the Assyrian king Ashurbanipal recorded: 'Cyrus, king of the country of Parsmash, heard of the mighty victories which I had won … he sent Arakku, his eldest son, with his tribute, to Nineveh, my residence, to declare his subjection.' This Cyrus was a forerunner of Cyrus the Great.

In the interval between Cyrus I's submission to the Assyrians and the birth of Cyrus the Great, Anshan became a Persian property and appears in Persian titles, a sign that the Elamites had been incorporated within the rising tribe. 'Anshan' was used not simply to signify the city, whose status at this time remains unclear, but a kingdom. This included the principal granary of Fars, the Marv Dasht plain, a large fertile expanse; the city of Anshan was on the western boundary of this plain.

With Assyria gone, Babylon's wariness of the Medes increased. The Book of Isaiah and other Jewish sources make it clear that the Jewish exiles in Babylon viewed the Medes eagerly as potential liberators. But whatever the Median designs on Babylon, Astyages was more and more distracted by events in Persia. Cyrus came to the Achaemenian throne around 559 BC. It is probable that by then all the Persian tribes in southern Iran had been united under the one king. Certainly, by the time of his accession, Cyrus had assessed the global politics of his day. Every subsequent move he made showed anticipation, a good intelligence network, and careful preparation. He clearly saw the problems facing the Medes: the distrust between Astyages and Nabonidus, the Babylonian king; the equally uneasy truce between Media and Lydia; and the apparent unrest in Media itself. Cyrus took advantage of an offer of alliance from Nabonidus to challenge Astyages on two fronts; while Cyrus organized his rebellion in Fars, Nabonidus attacked the Syrian and Levantine colonies of the Median empire. The Babylonians completed their campaign with ease; Astyages had his hands full with Cyrus.

At Pasargadae the defections to Cyrus from the Median army, including a brilliant general called Harpagus, were instrumental in his victory and were probably pre-arranged. The Median army, particularly its cavalry, was formidable. Their allegiance may have been swayed by a belief, carefully propagated by Cyrus, that he had a claim to the Median throne. This stratagem shows Cyrus's political skill, and his reluctance to rely exclusively on brute force when other means might produce the desired ends.

Once secure, he treated the captive Astyages with the reverence due to a royal line, and he preserved the military and administrative organization of the Medes. The appropriation of talent and ideas within the lands he conquered was a first principle of Cyrus's career; needless reprisal was always avoided, and his army was strictly disciplined. He was building very much from scratch. Before his employment of Median arms and minds, the Persians had probably enlisted the Elamites as a kind of resident intelligentsia to provide the skills that the nomads lacked. Elamite scribes were founding members of the Achaemenian bureaucracy.

Cyrus called himself the king of Anshan. And after his victory over the Medes, it was to Anshan that the riches of the Median court at Ecbatana were taken. His emergence as the leader of the united Medes and Persians broke the stalemate of power in the ancient world. The omens were noted with alarm in the Lydian capital of Sardis. Croesus – the king whose name is synonymous with vast wealth – consulted the oracles of Ionia, Greece and Lydia. The oracle at Delphi tantalized him most, with the cunningly ambiguous prediction that if Croesus moved against the Persians 'he would destroy a great kingdom'. There was another reason for Croesus to appreciate Cyrus's growing power: the Lydian king was married to Astyages's sister.

Fortunately for Cyrus, Croesus was not a man of immediate decision (a weakness encouraged by the quality of the seers). He hesitated for several years, years that Cyrus needed to harmonize his tribes and to construct his new army. Croesus, he knew, could not be underrated. The Lydian cavalry was superb. And Cyrus also knew from his intelligence that Croesus was not content merely to repel the Persian threat. He intended to expand his western rule and culture eastwards at least far enough to replace the Assyrians, possibly farther. Cyrus seems to have known when and where Croesus intended to attack. To forestall him, Cyrus crossed the Tigris in the spring of 547 BC, and moved west, gathering as he went mercenary contingents to add to the well-drilled core of his army.

Simultaneously, Croesus crossed the Halys into Cappadocia and there, in high summer, the Lydians confronted Cyrus at the head of the united Medes and Persians. The battle was indecisive, and costly to both sides. Croesus felt himself to be outnumbered. Perhaps the size of Cyrus's force had surprised him. He decided to cut his losses, not to risk another engagement on the second day, and broke camp to withdraw to Sardis.

This was not a victory for Cyrus. He was at the most dangerous moment of his life. One of his diplomatic ploys had failed: a delegation sent to persuade the Ionians to desert Croesus drew no response. Alliances mattered. Croesus intended to reinforce his own army by invoking treaties of support from Egypt, Babylonia and Lacedaemonia. He portrayed the Persian host as a spectre threatening the whole of the west. Cyrus had little choice but to risk all. His lines of communication were gravely extended; he was in a country of uncertain allegiance; winter was coming. If he paused, Croesus's augmented army would be too much for the Medes and Persians. Cyrus had one chance only: that Croesus would observe the conventions, and avoid battle in winter.

This is exactly what happened. Not only did Croesus advise his allies not to send reinforcements for four months; he even disbanded the mercenary units from his own army, and retired to the citadel of Sardis with only the standing army. The superstition-prone Lydian king was then confronted by another omen. According to Herodotus, a plague of snakes appeared in the meadows around Sardis sending the grazing horses and cattle into panic, and then entered the city's suburbs. Before Croesus had a chance to get the seers' opinions, Cyrus was at the gates. In Herodotus's majestic phrase, 'he was his own messenger'.

Although depleted, the Lydian army was still an impressive adversary. The cavalry, with their long spears, were an awesome prospect. They led the army that came out to meet Cyrus on the broad treeless plain before Sardis. To break them, Cyrus deployed a secret weapon: the camel. The Median general Harpagus had noticed that horses unfamiliar with camels went berserk at the sight and smell of them. As the Persian infantry advanced, led by bowmen in flowing saffron robes, it seemed that they would be easily cut down. But at a critical moment the lines of infantry parted and out swarmed the camels, brought up from the Persian baggage train. The Lydian horses reared, kicked and turned tail, unseating much of the cavalry. Into this chaos the Median and Persian archers poured a torrent of arrows. And then the Persian cavalry attacked. The Lydians exhibited great control and courage, but in the end were overwhelmed. The remnants of the army retreated into the citadel, surmounted by an acropolis believed to be impregnable.

Cyrus mounted a siege. At first it looked hopeless. A frontal attack on the city failed, at some expense. But then keen observation spotted a weak point. A part of the acropolis had been left lightly guarded because the slope beneath it was thought too steep for ascent, but an alert Persian noticed that when a Lydian dropped his helmet from the ramparts he was able to climb down and retrieve it. The point was stormed, the defences breached and the capital taken. The fate of Croesus remains conjecture. He may have attempted suicide to achieve immortality, only to be saved and proved mortal by Cyrus.

As Cyrus digested the triumph of Sardis, he was already an advanced student of civilization's earliest implements of government. His problem was suddenly imposing. From Lydia to his homeland there was a two thousand mile-long corridor to be controlled, and the lands around it. And he was without, as yet, the physical trappings of empire: a capital, a communications system and a structure of rule. Immediately he showed his capacity to adapt what he found and to create solutions of his own. His arrival as the new ruler of Sardis brought an eastern power to the Hellespont: an omen not only of risen power, but, to the developed world of the ancient Mediterranean, of a people and a culture with a different style and values. For Greece, especially, it was the beginning of an awesome shadow cast over her own ideas and culture for more than two hundred years.

The Greeks settled under Lydian rule on the Aegean seaboard of Anatolia soon felt the smack of firm government. Cyrus had become as rich as Croesus, the only true embodiment of the famous phrase, and he appointed a Lydian, Pactyes, to organize the shipping back to Persia of Croesus's great bullion treasury. On this one occasion Cyrus's trust in a conquered party was misplaced. Not only did Pactyes make off with the gold, but he also raised an army in revolt, among the coastal Greeks. This was put down with celerity. The worst reprisals fell on the Greeks and Ionians who were left in no doubt about where their new allegiance should lie.

The riches of Lydia were used for building and running the new empire, soon to become the biggest empire the world had seen. And there was another benefit. Cyrus's acquisition of Sardis opened his eyes and imagination to the vestments of power. Lydian architecture surpassed anything in Media or Fars. On the plateau the builders made do with rough-cut stone, mud-brick and wood, and were not too fussy about alignment. In Sardis, a western capital for half a century, had been developed all the refinements of Ionian and Lydian stonemasonry. Croesus's wealth had been expressed in opulent, colonnaded palaces, impeccably built. Cyrus's new stature required a capital city at least the equal of Sardis. With no native tradition of finely dressed masonry, he had no choice but to borrow. He had no doubt about *where* to build the capital of the Persian empire: on the Plain of the Water Bird.

The stonemasons of Lydia and Ionia were drafted and sent to Pasargadae, some from Ephesus, on the Aegean coast, where they were stopped in the middle of building the temple of Artemis. This raid on western architecture might, in other hands, have led to mere plagiarism. Instead, it produced a new cultural fusion, and a new sensibility. The palaces of Pasargadae (like the tomb that followed them) reflected the restraint of their patron. They were faultless in detail, and in harmony with their setting. This harmonizing of diverse skills into a new architectural idea reflects Cyrus's policy of reconciling diverse peoples to his own authority.

The British archaeologist David Stronach, who has done more than anyone in trying to transmute the stone of Pasargadae into the mind of Cyrus, points out that even details of the palaces which would never have been seen, once building was complete, still show a relentless demand for perfection: 'Cyrus brought back new levels of craftmanship, but he didn't just borrow. He fused the qualities of the developed stone architecture of Lydia with the ancestral architecture that he knew in Iran.'

The foundation of Pasargadae as the capital and symbolic root of the empire followed immediately the conquest of Lydia, probably in 546 BC. Cyrus was in his early forties. The western limit of his rule was set. He then faced a problem that lasted for the rest of his reign: the lack of a natural protective barrier to the north-east of the plateau. There

The setting of Cyrus's capital, Pasargadae, was open and unfortified, showing how secure the Persians felt. Only the lowest sections of the columns of Cyrus's residential palace have been found; the upper parts were probably of wood, covered in coloured plaster. The palaces were surrounded by gardens, believed to have inspired the idea of paradise.

The only trace of any representation of Cyrus is this figure, cut off at the waist, at the entrance to Cyrus's residential palace at Pasargadae. In one of the folds of the skirt is the inscription, in Elamite: 'Cyrus, the great king, an Achaemenian', believed to have been put there after Cyrus's death by his most celebrated successor, Darius, himself a less modest king.

were troublesome tribes on the steppes, particularly in the lands around the Oxus river. While Pasargadae was being built, Cyrus was repeatedly away on campaigns. In their campaigns the Assyrians had rarely gone more than five or six hundred miles; Cyrus had to assert his authority by taking his army five or six times that distance.

The control and allegiance of towns and cities was essential, and so, too, was the security of the routes that linked them. Between this very loose network of empire were large areas of dubious fidelity, in wild and often barely accessible regions. (Later, Alexander was constantly irritated by the intransigence of such places.) Cyrus had to ensure the security of the trans-Asian caravan routes which brought customs duties to add to the revenues which he drew from taxes.

Structurally, Cyrus's political solution to governing such a dispersed empire was the satrapy, a Persian word for province or kingdom. He employed *ad hoc* geography to determine the size of the satrapies, mostly retaining the boundaries of old kingdoms, rather than shaping new administrative units. He left the native peoples very much to run their own affairs, and he left the wide variety of religious life unmolested. Each satrapy was watched over by a man of unquestioned loyalty, who reported regularly to the great king. By this means, individual national identities could remain, and taxes went directly to the central treasury in Persia; there was no double taxation. But the price of living in a more secure and ordered world could vary. Where, as in the Fertile Crescent, the land was well-endowed, the taxes could be stiff.

The people who lived under the early Achaemenians enjoyed an immunity from the sudden irruption of war which was probably unique in the ancient world, and they benefited from the expanding opportunity for trade which this brought. Communications reached a high level of efficiency, and a speed not improved upon until the horse was made obsolete by the telegraph. The royal road which ran from Sardis to Susa, and branched to Pasargadae, was covered by post-stations spaced at the interval of one day's ride. Royal messages, with changes of horse and rider, could cover 1600 miles in a week. 'Nothing mortal travels so fast as these messengers,' says Herodotus, providing the credo for the later aspiration of the US Postal Service, 'these men will not be hindered from accomplishing at their best speed the distance which they have to go, either by snow, or rain, or heat, or by the darkness of night'.

One prosperous source of trade, the route to southern Arabia and the Red Sea, remained outside Cyrus's dominion. This was Babylon's sphere of influence. Cyrus's contemporary in Babylon, Nabonidus, has been vilified, perhaps unjustly, in the Babylonian chronicles. Certainly, in Babylonian eyes, he was an outsider, with Syrian parentage. Nabonidus came to the throne late in life, and instead of respecting the native Babylonian deities he worshipped the Syrian moon god, Sin, and advanced a peculiar lunar theology of his own. Also, contrary to the usual Babylonian preference for the climate and culture of the Fertile Crescent, he displayed an unusual interest in the life of the desert. He spent the best part of ten years away from Babylon, in northern Syria, and at the oasis of Tema in Arabia. His idea at Tema was probably to develop it as a commercial centre; it lay on the main caravan route across the desert.

Because of Nabonidus's prolonged absences, the people of Babylon were unable to celebrate the annual New Year festival which, by sacred rite, required the king's presence. Babylon was left in the care of Nabonidus's son, Belshazzar, a figure somewhat tarnished by legend as dissolute and neglectful, though his father's derelictions were clearly not helpful. Cyrus was well aware of the unrest in Babylon. The priesthood had made secret overtures to him to relieve the desecration, and the captive Jews, about forty thousand of them, were still hoping for liberation. Babylon was certainly Cyrus's patiently abided prize, the seal of his domination of Asia. But not yet. The east had still to be secured.

Six years were spent on far-ranging expeditions. An area of tantalizing doubt concerns India, and whether Cyrus reached the Indus. The great river would have been a natural boundary, and there is a suggestion in classical sources that Cyrus had a catastrophe in trying to reach it. Arrian, explaining Alexander's fatal decision to cross the Baluchistan desert, cites Nearchus's story that Cyrus had done the same thing and came out of it with only seven survivors. 'Alexander heard these old stories,' writes Arrian, 'they inspired him to go one better.' The impulse sounds like Alexander, not Cyrus. At any rate, it is certain that Cyrus preceded Alexander into the heart of Central Asia, reaching the river Jaxartes (now the Syr–Daryal) which, like the Oxus, drains into the Aral Sea from the great mountain barriers to the west of Sinkiang. A city named for him, Cyropolis, has been found in this region. With the completion of these expeditions, the Persian empire had been almost doubled in size; the colossus of Asia.

The new lands provided more contingents of able warriors for the polyglot army which Cyrus now assembled for the assault on Babylon. By 540 BC, when this campaign began, Nabonidus seems to have repented, and to have heeded his vulnerability. He sought restored popularity by resuming the New Year celebrations. The priests, however, continued to hope for Cyrus's intervention. A key province to the east of Babylon, Gutium, was already pledged to Cyrus, and its governor, Gobryas, was the agent, if not the architect, of the fall of Babylon. The legend of Babylon's downfall belongs to the great moralizing habit of western history, where one event produces the salutary deserts of the degraded society. Belshazzar's feast, the delirium in which the writing appears on the wall, and the retribution which followed, are good operatic material, but bad history.

The impregnable city was not breached by Cyrus draining the Euphrates so that his army could enter by the river bed. He deployed his own army as a decoy, to draw Nabonidus and his army from Babylon. Gobryas, who best knew the lie of the land, took the remaining defenders by surprise and entered the city without battle, on 13 October 540 BC. The priests, the Jews, and probably most of Babylon's population saw the invasion as relief. The temples were protected by Gobryas's men, and the city prepared for Cyrus's triumphal entry. On 29 October he led the Persians, the Medes and the rest of his armies into Babylon, down its great processional mall which was carpeted with leaves. He was careful to sustain the atmosphere of liberation, took the traditional titles of Babylonian kingship, and embraced the Babylonian gods.

What of Nabonidus? Whether, in his case, Cyrus could afford clemency and still fulfil the hopes of the Babylonian priesthood is open to doubt. According to one account, Nabonidus was spirited away to exile in Fars. Xenophon, on the other hand, offers a plausible drama, with Gobryas and another noble cornering the king in this throne room and knifing him to death. No matter. Cyrus was pronounced 'King of the Four Quarters'. With the conquest of Babylon he was beyond challenge as the primary power, and all the rich cities of Syria, Palestine and Phoenicia submitted to him.

The Cyrus who took Babylon was a more sophisticated politician than the Cyrus who humbled Sardis. He had learned the value of leaving his own record of events. In March 1879, archaeologists working for the British Museum on the site of Babylon found a small, barrel-shaped cylinder inscribed in cuneiform script, where the temple of Marduk had once stood. Transcribed, it turned out to be an extended account, by Cyrus, of the fall of Babylon and – more significantly – a justification of his assumption of the Babylonian titles. There is nothing self-effacing about it. Marduk is said to have despaired at Nabonidus's 'inappropriate rituals' and to have 'looked through all the countries for a righteous ruler'. He found him in the person of Cyrus, king of Anshan, whom he declared 'to become the ruler of all the world'. There is an account of the city's deliverance, and the joy of its people:

All the inhabitants bowed to him [Cyrus] and kissed his feet, jubilant that he had received the kingship, and with shining faces. Happily they greeted him as a master through whose help they had come again to life from death and had been spared damage and disaster and they worshipped his very name.

The cylinder goes on to confirm not only Cyrus's universal rule, but usefully his Achaemenian ancestry:

I am Cyrus, king of the world, great king, legitimate king, king of Babylon, king of Sumer and Akkad, king of the four rims of the earth, son of Cambyses, great king, king of Anshan, descendant of Teispes, great king, king of Anshan, of a family which always exercised kingship ...

He named also his son, Cambyses, 'The offspring of my loins'.

The Cyrus cylinder is sometimes called his 'Bill of Rights', because it shows the restoration of self-determination to the various peoples of Babylonia, whatever their creed. Recently, a missing fragment of the cylinder was examined at Yale University. The transcription of this has led some scholars to see the role of the cylinder less as a Bill of Rights and more a description of the works commissioned by Cyrus in Babylon. Be that as it may, Cyrus's proven record speaks eloquently enough of his tolerance, even if, in modern eyes, some of the cylinder's language seems hyperbolic. Long before the cylinder's discovery, the Bible bequeathed the accounts of Cyrus freeing the Jews and ordering (with precise specifications) the reconstruction of the temple in Jerusalem. This was more than magnanimity. There was a sensible political motive, too. An alliance with the Jews helped to maintain Palestine as a secure line against Egypt, as yet outside the Persian empire. The Book of Isaiah says: 'Thus says the Lord to his anointed Cyrus, whose right hand I have grasped, to subdue nations before him and ungird the loins of kings ...'

The absorption of Babylon into the empire brought a vast trading network under Persian control. We can only guess at how much this broadened the ideas and experiences of the Achaemenians and their subjects, and the relief that came after generations of irredentism. To the 'lateral' Asian trunk routes, reaching from the Indus into Europe, were now added the south-western routes through Arabia to the Red Sea, and therefore to the gates of Egypt and Africa. The land, not the sea, was the ocean of travel; the Persians were not (and never became) a sea-minded people, despite the strategic value of the Gulf, and its access to and control of the Indian Ocean (the monsoon winds were as yet unknown). Within the empire, the Phoenicians were the great seafarers, and naval mercenaries.

Cyrus was still vigorous and saddle-bound when he reached his sixties. Despite the submission and consent he had won over most of his empire, one area continued recalcitrant: the north-east. The Massagetae, a nomadic branch of the Scythians who ranged the steppes around the Jaxartes, continued to opt out of the great king's family. Herodotus alleges that the Massagetae women were notoriously promiscuous: 'If a man wants a woman, all he does is to hang up his quiver in front of her wagon and then enjoy her without misgiving.' It sounds like the reproof of the urban sensualist for the lusty pagan. Whatever the truth, it was a woman who led the Massagetae, queen Tomyris, who was spirited enough to warn Cyrus: 'Rule your own people, and try to bear the sight of me ruling mine.'

This was too much for Cyrus. He took his army across the Jaxartes and engaged the nomads. In an early encounter he captured Tomyris's son, who is then said to have committed suicide. The queen's grief turned into a vengeful passion. The Massagetae overwhelmed the hitherto invincible Persian army, and Cyrus fell. His men were hard pressed to recover the body, which had to be borne back to the tomb at Pasargadae.

He had ruled for twenty-nine years. David Stronach gives this judgement:

By the time of his death in 530 BC, Cyrus had changed the face of the civilized world, but I think the point that most deserves to be stressed is his judicious treatment of the many separate peoples under his rule. This introduced a new concept of benevolent government. For the first time, on a very wide scale, great force was used to protect, not degrade, the human condition.

Despite his achievements, western history seems seriously to have underrated Cyrus. The knowledge of his life which the work of scholars like Stronach is giving us serves to underline the omission. Sceptics will, of course, argue that behind the tolerance of Cyrus there was usually a political purpose. 'He was', says Stronach, 'an extremely able politician, and he saw that if he could win people to his cause, rather than force them in the way that earlier empires had done, he would secure the future – as he did – far more effectively.'

And it is this concept of security, against the previous turbulence of life in the ancient world, which needs stressing. Assured of peace, the cities could build over the ashes of more violent ages (as the layered sediment of Susa exemplifies) and develop the arts of government, commerce and the mind. The fragile agrarian economy needed to be free of the perennial risk of invasion. One bout of destruction could make an irrigation system useless for a generation, and bring famine. It is not surprising, therefore, that given this new climate of security there was not, on Cyrus's death, any hint of a serious uprising anywhere in the empire. Even the Ionic fringe, susceptible to antipathy towards Persia from the other side of the Aegean, seems not to have stirred.

In the search for the soul of Cyrus, it is the consistency of his ethic that demands an explanation: what *was* his faith? The religious world of the time was cult-ridden. Pagan gods of all shapes and sizes were bound up with myth and superstition, nowhere more than in Greece. In Babylon the tactless discrimination between cults had brought down Nabonidus. As political management came to involve larger numbers, and a perplexing range of deities, religion could be a serious source of friction within a large empire. Cyrus's wise solution was to permit diversity as long as it did not threaten his confederation. A more intolerant man would have sought to impose his own gods, whatever they were.

Was Cyrus simply free of that kind of fanaticism, or was he already influenced by a novel theological idea, one which was peculiarly consistent with the trend towards a society seeking to become stabilized in larger units – the idea of monotheism? Here is the nub of the mystery and, alas, the object of vigorous scholarly argument.

Monotheism was born on the Iranian plateau, with the coming of the prophet Zoroaster. That much, at least, is free of dispute. As far as Cyrus is concerned, the problem is *when?* Had the new faith of Zoroastrianism claimed its most illustrious convert, or had the two forces not encountered each other? Stronach is extremely cautious: 'I think that Cyrus subscribed to the stratum of religious belief that existed in Iran before Zoroaster. Very probably he also subscribed to certain of the new ethical teachings of Zoroaster which were prevalent in his own lifetime.' The elevation of Cyrus's tomb can be cited: the Zoroastrians decreed that corpses defiled the sacred element of the earth, and should be exposed above it. In the case of the great king, the tomb chamber would have complied.

A veteran authority on the Achaemenians, Professor Walther Hinz, believes Zoroaster to have been a contemporary of Cyrus, just a generation older. But Professor Mary Boyce, the highly respected scholar of Zoroastrianism, has now dated the prophet's time between 1400 and 1000 BC, which would allow ample time for the transmission and development of the creed before the existence of the Achaemenians and before the Persians even arrived on the plateau. As we shall see, Zoroastrianism supervened in Persian history, but there can be no question, with Cyrus, of the ruler promoting religious conformity. Stronach has established that, in a sacred precinct at Pasargadae, Cyrus ascended a stepped plinth to face and to worship a portable stone fire altar placed a few yards away. This was, he believes, the only sacred ritual performed at Pasargadae. Beyond this, speculation becomes futile.

Under Cyrus, the Persians built the first world empire. But what *was* their sense of the world? What would have been Cyrus's horizons? He had gone deep into Central Asia, but we know that centuries later Alexander believed that if he pressed on beyond the Himalayas he would find the end of the world, presumably a precipice. Herodotus, within the living memory of Cyrus, writes: 'The Caspian is a sea in itself and has no connection with the sea elsewhere, unlike the Mediterranean which the Greeks use, and what is called the Atlantic beyond the Pillars of Hercules, and the Indian Ocean, all of which are in reality parts of a single sea.' The Achaemenians knew, certainly, of

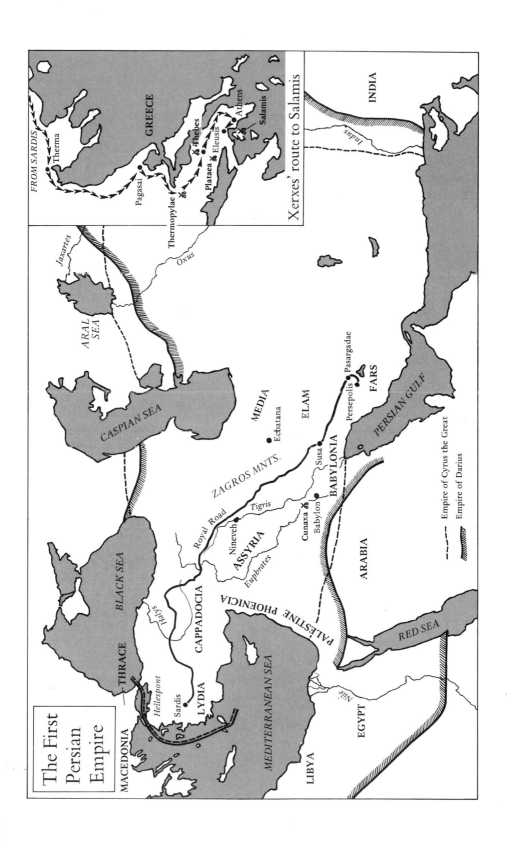

The First Persian Empire

Xerxes' route to Salamis

GREECE

FROM SARDIS
Therma

Pagasai

Thermopylae

Thebes
Plataea
Eleusis
Athens
Salamis

INDIA

Indus

Oxus

Jaxartes

ARAL
SEA

CASPIAN SEA

MEDIA
Ecbatana

ELAM

ZAGROS MNTS.

Susa

BABYLONIA

Babylon
Cunaxa

ASSYRIA
Nineveh

Tigris

Euphrates

Royal Road

Persepolis
Pasargadae

FARS

PERSIAN GULF

ARABIA

RED SEA

Empire of Cyrus the Great
Empire of Darius

BLACK SEA

THRACE

Hellespont

Sardis

LYDIA

CAPPADOCIA

Halys

PALESTINE PHOENICIA

MACEDONIA

MEDITERRANEAN SEA

LIBYA

EGYPT

Nile

Siberian gold. The Phoenicians knew of Italy, Spain and the western Mediterranean, and of north Africa. Egypt, we know, was next on Cyrus's agenda, his unfinished business. This was to be the work of Cambyses, his son who had already held office as his regent in Babylonia.

2

Worlds in Collision

530-336 BC

The first western subjects of the Persian empire were the Greeks on the eastern Aegean seaboard who were snatched into the same net as the Lydians, when Cyrus took Sardis. These Greeks in Asia appealed to Sparta, then the strongest of the European Greek states, but Sparta refused to go to their rescue. For the rest of Cyrus's reign the coastal and island Ionians accepted the new regime and, in their stonework at Pasargadae, helped to consummate the Greek and Persian cultures in a new architecture – the first marriage of the arts of east and west. Though the nation states of old Greece were nervous of the appearance of so vast a power on the facing shore, Cyrus showed no inclination to cross the Hellespont. He was preoccupied with the prizes of Mesopotamia and the insurrections in the north-east, on the steppes. There seemed no imperative for a war between east and west – military, economic or territorial. But the eastern and western societies were developing along divergent lines, in their styles of rule and, as Zoroastrianism gained influence in Persia, in their theologies.

With Cyrus gone, Persian ambitions were still directed elsewhere, towards Egypt and Africa. Cambyses, the crown prince, had served eight years' apprenticeship of power in Babylonia. From the outset, Cyrus had taken care to associate his own power with his son's: in the cylinder he proclaimed to the gods 'Cyrus, the king who worships you, and Cambyses, his son . . .'. When Cyrus's death was confirmed, Cambyses assumed the titles 'King of Babylon, King of Lands'. He then did something which scandalizes modern opinion: he married his two sisters, Atossa and Roxane. The Elamite kings had traditionally married their own sisters and Cambyses consulted his own high court as to the propriety of doing the same. They told him that under Persian law incest was forbidden, but they added that there was also a law allowing a king to do whatever he chose. This Cambyses did. There was a third sister, Artystone, but she was deemed too young for marriage.

It was a flagrant change of royal style; perhaps, the beginning of a falling reputation. There may have been a political motive: Cambyses might have been seeking to consolidate his own branch of the Achaemenian royal line because there was a powerful collateral branch of the dynastic family, and power in Fars was probably divided between them before Cyrus united the tribe. Certainly, as we shall see, they were an ambitious clan, and Cyrus's contemporary in this branch, Hystaspes, was still alive.

Hystaspes appears significantly in one of Herodotus's supernatural interventions. According to his story, Cyrus, on the eve of his last battle against Tomyris, dreamed that he saw the eldest son of Hystaspes wearing a pair of wings. One cast a shadow over Asia and the other over Europe. The spectre implied in Cyrus's eyes a possible usurpation. Hystaspes was straight away sent home to check on his son's loyalty (and so spared the battle). Nothing came of the suspicion, and Hystaspes continued under Cambyses to hold power as the satrap of Parthia, a crucial northern province. His son, Darius, was trusted well enough to take up a post alongside Cambyses as the royal spear-bearer, a position demanding both integrity and valour.

Cambyses spent four years preparing the invasion of Egypt. During this time the young Darius was at the centre of military and political affairs. He consolidated his position amongst the king's inner group by marrying the daughter of Gobryas, the satrap of Babylonia (not Gobryas the captor of Babylon, who had died a few days after the triumph).

The attack on Egypt was preceded by psychological warfare. The

Egyptian Pharaoh, Amasis, was heavily reliant on Greek mercenaries. They well knew the Persian strength, and their loyalty to Egypt was dubious, made the more so by Persian intrigue. Both sides needed a navy. Here, Amasis had acquired the services of the most redoubtable admiral in the Aegean, Polycrates of Samos. Cambyses could draw on the navies of Phoenicia and Cyprus. The sea forces seemed well matched, but on the eve of the invasion Polycrates defected to the Persians. Amasis died, leaving the parlous situation to his son, Psamtik. His cause was hopeless; the Egyptians were beaten and Psamtik fled to Memphis, where he was captured by Cambyses.

So Egypt fell into Persian hands with relative ease. It was a triumph bound to confirm Cambyses's authority in the whole empire. It also turned out to be useful for the Greeks for Cambyses continued the established and extensive trade between Egypt and Greece. Some of the most enterprising parts of the Greek world had now submitted to Persian control, and the Greek traders were, in effect, greatly assisting the Persian treasury.

Cambyses and his army pressed beyond Memphis up the Nile, driving towards Ethiopia. Another force was sent west to the oracle of Zeus at Ammon. In the course of this campaign part of the army fell to a great natural disaster. Herodotus says that Cambyses had detached fifty thousand men to burn the oracle and reduce the Ammonians to slavery. This force marched off into the desert and was never seen again, for 'a southerly wind of extreme violence drove the sand over them in heaps as they were taking their mid-day meal'.

On these events, Herodotus is convincing but a doubt still persists over his portrait of Cambyses. For these expeditions and for his behaviour generally in Egypt, Herodotus dismisses Cambyses as a madman. He is charged with wanton desecration and a catalogue of sins clearly intended to be the antonym of all Cyrus's stately qualities. Some scholars have gone so far as to diagnose epilepsy. But there is an alternative view. Discrediting Cambyses could have been mandatory as part of the re-writing of history to legitimize his successors. It is also more than likely that Cambyses had curbed the excessive power of the Egyptian priesthood, thereby inspiring some splenetic chronicles which later fell into eager Greek hands.

In any event, Cambyses lingered too long in Egypt for his own good. He was away from Persia for three years. At the end, he was undermined by a conspiracy which very nearly broke the empire.

The plot opens with a phantom: the second son of Cyrus. The fate of this son, Bardiya in Persian and Smerdis in Greek, remains a major mystery. Herodotus, following his line on Cambyses, alleges that Bardiya was murdered on instructions from Cambyses, who had dreamed that his brother had seized the throne. Early in 522 BC, while he was still in Egypt, word reached Cambyses of an uprising in Persia, in which Bardiya had miraculously materialized as the rightful claimant to the Achaemenian dynasty. Lively argument surrounds the following events. In the midst of it, three facts are salient: there was a serious *coup d'état*, with someone calling himself Bardiya at the head of it; Cambyses died before he could deal with it; there was a successful counter-coup in which Darius was proclaimed king. The pattern is familiar to modern as well as ancient history, and all history teaches us to distrust the accounts of involved parties. In this case, one of the accounts is the work of Darius himself.

The first caution is to remember that it is axiomatic that the victor of a counter-coup must validate his own role by stigmatizing the opposition. Here, both Darius and Herodotus sustain the idea that the risen Bardiya was, in fact, an impostor. They also agree that Cambyses had previously despatched the real Bardiya; 'but it was not known to the people' adds Darius, in explaining how the impostor was able to appear authentic. Certainly, the Bardiya coup had gained rapid acceptance. It began on 11 March, and by 14 April documents issued in Babylon bore the title 'King Bardiya'. By July most of the satrapies had followed suit, and – very significantly – there were no attempts to break away from the empire.

In contrast, the counter-coup faced a chain-reaction of revolt. The accounts of Darius and Herodotus emphasize the considerable military feat of putting down these revolts, but they do not mention how pacific the empire was until the counter-coup was launched. The 'Bardiya' regime won swift acceptance and popularity by promoting an anti-war policy. The Egyptian campaign had proved expensive; now the war taxes were suspended and further campaigns ruled out. The impetus for the coup came, apparently, from the priesthood. Darius, as a leader of the military lobby, can be assumed to have had a vested interest in opposing the new pacifism, and to have sensed the power of a lobby of disgruntled generals. He later asserted that the royal claimant was, in fact, a Magian named Gaumata. Although the Magian tribe provided priests, not all Magians were priests and

Gaumata was not, in this account, represented as one. Darius later carried out a vigorous pogrom against the Magi.

Things get curiouser and curiouser with the death of Cambyses. This is left exasperatingly opaque. Herodotus says it came from blood poisoning after Cambyses had accidentally gashed his thigh with his own sword; Darius says 'Cambyses received his own natural death.' This apparently happened during a rapid march home from Egypt. The trail then goes cold.

What were the army's sentiments? Here was the most seasoned body of fighters in the empire, suddenly proclaimed redundant by the anti-war lobby, against all the martial traditions of the Persian empire. Darius, presumably, was with the army when Cambyses died. And yet the next we hear of him is that he has joined, at the last minute, a plot hatched by six nobles to assassinate the usurper.

At this moment Darius's nature and skill assert themselves. He is only twenty-eight years old. The empire which had seemed so secure at the death of Cyrus is wobbling; the aura of monolithic kingship which had bound it together has clearly, for the moment, lost its spell. The resurrected heir has been six months on the throne. Six hardened aristocrats are intriguing, supposedly because they have finally concluded that the king is a fake. The young 'spear-bearer' appears, the youngest of the three possible heirs from the Hystaspes branch of the Achaemenians; both Darius's father, Hystaspes, and his grandfather, Arsames, are still very much alive. Amongst the six conspirators (was it he who admitted Darius to the secret?) is Gobryas, Darius's powerful father-in-law. Darius, the apprentice, does not hesitate: he urges action. On 29 September he and the nobles pass, apparently without challenge, into the inner sanctum of the court and slay Bardiya/Smerdis/Gaumata.

Why was it so easy? Where was the army? What was the arrangement between the conspirators? ('You who shall be king hereafter, preserve well the families of these men' said Darius later, and in all but one case their noble families flourished.) A royal claimant of singular energy, with a precocious grasp of politics and warfare, was reaching for the Achaemenian crown, and secured it with simple-minded ruthlessness. His account of how he did so, however disputed, is an historical document without parallel. It shows with what manner of mind we are dealing.

The modern road runs north-east from Kirmanshah to Hamadan

(ancient Ecbatana) and follows much the same line as the old royal Achaemenian road that linked Ecbatana with Babylon. On its northern side stands, for twenty miles or so, a sheer rock face which breaks suddenly into an alluvial plain. Just before this break, where the peak rises to three thousand feet, an angular crevice faces the road. About three hundred feet above the road, one face of the crevice has been polished into a rectangular frame, rather in the size and proportions of the screen of a drive-in movie theatre. From the road it is hard to make out any detail and, indeed, the site goes unheeded by most of the passing traffic. A steep flight of steps (a modern addition) weaves up through broken rocks to within fifty feet of the carving, and from there it is possible to make out a line of twelve figures, and below them a densely packed inscription in several broad columns of cuneiform. This was the medium chosen by Darius to ensure that he had the last word on how he gained the universal power of the Persian king – an autobiography cut into stone and, even now, mostly still legible. This is the epic inscription of Bisitun, carved in the three languages of Persian, Elamite and Akkadian. It was copied down in the nineteenth century, and has been progressively transcribed ever since, a definitive version coming only a few decades ago.

In view of this cliff face, Darius had won a great prize in the journey to the throne: the submission of Media. This was one of nineteen rebellions he had to suppress within less than two years after the counter-coup, and some of the battles were critical. They are all described at Bisitun in quite unabashed, grisly detail, as though one purpose was deliberately to deter any further challenges. The account includes repeated invocations of the newly acknowledged deity, Ahuramazda: each victory is 'by the favour of Ahuramazda' and the divinity and king are as one on the battlefield: 'Ahuramazda bore me aid; by the favour of Ahuramazda my army smote that rebellious army exceedingly.' This is the first formal alliance of church and state in the Achaemenian records, and the fact that it seems suddenly to have materialized underlines how incomplete is our knowledge of Zoroastrianism's advance. Bearing in mind that Darius had already suppressed the political ambitions of the Magi, his invocation of Ahuramazda is less a gesture of piety than a pragmatic way of giving a divine blessing to his own actions – and of leaving nobody in doubt as to who was the supreme mortal agent of the lord. Darius was in no sense a sudden 'convert' but he saw the value of promoting

Darius's battles of accession were recorded in this tableau at Bisitun, where the rebel leaders, bound and captive, await the new king's revenge. An extensive cuneiform inscription under the figures lists each rebellion and its suppression. The site overlooks the scene of the battle in which Darius reclaimed Media: 'My army smote that rebellious army exceedingly.'

what was, by then, probably the established grass roots religion of Persia.

As with all mandated history, the Bisitun inscriptions have to be treated warily. The paucity of alternatives makes their comparative volubility very tempting. Their partial transcription in the nineteenth century did much to restore Herodotus's reputation just when he was under attack: his list of those who overthrew Gaumata differs in only one name from the inscription. But against the preceding history of the Achaemenian empire, the inscriptions propose one inescapable question which they do nothing to answer: why, with the declaration of Darius's kingship, *was* there such a determined rebellion; risings in every one of the most ancient provinces of the kingdom, including Fars and Media? Elam rose twice, once within months of the start of the new regime, when the rebels changed their minds and delivered their leader to Darius, and again more seriously under a new rebel, Atamaita. His fate is recorded at Bisitun: 'Gobryas with the army marched off to Elam; he joined battle with the Elamites. Thereupon Gobryas smote and crushed the Elamites, and captured the chief of them; he led him to me, and I killed him. After that the province became mine.' Parthia, under Darius's father Hystaspes became so troublesome that reinforcements had to be sent there at a moment when depletion of the army might have been fatal. Even the king's bow-holder, second in allegiance only to the spear-bearer – one Vindafarnah – had to be executed. Fortunately for Darius the risings were unco-ordinated. Otherwise he could not have prevailed.

Were the risings a sudden attempt to exploit the supposed weakness of the centre, or a deeper conviction that Darius, not Bardiya, was the usurper? The most far-fetched theory, that Bardiya *had* survived and that the next in the direct line from Cyrus was supplanting Cambyses because of his Egyptian folly, gains some credibility simply because of the absolutism of Darius's rock-hewn propaganda, and by the damaging fact that although he gives a genealogy of his collateral branch of the Achaemenians he conveniently omits Cyrus the Great from it, and mentions Cyrus elsewhere only perfunctorily when explaining Bardiya's 'false' claim to illustrious parentage. This could be, of course, the jealousy of an overweaning and as yet immature ruler towards a man he had still to surpass, both in achievement – and perhaps more consciously – in the affection of his people.

Scores of thousands died in the rebellions and their suppression. So

ABOVE Persepolis, looking north-west across the great plain of Marv Dasht. The covered building (foreground) is the modern museum; to its right is the site of the ancient treasury. In the north-western corner is the Gate of All Nations which led to the huge hall of audience, the Apadana; beyond that, to the left, is Darius's palace and his private apartments.

BELOW Professor Friedrich Krefter has reconstructed, to exact scale, the Apadana at Persepolis as it looked when completed. Up to 10,000 people could be gathered in this hall, to pay respect to the great king who sat on an elevated throne. The ceiling was of cedar of Lebanon; the columns were covered in painted plaster and the whole glistened with gold and jewels.

far, Darius had shown exceptional ability as a soldier. At the start his loyal armies had not been large. Darius moved carefully to cement the dynasty. He married Cambyses's widow (and sister) Atossa, and Artystone, the younger of Cyrus's daughters. Gobryas's daughter had borne him three sons already, but now the offspring of Cyrus's daughters took precedence. This did nothing to diminish Gobryas's status, or his loyalty. He appears at Bisitun alongside Darius as the king's spear-bearer. A royal harem was already an institution; Darius acquired that of Cambyses.

A new court structure, trustworthy and vigilant, had to be devised. The administrative power was invested in a Lord Chamberlain, or Marshal of the Court, an office taken by a Mede, Farnaka. Once freed of his military preoccupations, Darius showed an acumen approaching genius for the organization of empire. Where Cyrus had improvised, albeit brilliantly, Darius formalized. The satrapies – Herodotus names twenty of them – were rationalized into more balanced units, less tied to the former territorial boundaries, although many of them were vast, incorporating more than one old kingdom. To ensure the integrity and, most of all, the loyalty of the satraps Darius instituted a network of surveillance, part of it overt and part covert, the 'eyes' and the 'ears' of the king. The eyes were those of an inspectorate, whose authority came not from the satrap but directly from the court. The ears were not identifiable; they could be anyone's.

Darius soon proved to be scrupulous about legal precedents, and about equity in law. In 520 BC the Jews in Jerusalem appealed to him after the satrap of Syria curtailed work on their new temple. They quoted the edict of Cyrus, made at Babylon in 534 BC, authorizing the reconstruction. The edict was unknown to Darius, but he ordered that the archives should be searched, and it was found. The satrap was told briskly to observe it: 'Whosoever shall alter this word, let timber be pulled down from his house and being set up, let him be hanged thereon.' (Ezra 6:7, 8, 9, 11.)

Darius's military talent was matched by a burst of creative energy, directed at the dynastic architecture. As the site of his first palace he chose Susa. Symbolically, he was rubbing home his interment of Elamite independence. Practically, he was confirming Susa's value as a junction of the imperial routes. Politically, he was showing the eclecticism of the empire: Ionians and Lydians carved the fine grey limestone of the Zagros; Medes and Egyptians fashioned gold ornaments from Sardis and Bactria; cedar wood was shipped from the Lebanon to Babylon by Syrians and then taken by Carians and Ionians to Susa; the rare Sissoo tree was brought from Carmania and Gandhara; turquoise from Chorasmia and lapis lazuli from Sogdiana. Darius was to out-build Cyrus, something more lavish, more grandiose than Pasargadae, an imperial style marking a distinct change of tone in the manner (and aura) of Achaemenian rule.

Because of the size and weight of the planned palace at Susa, and because the historical detritus of the old city formed a mound, or tepe, a vast pit had first to be dug to rock level, and then a foundation of compressed rubble and gravel laid to a depth of 40 cubits (26.6 feet). The platform was 820.5 feet long and 492 feet wide. And the centre-piece was a towering audience hall, or Apadana, with 36 columns in 6 rows of 6; at the top of each column was a bull capital. The walls were decorated with polychromatic glazed bricks, with portraits of archers of the royal guard in their Elamite-style robes.

But even before this project was finished, the restless patron had begun planning his *magnum opus*, the work which more than anything else survives as his personal mark on Persia and its empire: Persepolis. Like Cyrus, Darius wanted one capital which from the start was his own, not, like Susa, an increment to a past site. The decision to build in Fars, within a morning's easy ride of Pasargadae, could be no clearer pledge of Darius's fidelity to the historical roots of the dynasty. The old association with Fars had not been neglected since Cyrus: Cam-byses, before he left for Egypt, ordered his own tomb to be started – apparently identical in form to that of Cyrus – only a few miles from the site in the Marv Dasht plain now chosen by Darius.

The choice of site had more than sentiment to commend it. Perse-polis was not a great junction city like Babylon, but it was the terminus of the royal road which was extended to it from Pasargadae. Darius took the apron of a limestone mountain, sacred by tradition, and extended it to form a massive platform rising up to fifty-two feet from the plain. The platform, facing south-west, was really an elevated stage on which to display the assembled glories of the king, court and the élite of the army. Today, the once forested plain is mostly crop-bearing and open as far as the distant lower ridges of the Zagros. The platform of Persepolis merges with the promontory of the mountain so that from a distance the mark of man and nature are indis-tinguishable. Only within half a mile can the scale of the statement be grasped, and then we are left with nothing but a kind of monolithic rib-cage in stone. Walls and roofs have gone; columns rise to nearly sixty feet; a few vestigial capitals remain.

Doorways of great bulk, lintels and cornices, and a staircase wide enough to take an army (which it did) ascends from the road to the surviving piers of a ceremonial entrance, still bearing the headless trunks of the great stone bulls which guarded this, the Gate of All Nations. Gone is the restraint of Pasargadae: from the first steps through the gold-plated doors the design was to awe the subject mortals with the power of the king, in textual alliance with Ahuramazda. The remnants of Persepolis may convey the ego behind the stone, but they do not begin to suggest the original repertoire of ornament, stonework and ceramic – the display of monarchy *excelsis*. The modern eye might well have found it all too much – vulgar megalomania. We can only stand and wonder; Persepolis may be more digestible in ruin than it was when replete.

The role of Persepolis is still disputed by scholars. Clearly it was a shrine of the temporal power; religious observance was secondary to the obeisance demanded by the king. Was it, too, a capital *city*? A seat of permanent government? Achaemenian kings from Darius onwards divided their time between Persepolis, Ecbatana and Susa. The question is for how long, and to what purpose in each? Susa, in the humid lowlands, was comfortable only in winter, and that would have been its normal time of royal occupation. Ecbatana, in the cool Zagros highlands, was temperate in high summer. At the least, it is held that Darius used Persepolis only to celebrate the festivals, either in the spring or in the autumn, when the climate in Fars is at its best. But Professor Hinz argues persuasively that Darius was not so cursory in his affection for his own creation (which kept occupied a substantial labour force throughout his reign and was unfinished when he died). Hinz points to administrative records found on clay tablets at the site and transcribed in 1969, which indicate the king's presence there, when he was not campaigning, in both summer and autumn, although not to a regular pattern.

Persepolis is not intolerable in the heat of summer, and the far more extensive vegetation at the time of the Achaemenians would have made it more temperate still. The palaces were lofty and open, affording plenty of shade and ventilation.

An area next to the site and extending north-west beyond the

The Apadana as seen from the Gate of All Nations, facing south-east. The stairways of the Apadana were covered in carvings portraying the bearers of tribute, coming to Persepolis from all over the empire. The columns of the Apadana were nearly sixty feet high, and each drum making up the columns weighed up to forty tons – how installed is unknown.

stunted tomb of Cambyses was developed into a royal park, in the manner of Pasargadae, but more extensive. Nobles, military commanders and a swelling bureaucracy lived here with their families. On the north-western fringe of this park a line of cliffs overlooks the royal road. Here was created a royal burial place, with the tombs cut deep into the cliff face in a manner not unlike the Valley of the Kings in Egypt. The place became known as Naqsh–i–Rustam, and the tombs retain an ethereal atmosphere, though they have long since been ravaged.

As Persepolis rose, Darius embarked on a new phase of Persian imperialism. Transcending Cyrus was no doubt a powerful drive, but he has also left an impression of messianic direction: 'Ahuramazda chose me as his man on all the earth, he made me king of all the earth.' India was the big prize. In 517 BC he campaigned into the Punjab, drawn there by tribal wars, and then plunged south into Sind, which matched Sardis in its troves of gold. Its fate was to become the highest-taxed satrapy in the empire.

The Indian adventure produced a geographical discovery. Darius despatched an expedition in boats down the Indus towards the sea. Thirty months later they arrived on the north African coast, at Libya, having circumnavigated the Arabian peninsula and reached Suez, via the Red Sea and the Nile. They were led by a shipmaster called Scylax of Caryanda (near Herodotus's birthplace) who later published, in Greek, his log called *Periplus*, or *Circumnavigation*, which gave the west its first certain knowledge of the great sub-continent and the sea routes. The Scylax voyage was able to use one of Darius's engineering feats. He had decided to complete a plan aborted by an Egyptian king one hundred years earlier for a canal linking the Red Sea and the Nile. And so, two thousand four hundred years before the Suez canal was built, a navigable link was established between east and west. When finished, Darius's canal was one hundred and fifty feet wide and boats could pass through it in four days. At its edge Darius left a typical inscription: 'Saith Darius the King: I am a Persian; from Persia I seized Egypt; I gave order to dig this canal from a river by name Nile which flows in Egypt to the sea which goes from Persia. Afterwards this canal was dug thus as I had ordered, and ships went from Egypt through this canal to Persia thus as was my desire.'

'*Thus as was my desire*' ... and so it went. As Herodotus says: 'The greater part of Asia was discovered by Darius.' But what of the west?

With Egypt and the north African coast as far as Libya secured, and unchecked adventure becoming a habit, Darius looked towards the Mediterranean – and Europe. The terrain and climate were different, but not apparently more forbidding than the Central Asian steppes which seemed, at last, to have surrendered their fate to the empire. Early in his reign Darius sent a sea-borne spying mission as far west as southern Italy, which yielded little except hazy geography. In 512 BC Darius decided to invade Europe. He took an army across the Bosphorus, marched north, and crossed the lower Danube. The local Scythian tribes, fleet with horse, withdrew and burned their crops to deny supplies to the invader.

Darius was forced to withdraw. The campaign was the lowest point of his reign, and for a while damaged his standing. His objective is disputed. Was it a conscious probing of Europe's 'soft underbelly', or a flanking movement around the north of the Greek states? The Greek fringe was a constant irritation. As the Persians drew back from the Danube they secured the submission of the Greeks on the Aegean coast of Thrace and of the king of Macedonia. Thus a buffer of Greek thraldom was secured in the eastern Mediterranean. And with it, an enduring western resentment of Persian imperialism.

The fractious Greeks, feeling the divergent strains of the old, high conservatism and the experimental democracy, should have been easily consumed by the armies of Darius. That they were not is miraculous; *why* they were not is perplexing; one of the great speculations of history. For one thing, water disconcerted Persian commanders. Its treachery broke them more than once; dependent always on others to be their sailors they lacked in naval matters the experience that made them so confident on land. But they bungled badly on land, too, perhaps because the Greek campaigns forced them into littoral engagements – awkward, constraining and alien to their tactics (and their whole background).

But at the end of the fifth century, when the Persians faced their first really serious uprising in the west, the Ionian revolt, there was little sign that the colossus could be checked. The Ionians were adept at sea, and if their western kinsmen had provided unstinting support they might have proved more of a challenge. As it was, the Greek revolt and invasion of the Persian empire as far as Sardis proved to be ill-timed and disastrous. After it collapsed vicious skirmishes continued around the Aegean for five years, until the cause passed beyond hope. At the end the islands of Chios, Lesbos and Tenedos were each swept by an advancing line of Persian soldiers who hunted down whole populations as though they were game.

In 492 BC Darius sent his son-in-law Mardonius, the son of the invaluable Gobryas, to take over the final pacification of the western provinces. To some degree the revolt had been encouraged by conservative, land-owning elements, not by radicals. Deciding to purge this faction from the empire, Darius instructed Mardonius to encourage the nascent democrats. Herodotus, with justice, remarks: 'this will come as a great surprise', especially to the Greek propagandists; the removal of despots and their replacement by democratic governments, under the aegis of the Persian king! At the least, it is an early example of the political technique of stealing the opposition's clothing, doubtless with designs on the sentiment of the mainland Greeks.

Had Mardonius stayed in the west, Persia's first humiliation at Marathon might have been avoided. But after an injury he returned to Persia and was replaced by a Mede, Datis, and the king's nephew, Artaphrenes. They captured Eretria, only to be beaten by the tardy Athenians on the plain of Marathon in 490 BC. Speculation over the quality of leadership saves nothing; the Persians, notably punished in reputation, went home to plan retribution.

Persepolis was remote and insulated from the hardness of war. In none of its hundreds of friezes is there any portrayal of war (or incidentally, of women). As it rose, column by column, over the Marv Dasht plain, Persepolis was the symbolic heart of Persia and of the empire. More materially, it was also the treasury. With each conquest the flow of tribute became a torrent. Despite the cost of maintaining the huge army, and of running the empire, as well as the epic building works, the Achaemenian court accumulated unprecedented wealth. But the economic potential of such wealth went unrealized. Hoarding became a congenital weakness of Achaemenian kings.

In other ways Darius was progressive however. He standardized money by following the Lydian innovation of coinage. After the acquisition of Indian gold he introduced the *Daric*, ninety-eight per cent pure gold, and lesser coinage of silver. The standardization of money was part of a general alignment of weights and measures. This attention to detail produced a rather caustic epithet: 'Cyrus was a father, Cambyses a master, and Darius a shopkeeper.'

The theme of many reliefs at Persepolis is of an empire unifying peoples of diverse origin, who sent their delegates and tribute to honour the great king. RIGHT Medes, in rounded hats, acted as court ushers.
BELOW Two rams are brought as tribute by Syrians, wearing cummerbunds over their long robes. Fallen debris, after Persepolis's destruction, helped preserve the carvings.

Equity and standardization were themes of Darius's reign: not so much the equity of citizenship that Cyrus allowed, but the equity of duty which Darius demanded. *Ad hoc* methods were no longer good enough. The reformer was less paternal, more authoritarian. But there had always to be doubts about how even-handed the king's laws could really be when they had to be dispensed over an empire of such span. The concept of the casebook as a body of law had been established as early as 1758 BC, by Hammurabi the king of Babylon. Drawing on this Mesopotamian tradition, Darius promulgated his own universal laws. Their tenor comes over clearly from an inscription at Naqsh–i–Rustam: 'Saith Darius the king: by the favour of Ahuramazda I am of such a sort that I am a friend to right, I am not a friend to wrong. It is not my desire that the weak man should have wrong done to him by the mighty; nor is it my desire that the mighty man should have wrong done to him by the weak. What is right, that is my desire.'

The Old Testament confirms the consistency of Darius's law: 'Now, O king, establish the interdict, and sign the writing, that it be not changed, according to the law of the Medes and Persians, which altereth not.' (Daniel 6:8.) But little of these laws, put together under the title of the Ordinance of Good Regulations, survives in detail, nor is there enough evidence to judge how successfully they were applied. The nature of the man suggests stern application: 'What things develop in my anger, I hold firmly under control by my thinking power. I am firmly ruling over my own impulses.' It was a creed under which men knew where they stood, and could expect salutary punishment for a lapse of duty.

Professor Richard Frye sees Darius's codification of the laws as an important stage in the organization of societies:

It is probably the beginning, for example, of the Jewish Torah as the law of the Jewish people. The king wanted a system of international law, which was the king's law above the local laws, but he wanted the local laws also to be in good order. This is, in my opinion, the real background of Roman law, which is the background of all western law.

But how, in such a variegated empire, could the law be transmitted? It was put down on parchment or papyrus in the Aramaic language which by force of its superior fluency became the empire's *lingua franca*. But royal inscriptions continued to be trilingual, in Elamite, Akkadian and the Persian cuneiform which Darius tried, rather vainly, to make the equal of the others. Fortunately, because the bureaucracy's records were often not in Aramaic but in cuneiform on baked tablets, they have survived to give an extensive picture of the minutiae of Achaemenian court life and business: what the workmen at Persepolis were paid, where they came from, tallies of the taxes.

Literature as we know it was a tool of the Achaemenian court, not a part of its culture. It was employed for the *ex-cathedra* royal pronouncements, for the records and for the laws. Otherwise communication was oral, dependent on a highly developed sense of memory. The king, probably illiterate, would have all the documents read to him and, far from feeling inferior because of it, regarded the scribes as we regard plumbers: the providers of a useful service but not a skill in need of emulation.

Zoroastrianism was defined, transmitted and sustained entirely within this oral tradition; it had no recourse to a written gospel. No priests appear in the Achaemenian reliefs showing the king and his courtiers, and the place of priests at court is unclear. The nomadic heritage still greatly influenced royal ritual. We know from Plutarch that Achaemenian kings returned to Pasargadae for a coronation ceremony supervised by the Magi in which they had to eat a cake of figs, chew turpentine wood and drink a cup of sour milk. Zoroastrianism was in no sense the state religion it was later to become. The king had the sole power to impose order, to judge between good and bad, and as long as this was reasoned or enlightened despotism it was probably consistent with Zoroaster's ethic. The trouble came with the variability of kings.

Under Darius, there was no doubt to which authority the many peoples of the empire gave their tribute. When the king was resident at Persepolis gifts symbolic of each nation's obeisance were paraded past the throne in the Apadana, a hall large enough, it is said, to have held ten thousand people. On the eastern staircase of the Apadana a detailed protocol of the delegations is carved in relief. Twenty-three peoples are represented, and the leader of each is led by the hand by either a Mede or a Persian, the ushers of the court. The gifts – dromedaries, horses, rams, textiles, bowls, bracelets, gilded weapons – are as exotic as the empire. Each group on the reliefs is punctuated by small cypress trees which grew on the Marv Dasht plain. Allowing for the propagandist element in these decorations, the harmony of so diverse an empire is still very impressive: Indians, Syrians, Ethiopians, Libyans,

Sogdians, Babylonians came to Persepolis from all the corners of Asia to feel a common tie under the Achaemenian king. By the end of Darius's reign twenty-nine separate peoples gave him their allegiance. The regime had transformed a warring rabble into sensibly interdependent provinces. The consequences of submission to the central authority were stability, an expectation of equity in law, and a great development of agriculture and trade.

In 486 BC, while he was laying the plans for a renewed and far more ambitious campaign in the west, Darius fell ill. He had always been vigorous in health, but this illness gained a hold and within thirty days the great king was dead, at the age of sixty-four. Naturally, he had left his own epitaph, carved above his rock-tomb at Naqsh–i–Rustam:

> Ahuramazda, when he saw this earth in commotion, thereafter bestowed it upon me ... the spear of a Persian man has gone forth far; then shall it become known to thee: a Persian man has delivered battle far indeed from Persia. ... Me may Ahuramazda protect from harm, and my royal house, and this land. ...'

This time the lineage was secure in the issue of both wings of the royal family: Xerxes, son of Darius and Atossa, Cyrus's daughter. Cyrus's youngest daughter, Artystone, had been so close to Darius's heart that he always carried a gold portrait of her. None the less, of all the aspirants to the throne (Darius had at least twelve acknowledged sons) it was the eldest of the direct line, Xerxes, who could not be denied. His inheritance was formidable. In only a few more years' reign than Cyrus, Darius had extended, consolidated and codified the systems of world empire. How much further could the Persian arm reach? In the east, the riches of Hindush, as the Indian satrapy was called, were enough; but in the west the Greeks were celebrating their victory at Marathon by laying the foundations for the Parthenon on the acropolis at Athens. One voice, that of Themistocles, warned against euphoria. He knew that the Persians would be back.

But before Xerxes could renew his father's plans for invasion there were more pressing challenges. A change of kings again tempted rebellious factions. Successors, it seemed, must prove themselves by repression. This Xerxes swiftly did, in Egypt. An uprising broke out there in 486 BC. Xerxes conducted the campaign personally, and within two years had left no doubt that his rule would be as harsh as his father's. And in one respect it was harsher. The conciliatory device of

Darius was buried, like several other Achaemenian kings, in a tomb cut into the cliff face at Naqsh-i-Rustam, near Persepolis. An inscription on Darius's tomb reads: 'What is right, that is my desire. I am not a friend to the man who is a Lie-follower ...' In Zoroastrianism 'the Lie' was an anti-force associated with Ahriman, the devil, and opponent of the king.

the king taking, in each province, the indigenous titles was abandoned in Egypt. Xerxes chose to remain the alien king. In Babylon, where Cyrus had judiciously appeared as the chosen agent of Marduk (as recorded in his cylinder inscription), Xerxes inserted 'King of Persia and Media' before the traditional local titles.

In 482 BC, bridling at this new assertion of central authority, Babylon rose in revolt and Xerxes's satrap was killed. That polyglot Babylon felt able to combine its forces against the king suggests a deep resentment, but it was folly. In the manner of the new regime, the rising was crushed mercilessly. Much of historic Babylon disappeared: fortifications, temples and the eighteen-foot golden statue of Marduk, weighing nearly eight hundred pounds, which was taken off and melted down for bullion. As a final ignominy, Babylon was merged with Assyria into a new satrapy.

Should Xerxes, therefore, be held in awe, or contempt? Because of his later conduct in the west, it is not hard to see why he should be reviled from that quarter. But the vilification of Xerxes has been inconsistent. He is variously called a higher form of Achaemenian megalomaniac, a weakling, a religious bigot, an unmanly aesthete, and a satyr of the harem. It is fairer to see in him all the strengths and weaknesses of the dynasty in a new concentration – a personal epitome of established trends. His refusal to pay lip-service to provincial deities was simply confirming the inevitable: central power was absolute. Darius felt less need to conciliate than Cyrus, Xerxes less still. No doubt his father had drilled into him the moral expounded at Bisitun, that dissent should be eliminated at root. When he took the throne at the age of thirty-five, Xerxes was already an experienced administrator, having spent twelve years in the crown prince's seat as regent of Babylon. A foundation plaque at Persepolis shows his confidence: 'Thus speaks King Xerxes: After I became king, there were some among these countries which revolted but I crushed these countries, after Ahuramazda had given me his aid. . . .' A chip off the old block indeed.

In the same inscription (transcribed in 1938 a few years after the plaque's discovery) comes evidence that Darius's ersatz piety was being superseded in his son by a more conscious orthodoxy: 'There were among these countries some which performed religious service to the Evil Gods but by the grace of Ahuramazda I destroyed these temples of the Evil Gods ... and wherever formerly service was performed to the Evil Gods, I, myself, performed a religious service to Ahuramazda and the arta [cosmic order] reverently.' This is quite a new tone; whether religious conformity sprang from closer ties with Zoroastrianism, or whether it was used as an excuse to enforce political conformity, is open to question. The Jews, who shared the tidiness of monotheism with the Zoroastrians, were usually looked upon with favour by the king. Just who were the 'Evil Gods' was a pragmatic decision. Some of the gods and temples stripped from Babylon were later restored. When Xerxes talks of Ahuramazda's role he means an enveloping, amorphous spirit engaged in the conflict with Evil, an enemy which the king can identify at will – and whim.

Whether, in this definition, the pagan gods of Greece were 'Evil' we do not know. But Greece's second experience of Persian invasion was coming. Xerxes marched out from Susa in the spring of 481 BC. The years spent planning the invasion of the west produced the most extensive war machine ever seen in Asia. Its new feature was the co-ordination of land and sea forces. For months the harbours of the eastern Mediterranean were thick with assembling warships. The real size of the invasion force is still subject to learned dispute, although nobody now doubts that Herodotus's total of 1,800,000 men for the army is absurd. Modern studies suggest between 80,000 and 100,000 – still a large enough host with its cavalry horses, baggage camels and supporting personnel to require great skill in assembly, movement and supply. The strength of the navy, again inflated by Herodotus, was probably about 600 triremes.

Darius had organized the Achaemenian army on a decimal system, with divisions of 10,000 men (myriads), themselves divided into units of thousands, hundreds and tens – commanded by a hierarchy from the myriarch at the top to the dekarch at the bottom. The army's élite were the 10,000 Immortals, recruited only from Medes and Persians. They provided the king's bodyguard, and their number was kept constant by automatic replacement. The training of the Immortals epitomized a traditional Persian objective, 'to ride, shoot and tell the truth'.

The command of army units went to the heads of those families who had distinguished themselves under Cyrus and Darius, none more valued than the family of Gobryas, whose son Mardonius had returned, after his injury, as a commander of one of Xerxes's divisions. For the expedition to Greece eleven of Darius's sons were given commands; the prestige and importance of the campaign was enormous. If Greece (and Europe?) were to fall, there would be no shortage of Persian princes to govern.

A pontoon bridge constructed of obsolescent triremes was strung across the Hellespont, and a canal dug across the peninsula, to speed the passage of both army and navy. Strict synchronization was needed to keep the land and sea forces in contact. The navy, in which the Phoenicians and Egyptians were crucial, was not only an armada but also a vital source of supply if the army ran upon barren ground.

In Greece Themistocles's brilliant oratory had some effect at last: the bulwark of defence was to be the navy. Themistocles shrewdly guessed that the Persian fleet would be vulnerable in waters which were unfamiliar, lacking in harbours and beaches, and subject to capricious weather. On land the first stage of the Persian invasion was allowed to go unopposed. Alexander, the king of Macedonia, supported the Persians and assured them of an easy passage through his territory. The first serious resistance came at Thermopylae, where Leonidas, King of the Spartans, fought his legendary but futile action; a rare moment when the Spartan commitment was not equivocal. But the sweetness of this victory for the Persians was soured by a near-catastrophe at sea. A storm, unusually severe for the season, caught the Persians unprepared and many ships and men were lost. The disaster was compounded by Themistocles, whose navy raided the Persian anchorages in the confusion. Nothing, though, could stop Xerxes's army. They swept through Attica, burning the towns and villages. Finally exultant and apparently sure of conquest, they took Athens (whose population had fled across the narrow strait to Salamis) and, after a struggle, stormed the acropolis and burned the emerging Parthenon, where the scaffolding greatly assisted the inferno. Watching from their sanctuary on Salamis, the Athenians were much demoralized. Xerxes sent a message back to Persia, indicating victory.

But there was still the Greek navy, pulled back by Themistocles into the bay lying to the north of the strait of Salamis. The Persians were tricked into thinking that the Greeks intended to run, fugitive, through the strait. The entire Persian fleet was launched, at night, to stop them. What happened instead was that the Persians were caught, bunched and without scope for manoeuvre, by an encircling Greek fleet. Xerxes had installed himself on a throne above the strait, a grandstand position for what he expected would be a *coup de grâce*. So it was, but by the Greeks. The two fleets, after the ravages of the storm inflicted on the Persians, had been roughly equal in number. But Themistocles's tactics rendered many of the finest units of the Persian fleet helpless. After this fiasco, Xerxes left Athens in the hands of Mardonius and went back across the Hellespont to Sardis, followed by the remnants of his fleet. He never returned.

For the winter, Mardonius prudently withdrew north from Athens. Without the king, and shorn of many mercenary contingents, the Persian land force was still thought to be a serious enough threat to intimidate Athens into surrender. Alexander of Macedon appeared as mediator and urged it. He was rebuffed, famously. 'We know quite well the power of Persia ... but we desire to be free, so we will defend ourselves as best we can. ...' In the summer of 479 BC Mardonius descended again on Athens, and again the citizens evacuated to Salamis. Xerxes, content to remain in Asia, knew that the southern Greeks were still divided and, furthermore, that they had dropped Themistocles in spite of (perhaps *because* of?) his success. Mardonius could bide his time. The strength of his opponents depended on the Spartans, who calmly held a religious festival while their allies waited for help. When a new Greek army was finally mobilized it was led by an unknown quantity, the Spartan prince Pausanias.

Both armies moved north, to meet on the Thriasian Plain before Thebes. It was a set-piece battle, with Mardonius and Pausanias each able to spend days surveying the dispositions of the other and making raids of attrition. After thirteen days the armies fully engaged at Plataea. It was a finely balanced and viciously fought collision of worlds. Psychologically the turning-point came when Mardonius, prominent on his great white horse and supported by a thousand of the Persian elite, was felled. According to Plutarch his skull was broken by a hurled rock. Of equal psychological importance was that the Greeks were fighting with their backs to their homelands. With Mardonius's death the Persian army was broken, and it fled. The profane victors stayed on the battlefield for ten days, scooping up their spoils and celebrating to the gods.

Intermittent conflict persisted, but Plataea was decisive. From that moment the west was lost to Persia. The jubilation of the west has been passed through Herodotus downwards and still rings in the classic perspective of history. Inadvertently, Xerxes had made a point about the Greeks that they seldom respected themselves: that when they optimized instead of dissipated their power and convictions they could humble the world's most feared military machine. A Greek army patched together, totally unrehearsed in combination on this scale in the field, had stopped a monolith that had years of hard campaigning behind it, was impeccably drilled and instinctively responsive to command. Easy, then, to draw a political parallel and to read from it a moral in favour of free men hastily convened proving superior to a monarchy in which, to quote one scholar, 'even the noblest of his own Persians were no more than his slaves'.

But...

Greece was ungrateful to her heroes. Themistocles, always prescient, was ostracized and then driven into exile for promoting the idea of an armistice, having judged the line between east and west to have been sensibly settled. He was accused of defeatism, collaboration or worse (credible in so fine a patriot?). His congenial fate was to rule over Magnesia, with ample tribute, under a *Persian* king. Pausanias, altogether a more complex and headstrong figure, was killed while on his way to ask favours of the Persian king. And what of the 'Medizing' Greeks, like Alexander of Macedonia, who were pledged to Persia for a variety of reasons, all to do with self-interest and the internecine Greek struggles? Even when defeat stared them in the face, there had not been one significant defection from the Persian king, although Alexander switched sides afterwards and massacred a retreating Persian contingent. Where there was continual unrest, on the Ionian seaboard of Anatolia, it had more to do with schisms within the Greek culture than with a distaste for the Persian overlords. The conflict of tyrant and democrat was more acutely felt *within* the Greek world than outside it.

If the political indictment of the Persian system is partial, the military doubt is not so contentious. There was no failure of nerve. Accounts of Persian vassals having to be whipped into battle are at odds with their behaviour on the field. On land both the strategy and tactics were considered and efficient, although there was, in the Greek campaigns, a marked lack of *dash*. The weakness seems partly to have been technological. The lessons of Marathon had not been learned. Persian archers, previously devastating, had failed against the phalanx of the Athenians. In hand-to-hand combat, which the Persians disliked and which both their cavalry and archers were intended to forestall, their lack of body armour was fatal against the Greek citizen infantry, the hoplites, who had helmets, corslets and greaves, carried spears and short swords and who fought shoulder-to-shoulder with their shields interlocking. The Greeks were astounded to encounter opponents wearing caps and flowing gowns, some of them directly handed down from the Elamites. The Immortals, notes Herodotus, had shorter spears than the Greeks. The cavalry, pivotal in any Persian tactic, might have been impaired by the wickedly sharp stones, since the horseshoe had not yet been invented. Faced with the impregnability of the phalanx, the mounted archers soon exhausted their arrows.

Topography was also crucial. The constrictions of Greek terrain were against the sweeping and fluid patterns which the sheer size of the Persian army made essential; instead of making an arc, they were often forced into a funnel. Because both Greece and Persia are mountainous, military historians seem sometimes at a loss to explain the Persian failures in Greece. This is to confuse two very different kinds of mountain terrain. The plateau was a wholly different environment to Attica, unfamiliar and alien. According to Herodotus, a Persian noble once proposed to Cyrus that the tribe should migrate to easier pastures. The reply, apocryphal or not, says a lot about the peculiar qualities of Persia: 'Cyrus listened, and did not think it a good idea. He said "Do, if you will; but if so prepare to be not masters but subjects . . . for it does not happen that the same lands produce splendid crops and good fighting men."'

Perhaps the new tracts of the empire had already softened Cyrus's successors. Certainly Xerxes had permitted himself the observation that all empires expand until they are checked, and Greece had checked him. With the final years of his reign, Persian expansion is over and the struggles are, instead, to keep territory. At Persepolis Xerxes completed his embellishments of his father's grand scheme, adding a palace of his own and the Gate of All Nations: 'Saith Xerxes the king by the favour of Ahuramazda this colonnade of all lands I built. Much other good construction was built within Persepolis which I built and my father built.' Xerxes the aesthete appears as the patron of a series of finer, slightly more effete carvings; Achaemenian art becomes, under him, more sensual.

He spent his remaining thirteen years, as often as he could, in regal pleasures. The harem at Persepolis expanded. Intricate polygamy and in-breeding caused fanatical jealousies; the 'terrible' royal women gained great influence. In 465 BC Xerxes was assassinated in a plot led by the commander of the guard, Artabanus, and the eunuch chamberlain, Aspamitres. Nothing better shows the degeneration of the court than that a chamberlain could succeed in king-making. Darius, the eldest son, was slain and the throne went to the eighteen-year-old Artaxerxes. The spasm of murders ended with Artabanus overreaching himself. The young king had him killed, and went on to rule for forty-two years. He achieved significant diplomacy by coming to terms with Greece in an armistice called, after its Greek negotiator, the Peace of Callias.

The Athenians and the Persians each conceded territory, Persia the Asian cities which had been drawn into the Athenian orbit, and Greece gave up Cyprus and her alliance with Egypt. The Persian fleet was withdrawn from the Aegean. In modern terms it was a military disengagement, creating a neutralized zone between east and west. Athens, with the Peloponnesian League of Sparta to worry about, did not need further distractions. And Artaxerxes was left to concentrate on policing his subject states, of which Egypt was still troublesome. The Peace of Callias was unusually enlightened for its time, and gave fuel to the jingoists. A rational case could be made that Persia's empire had long ago reached viable limits for the communications of the time. Dreams of Europe had been a fantasy. Compared with the established logic of the rest of the empire, Greece was peripheral. Despite the ideological gulf, there was really no political reason for war. This is not to minimize Xerxes's defeat, as some do, by saying that set alongside the empire's achievements it was not important. Why, in that case, had virtually the whole court gone on the expedition? The king had spent years planning it, the army was directed at nothing else. Perhaps, watching the débâcle of Salamis from his throne on the knoll, Xerxes *had* come to terms with the geo-political realities, but only the hard way.

Artaxerxes was not to repeat the error. And he was wise in another matter. Babylonia, which had inspired Darius's universal code of laws, now produced the new Jewish lawbook, the Torah of Moses. This was compiled in Babylon by Ezra, the leader of the city's Jewish community, who was responsible for them to the king. Ezra's lawbook formalized and organized the spiritual and social order of the Jews, and so endeared Ezra to Artaxerxes who, in the Achaemenian tradition, disliked ambiguity in all things. Ezra, in turn, would have seen how Darius's Ordinance of Good Regulations had supplanted anarchy. In the Old Testament (Ezra 7:25–26) the Great King says: 'And thou, Ezra, after the wisdom of thy God that is in thine hand, appoint magistrates and judges, which may judge all the people that are beyond the river, all such as know the laws of thy God; and teach ye him that knowest them not. And whosoever will not do the law of thy God, and the law of the king, let judgement be executed upon him with all diligence. . . .'

This theological turning-point emphasizes the interchange of ideas as civilization gained a hold in the ancient world. The intellectual curiosity of east and west overlapped and fused. In philosophy, mathematics, astronomy and literature men were seeking to match reason with knowledge. Egypt and Babylonia were very important in this process, and the ease of communication within the Persian empire helped the fusion. Babylon, in particular, became a place where ideas as much as commodities were exchanged. And the Peace of Callias in 499 BC greatly extended the dialogue to include Greece. At least two of the men who in this period moved eastwards were to show the value of freer movement. Democritus of Abdera was the first Greek scientist to visit Babylon, after being also in Egypt. In mathematics and astronomy he was a pathfinder. And at the moment when Ezra took his lawbook to Jerusalem, a vigorous young Greek who had been raised in a vassal province of the Persian empire began wandering western Asia, much of it on foot, improvising subsistence much as a modern hippy hitch-hiker does, passing along a network of Greek-speaking traders.

He worked his passage across the Black Sea, then followed the routes into Egypt, then to Tyre and then into the Persian empire to Babylon. He would have stood out as an assiduous listener, pursuing and encouraging tales from first or second-hand about the great Persian wars and the figures who rose and fell in them. This was Herodotus of Halicarnassus, planning the first systematic historical work or, as he named it, his *Researches*, 'set down to preserve the memory of the past by putting on record the astonishing achievements both of our own and of other peoples; and more particularly to show how they came into conflict'. Note *'and of other peoples'*; unlike some of his publicist successors, Herodotus is notionally impartial, no chauvinist. After his grand trek he went to Athens where he was welcomed as a partisan of democracy. But later, feeling the fickleness of that volatile community, he failed to qualify as a naturalized Athenian and left to live in southern Italy. His heart was Athenian, his fate that of the transient.

In contrast to the vigour of Mesopotamian intellectual life, the Persian court was more and more riven by dynastic jealousies. Neither Persepolis nor Fars kept their hold on the affections and character of the Achaemenians. Artaxerxes spent most of the last period of his reign at Babylon, in the humid and enervating lowlands, and there he died (although he was buried at Naqsh–i–Rustam). Again, regicide erupted. The heir, Xerxes II, survived only months. Sogdianus, the next in line, went even faster. The mendacious ascendant prince was Darius II, aided and abetted by his queen, Parysatis. Perhaps the ways of the harem had diluted the royal blood line: the head of Artaxerxes on his coins shows a most un-Achaemenian nose, short and curved, and instead of the normally manicured beard, a rough one. Darius II and Parysatis were both half-Babylonian by birth.

The only achievement of Darius II's reign was some cunning diplomacy in the west, principally the support of Sparta. But it was too clever, and bought time, not peace. The great empire had become otiose, and the Greeks knew it. Aside from the declining character of the court, there were two persistent flaws. Firstly there was Egypt, which was a costly distraction, sapping manpower and not worth the effort. Secondly, although tribute and taxes still poured into the treasury, very little ever came out. Economic stagnation persisted without any just cause.

The Greek problem was the reverse: not stagnation, but constant political turbulence; not unquestioning fidelity to a central authority, but a quarrelsome search for consensus. Amid all the currents of Hellenic life, the imaginative leap of democracy was persisted with. In contrast, life around the Persian throne was paralysed by certitude. The loose ends of the empire, entangled in the west with Greece, were waiting to be snatched up and worked into a noose around the king. They very nearly were, and by a Persian prince. Before Darius II died, in 405 BC, Parysatis had advanced the fortunes of her favourite son, Cyrus, by having him appointed, at the age of eighteen, commander of all the Persian forces in Asia Minor. It was a position which could soon be cultivated into a powerful personal constituency, not only amongst Cyrus's own Persian troops but also in the Greek colonies and particularly with a Spartan, Lysander, who became his confidant. From here it was easy to foment criticism of the distant court and king.

Beware the event that becomes a parable, especially one beloved of Greeks *and* Persians. But the story of Cyrus the Younger is seductive: it serves well to illustrate the Persian lament of kingship gone to seed, and of the noble pretender who fails, and it well amplifies the Greek intolerance of Oriental manners. Two pieces of Greek literature in particular have exploited this opportunity: Xenophon's *Anabasis*, and Plutarch's *Life of Artaxerxes*. The solution, begging reliable account, is to see Cyrus and his revolt as important in themselves but even more telling in the attitudes they provoke. The portrayal is larger than the event.

Parysatis lurks at all times in the wings, scheming and switching loyalties. Plutarch has her thus at Pasargadae as her son Artaxerxes II is prepared for the coronation rites. Cyrus, the favourite, is there too, waiting to knife his brother before he is sanctified by the robes of Cyrus the Great. But the plot is betrayed. Artaxerxes orders his brother's execution but Parysatis 'by much lamentation and entreaty' wins a change of heart. Cyrus is spared and, astonishingly, sent back to his headquarters at Sardis.

So, the prelude. What of the respective characters? Cyrus is not misnamed. We are told of Lysander discovering him at work in his own park at Sardis, planting trees and landscaping in the classic Pasargadae style, and Lysander is, of course, incredulous. To the political shrewdness and military daring has been added gentility, surely rounding the character nicely. Xenophon says that under Cyrus's viceroyship travellers, Greek and Persian, could move without fear. And he sums up unequivocally: 'There has never been anyone, Greek or foreigner, more generally beloved.' Of Artaxerxes Plutarch writes: 'There was a certain dilatoriness which most people took for clemency ... he appeared to be altogether emulous of the gentleness of the Artaxerxes whose name he bore.' Examples are given of tolerated insubordination, surely an outrage in Persian courts. And Plutarch cites Cyrus, declaring his own *machismo* and damning his brother as 'too effeminate and cowardly either to sit his horse in a hunt or his throne in a time of peril'.

The brothers met in battle at Cunaxa, north of Babylon, in September 401 BC. Cyrus led a multi-national army of which the largest and toughest element was Greek. Amongst its officers was the young Xenophon, an adventurer disaffected by the democratic trends in his homeland. Initially the Greeks, though erratic, badly punished the

Persians. But Cyrus was personally over-bold, got trapped, and was killed. Artaxerxes also fell, wounded, but was revitalized by the news of his brother's death, and he ordered the body to be displayed. The insurgency was smashed and the surviving Greek mercenaries began their epic march home which is the substance of the *Anabasis*. Xenophon's story is self-serving, but the stuff of legend. Significantly the Greek accounts are at their most virulent on the subject of motivation. In one version Artaxerxes is so anxious to claim the battlefield honours that he eliminates anyone with a claim to having killed Cyrus; in another the same killings are attributed to Parysatis as revenge for the death of her favourite. The durable queen mother ingratiated herself with Artaxerxes and continued to arrange gruesome deaths for all who crossed her. But the king long outlived her, presiding over empire and dissolute court for forty-six years. At the end the whole edifice was undermined. Two kings, Artaxerxes III and Arses, followed in twenty-three years. Their successor was Darius III, last of the line.

A new force had risen in the west, Macedonia. The parable of Cyrus the Younger, whatever its colouring, rested on facts damning to Persia. The ruling family was corrupt, and prone to regicide. The empire's western provinces were fertile ground for revolt. And the weaknesses of the army exposed at Marathon and Plataea had not been remedied: in their first penetration of Babylonia the hoplites at Cunaxa had barely been contained by the Persians. From Macedonia all these debilities were very clear. Panhellenism, the doctrine of Greek Imperialism, waited on only two things – a resolution of Greece's own political schisms, and a leader to rip the Persian empire to pieces. In Philip of Macedonia came the answer to both. Philip had slowly intimidated the southern Greek states into quiescence, forging the conciliation necessary before beginning an eastern expedition. As Darius III came to the throne the first phase of an invasion was launched, a path-clearing operation into western Anatolia under the generalship of Parmenion. It was instantly successful. The Greek offshore islands and the coastal cities rose in revolt and were enrolled in the Hellenic League. But before this tentative liberation gained more momentum a tragedy intervened: the assassination of Philip. For a moment Panhellenism was forgotten, as Macedonian unity was threatened. Philip and his heir had been estranged, the court was thick with intrigue. The assassination has never been adequately explained. The heir had thought, probably from paranoia, that his succession was in jeopardy. Now he seized it, and this ceremony delayed resumption of the invasion which it fell to him to lead. His father had been a commander of rare qualities. Alexander had much to emulate.

3

Legend as History:
Alexander in Persia

331-330BC

Partiality is not prejudice: it hovers delicately
between preference and bias. The legend of
Alexander the Great has loaded history against the Persians. And it has
greatly reinforced the western preference for the Greeks, who called
everyone who did not speak their language barbarians. The propaganda began quite deliberately with Alexander himself. In Greece,
support for the expedition was lukewarm, in spite of the campaign
whipped up by the Panhellenists. Alexander anticipated the modern
art of news management by taking with him an official historian,
Callisthenes, whose priority was to enthuse opinion back in the homeland. He was but part of Alexander's itinerant academy: the retinue
included scholars, scientists, poets and – as the conquests grew – more
historians. But the later legend of Alexander fermented into idolatry
through the pens of western biographers. It was fed on material far
sounder than mere official propaganda. Alexander's battle companions wrote their own memoirs and those of two of them, Aristobulus and Ptolemy, survived in detail. They were written after
Alexander's death and Arrian, 450 years later, carefully drew on them
as sources.

Alexander looks different through Persian eyes. It is the same man, but with different ends. His genius is not disputed (he has entered Persian mythology, too). But to accept him also as an *exemplar*, as the paragon of Hellenic civilization, that is too much. For one thing, there are the ruins of Persepolis to remember. In fact, to counter the adoration of Alexander, Persian history has to fall back on stone fragments and fallible oral traditions. With no contemporary literary tradition to summon, Persians rely on the relatively recent sciences of archaeology and epigraphy to redress the picture, and their help is still sparse.

Professor Frye, who has been at pains to balance the Greek and Persian virtues, points out that Alexander was engaged in the political conquest of the world and that, therefore, he became, *de facto*, the symbol of Hellenism's penetration of the east. This is ironical, because Alexander was far from being the unalloyed ambassador of Athenian democracy. There are striking similarities between the Macedonia of Philip and Alexander, and Achaemenian Persia. Both were tribal kingdoms which had been unified by hereditary monarchies, and both benefited in battle from the toughness which the terrain had bred into their people. Macedonian kingship, like Achaemenian, was a parlous game and depended on the continued support of powerful sub-chieftains. But Aristotle had marked his pupil Alexander in a way that tempered this Macedonian background with new enlightenment, and a new respect for the principles of the Greek city-state. Perhaps this is why, when he encountered the very different Persian concept of cities, Alexander never quite managed to understand them, or the pastoral nomadic world beyond them.

And yet when the conquest was complete he made great efforts to be accepted by Persia and the Persians. He adopted Persian habits and even the imperiousness of Persian kings. It was this offence to Greek sensibility that provoked reproof from Cleitus, the lieutenant who had once saved Alexander's life in battle. In a famous scene, Cleitus could no longer stomach Alexander's regal airs, especially the Persian fashion for prostrating before the king, and accused him of betraying his own nationality. In an impulse he instantly regretted, Alexander slew Cleitus. In his subsequent remorse he realized how greatly he had offended his loyal companions. But he persisted with the idea of fusion, adopting Persian court dress, protocol and offices. Persian collaboration remained tepid. Robin Lane Fox, a biographer of Alexander, holds that the conqueror was attempting to graft Greek culture to the Persian machine: 'He felt that Greek culture was in some sense superior and should be encouraged as the culture of the court and of the king of Persia, which he became.' Professor Frye sees Alexander's policy as pragmatic: 'He would have had to conciliate the people who ran the empire, the bureaucracy.' Even more cautiously, Dr Shapur Shahbazi, the custodian of Persepolis, says that those Persians who did collaborate were never trusted; each was shadowed and guarded by a Macedonian: 'When Alexander went to India he took young Persians with him, allegedly to train them as soldiers, but actually as hostages.'

Much hinges on this matter of kingship. The Persian style of court has never been much regarded in the west: simply to use the phrase 'the barbarian king' is to damn it. Intriguingly, Herodotus goes to imaginative lengths to sustain the rationale behind Persian kingship, through the lips of Darius. In Herodotus's story of the succession, Darius examines the rival claims of democracy, oligarchy and monarchy and, naturally, extols the latter:

> One ruler: it is impossible to improve upon that – provided he is the best . . . where did we get our freedom from, and who gave it us? Is it the result of democracy, or of oligarchy, or of monarchy? We were set free by one man . . . we should refrain from changing ancient laws, which have served us well.

The rhetoric is suspiciously Athenian; from what we now know of Darius it is *most* unlike him. But Herodotus, alas, knew nothing of the adamantine inscriptions of Bisitun and had, instead, ascribed Darius's selection to a trick played with a horse's genitals!

Herodotus is always at his most aberrant when tempted by the supernatural. In the case of the Darius conspiracy he fused fantasy and, as it turned out, a good deal of circumstantial truth. But he is never phobic towards Persian kingship in principle (he lived under it) although his sympathies were elsewhere. We should remember that Herodotus lived at a time of truce between the two great powers. From the Aegean coast, where he was born, both the strengths and weaknesses of Greece and Persia were clear. Cyrus the Great fascinated him, and his portrait of him is heroic, almost Homeric. Supernatural events attend Cyrus's survival as a child, supernatural prescriptions attend his death. Cyrus can usually do no harm in classical eyes. The tendency is to see the Achaemenians as a power with benign origins which turned bad as soon as that power impinged upon Greece. Xenophon's biographical attempt, *The Education of Cyrus* (revered it is

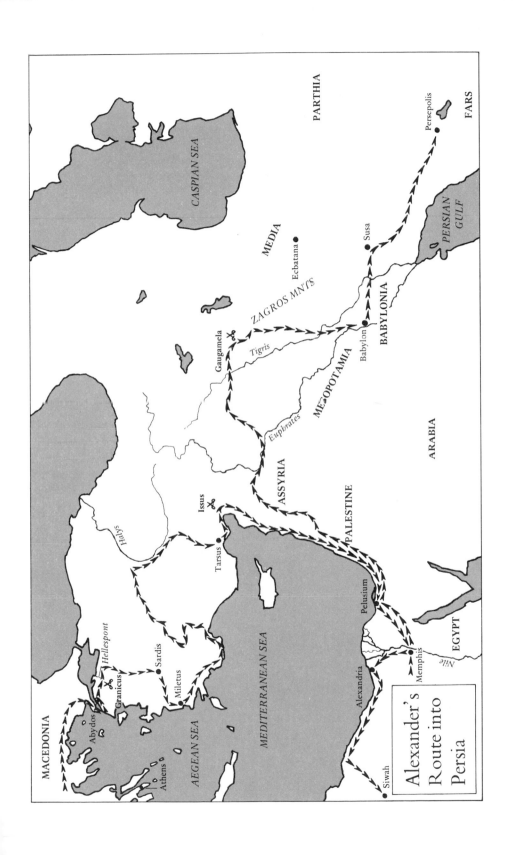

Alexander's Route into Persia

said by Caesar), is tedious hagiography, but in its epilogue it changes heart with indecent haste: 'No sooner was [Cyrus] dead than his sons were at strife, cities and nations revolted, and all things began to decay.' Well, Xenophon had a grudge. Arrian, who did not, reports that when Alexander, away on a campaign, was told that Cyrus's tomb had been robbed (by a Macedonian nobleman) he was so distressed that he broke away from the army and rode by the fastest route back to Pasargadae, where he ordered the tomb restored and the culprits caught and executed. Unfortunately the real culprit went free, having 'framed' a Persian prince. To Alexander, Cyrus was more than a monument. He was an exact forerunner, the first world conqueror and architect of syncretic rule. As the new king of Persia, whatever the tarnish of the later Achaemenians, it was natural for Alexander to look to the founding father for values and inspiration.

How far the royal line had deteriorated since Cyrus was made amply clear to Alexander. Before he crossed the Hellespont the extent of his ambitions was in doubt. The Panhellenists had posed three options, according to the capacity to achieve them: to liberate the Greek colonies in western Anatolia; to take the whole of Asia Minor; or – a seemingly fantastic extreme – to take Asia itself. The first two options were soon made tangible not only by conquest, but by Persia's reluctance to fight. Twice Darius III offered to cede territory, the first time all of Asia up to the river Halys, the second time 'all the territory from the Euphrates to the Greek sea'. Instead of accepting, Alexander disgraced Darius on the battlefield. First at the battle of Issus, on the hinge of Asia Minor and the Levant (the loss of his harem during this encounter had heightened Darius's taste for surrender) and then at Gaugamela in Babylonia, where Darius fled the field, surrendering his empire, and at the same time, drawing Alexander towards the realization of the final of the Panhellenist dreams.

At Gaugamela Alexander had been demonstrably outnumbered. Darius's army, concentrated on cavalry, overlapped the Greek front-line by a mile. A tactical plan of genius, later borrowed by both Marlborough and Napoleon, overcame the odds. It should be stressed that nothing less than genius would have been enough against the Persians. The two major battles and a lesser opening one at Granicus were marginal and Darius, for once, learned from mistakes at Issus well enough to daunt Alexander on the eve of Gaugamela. The horsemen whom Darius called from the reaches of the empire, particularly those from the north-eastern steppes, were the best cavalry in the world. Given finer leadership the work of genius on the other side might not have been enough.

There was another, much neglected, encounter to come as Alexander plunged through the Zagros mountains towards the heart of Fars. At the pass subsequently called the Persian Gates he was opposed by the satrap of Persia and governor of Persepolis, Ariobarzanes. The men of the original Persian lands had kept their toughness. Like the Spartans and Athenians at Plataea they had their backs to the roots and shrine of their nation. The Macedonians faltered, jammed in the pass, until a typical Alexander flanking movement, made with the help of a shepherd, caught the defenders from behind. What then lay ahead of Alexander was the site of old Anshan, the Marv Dasht plain – and Persepolis.

The sacking of Persepolis is Alexander's war crime. 'Bad policy,' says Arrian, in a rare moment of misgiving. 'It was absolutely necessary for Alexander to destroy it,' says Dr Shahbazi. 'As long as Persepolis was alive the Persians would not have submitted completely to Alexander, it would have always been a cradle to which the Persians would have looked.' The dilemma is crystallized in a fragment from Plutarch's Life of Alexander:

On seeing a huge statue of Xerxes, overturned by the hordes which had forced their way into the palace, Alexander stopped beside it and addressed it as if it were alive. 'Are we to pass you by', he said, 'and leave you lying on the ground because you campaigned against the Greeks, or are we to set you up again, because of your otherwise high-minded nature?' For a long while he stood by himself and thought the matter out in silence, but finally he passed on by.

Like all conquerors, Alexander had to choose between private sentiment and what was necessary for the public psychology. It went more deeply than avenging the burning of the Parthenon by Xerxes. Was Persia the barbarian redoubt his men had imagined, or something far less primitive and more impressive? The European army on its march must have sensed the difference in worlds as they reached Babylonia. After the hardness of their own mountain lands the Fertile Crescent was more bountiful than anything they had known. Greece, in comparison, was impoverished. Panhellenism had been fed on a version of *lebensraum*, and the invasion was advanced partly as a remedy for hard times. Alexander's men, once upon Persia, could not doubt it. At Susa, which they took without a fight, the treasury yielded fifty thousand talents of silver (they did not know this was merely the hors d'oeuvre) and many treasures which Xerxes had taken from Greece, including the bronze statues of Harmodius and Aristogeiton. Susa was certainly not the mark of a backward culture: there had been sophisticated urban life there for more than two thousand five hundred years before Alexander arrived. Darius's palaces had familiar Ionic touches. It was not a stage which the Macedonians could strut with any feeling of contempt. It was, in the most impressive sense, imperial. It was respected, and preserved. Why, then, was Persepolis marked out for harsher treatment?

It is said that Alexander described Persepolis to his troops, in advance, as 'the most hateful city in the world'. It is probable that as the Macedonians advanced across the Marv Dasht plain they liberated Greek prisoners who had been mutilated, as was the Persian habit, by the removal of their ears and noses. A mood of reprisal probably ran strong, and became uncontrollable. Before Persepolis itself was taken, many people, soldiers, women and children, living in the surrounding garrison and settlement were massacred. This episode was so repugnant to Arrian that in one of his rare acts of self-censorship he excluded it. The treasurer of the royal complex, watching the devastation from the high and fortified platform of Persepolis, decided that the palaces stood more chance of surviving if surrendered, and he opened the gates.

Alexander was able to march up the ceremonial staircase in triumph. The gold-plating on the rim of the roof and on the doors indicated an opulence surpassing anything he had yet seen. Inside, each of the hundreds of reliefs was hand-coloured, with real gems set into the costumes, and the necklaces, rings and amulets. Over the king's bed was a golden vine, dripping not with grapes but with jewels. But this was merely show. In the treasury lay another one hundred and twenty thousand talents of silver and eight thousand talents of gold, thousands of times the wealth of the wealthiest state in the Greek world. Economic conservatism had rendered Achaemenian riches nugatory; now, for Alexander, financing the conquest of the world was no longer a problem. He ordered ten thousand baggage animals and five thousand camels to carry off the loot, not to Greece but to Susa and Babylon, which already he was planning to use as the metropolises of the new world empire. Because of its remote location, Persepolis was of little use either for strategic reasons or for trade. Its fate – or use – therefore rested on its symbolic value, either to Persia or to Alexander.

The chronology leading to the destruction of Persepolis is unclear, but the systematic removal of the treasury suggests that Alexander lingered in the palaces wondering whether they could serve his reputation as well as they had that of the first Darius. The most histrionic version of his arson has a courtesan, Thais, urging it upon him during the dissipations of a banquet. Recent evidence postulates a far more prepared spectacle. High on the mountain behind Persepolis, at the site of the old defensive wall, archaeologists have found several replicas of the bulky inscribed foundation tablet of Xerxes, taken there from the treasury, curiously lying side by side. Dr Shahbazi believes they were used as grandstand seats while the palaces below burned and collapsed. No trace of burning has been found in the hillside garrison quarters, again suggesting that the army, having stripped the royal quarters, kept their own area for use afterwards. On the other hand, residential palaces some distance from the great platform of Persepolis and separated from it by a deep and wide dyke were burned, again indicating selection and control, rather than accident or impulse.

Forensic archaeology is not well advanced, but current evidence weighs heavily against Alexander. And this, in turn, inevitably hardens Persian opinion. As Dr Shahbazi puts it: 'I have every day to look at Persepolis and be reminded that it was built and it was burned. Alexander came and destroyed an empire. He took many things from us, and he gave us practically nothing.' Professor Frye is more generous: 'Alexander ushers in a new age into world history, the bringing together of different outlooks on life, of east and west. No matter what you say about him as a man, the consequences of the conquest brought together ideas and institutions in such a way that the world was changed.'

But one trophy eluded Alexander: Darius, alive. Fighting rearguard actions, accompanied by remnants of his army, the king had fled first to Media and then, when Alexander moved out from Persepolis in the spring of 330 BC, into the steppes of the north-west. His praetorian guard of nobles grew weary of the king's unwieldy entourage, and of the king himself. They slew him and ran into the mountains where, for a while, they proclaimed a new Achaemenian dynasty, which Alexander soon eliminated. A Macedonian advance party recovered

Darius's body, and Alexander had it interred in another rock-cut tomb at Persepolis, though at an undistinguished site. Darius was in his mid-forties when he succeeded to the already gravely jeopardized throne, and he occupied it for only six years. Unlike his illustrious forbears, he had not been seasoned in war and he had the bad luck to meet the ablest general in history. He is, inevitably, recorded as a coward. Ironically, he had taken the trouble to learn Greek, a sign of the increasingly cosmopolitan influence of Babylon and how the Greek and Persian worlds had intermingled well before Alexander's coming.

In the few years Alexander survived to spend in Persia he, too, realized the value of cross-fertilization. As the most extreme of several steps he took to encourage it, he organized at Susa a mass marriage between Macedonian soldiers and Persian girls. The ideal, about which he was probably sincere, was clear: Hellenism and the sensibility of Persia in concert; a dream beyond the savagery of conquest. But history was against him; the national identities were inimical.

4

The Guardians of the Sacred Flame

323BC-AD640

Weakened by wounds and gripped by fever, Alexander died in Babylon on 10 June 323 BC. He was thirty-two. He had not matched his own dreams, but he died a demi-god and became the most pervasive of legends. His immediate earthly succession was unprepared. His dominions were extensive: garrison cities had been founded in a chain across the northern reaches of the old Achaemenian empire, from Anatolia to India. But by the time he died these outposts had barely got their roots down; now the colonizers were left headless. For forty-two years Alexander's generals squabbled over possession of the empire. An effective settlement came only after a series of battles which left the inheritance divided: Egypt went to Ptolemy, the remainder was seized by Seleucis, Alexander's Macedonian cavalry commander.

Nominally, Greece had conquered the world. To the Seleucids fell the task of upholding Alexander's vision of civilizing the barbarians, of incorporating the subject peoples into a super-state governed by the Greek ideals, ordered by Greek laws, communicating in the Greek language and shaping its face with Greek art. But it was not to be all one-way; Alexander had, after all, succumbed to Persian ways and his master, Aristotle, had cautioned him: 'If you destroy them, you will have overthrown one of the greatest pillars of excellence in the world.' None the less, the Seleucids were convinced of their own supremacy, and they admitted local influences only as a garnish. Just how undiluted the Greek culture was in their colonies has been shown emphatically by the recent excavation of a city on the banks of the Oxus, straddling the border of Afghanistan and Russia, in what was once ancient Bactria. The place was replete with the classic Hellenistic institutions: Acropolis, palaces with Corinthian porticos, statuary, gymnasium, theatre and stadium, as well as a building dedicated to Hermes and Heracles, the gods of cleverness and *machismo*. All this more than three thousand miles from the Greek homeland, the Seleucid equivalent of British Gothic in India. In fact, the feeling is of a kind of Hellenistic *raj* in Asia – civilized, tolerant, but irredeemably patronizing. As with the *raj*, the 'natives' could be encouraged into emulation, into aping the style and manners of their rulers – but would the graft really take?

While it is true that neither the Seleucid cities nor the Persian life around them were mutually exclusive (nor mutually unimpressionable) the ultimate test of colonization was in the Greek order of urban society, the *polis*. After all, had not Aristotle inspired his brilliant pupil with the idea that the *polis* was the trigger to distinction, and the seed corn of the new world of Hellenism? Although the Seleucids reigned, with variable success, for one hundred and ninety years, nearly as long as the Achaemenians, the *polis* never took root in Persia. The cities were Greek islands in an Oriental sea. Perhaps there was something eternally different in the Persian idea of a city. Although they built 'imperial' cities, like Susa, the Persians did not create cultural capsules, micro-societies in the Greek manner. A Persian city was usually a junction of worlds, not the distillation of one world and, like Persia itself, a place between worlds, not of them.

There was also an inherent contradiction between the political and economic functions of these Seleucid cities. On the one hand, they were meant as models of the *polis*; on the other hand, they were strung out from west to east along the inter-continental trade routes and, therefore, constantly exposed to exotic ideas. They could not be confidently chauvinistic under such conditions. Their identities were apt to get confused, and those cities at the global extremities were pulled in opposite directions. At the eastern extreme the colonies in

Bactria went as far as declaring their independence and developing an association with the Buddhist empire of the Mauryans which dominated India. In the west, Seleucid power was threatened by hostility from Egypt, and by the appearance from the steppes of a tribe called the Parni.

Moving down from the eastern side of the Caspian, the Parni settled in Iran after the death of Alexander. Although semi-nomadic, they began to absorb the culture of the plateau and founded their own cities and a Persian-style hereditary monarchy, the Arsacids. The Seleucid kings were poorly placed to handle problems on such a broad front; with Egypt and Bactria on their minds they could little comprehend that the Parni were, in embryo, a resurgent Persian empire. In the Seleucid centres at Antioch in Syria and Seleucia on the Tigris in Babylonia the idea of such a phenomenon being possible was probably fantastic.

From the nucleus of their first settlements the Parni gradually extended the territory under their control until they swallowed the whole of the old satrapy of Parthia. And they took this name for themselves. Between 228 BC and 200 BC, two Seleucid kings were forced to lead armies against the assumptive Parthians to contain their expansion. A truce was struck which held for several decades, in which Seleucid power recovered under King Antiochus IV. In 171 BC the Parthian throne passed to a new king, Mithradates. At first, Mithradates was circumspect, knowing the strength of Antiochus. But after the Seleucid king's death in 163 BC the Parthians were led on a series of campaigns of conquest, first in the east and then in the west, where they gained control of Media. This severed the main artery of the Seleucid empire. More important, it brought the north of the plateau into contact again with the south, after a long period when the band of Seleucid settlement had divided them. Persia's north–south axis, symbolized originally by the union of the Medes and Persians, had been broken by the Greeks, on the principle of divide and rule.

By the time Mithradates acquired control of Media, the Achaemenians could have been little more than a hazy, distant memory, but it was memory that kept alive Persian history through the western occupation. In the hundred and sixty years since the humiliation of Darius III, the Greek veneer had replaced the Persian fabric but it had not seduced the Persian heart. By what means the national epic was nourished is not clear, but the oral tradition was crucial. Only as they first penetrated the plateau could the Parthians have discovered the juxtaposition of two inimical legends, those of Alexander and Darius the Great. In Media, at Bisitun, they would have found evidence of both at the same site: by the road a bibulous Heracles, reclining on a lion, and above, on the cliff face, Darius's great inscription. Here was both an interloper to assault and an 'ancestor' to venerate. Sure enough, the Parthians suddenly appropriated an Achaemenian royal lineage.

The Parthians have been overlooked and underrated by history, possibly because they are caught between the afterglow of Alexander, and Persia's last pre-Islamic dynasty the Sasanians. Some historians believe that the Sasanians, when they could, deliberately erased the record of the Parthians to consolidate their own place in the folk memory – and as the rightful heirs of the Achaemenians. There is now a mood of redress: 'The Parthians,' says Dr Shahbazi, 'were the most noble of all the Iranians.'

They owe what prominence (or notoriety) they have enjoyed in the west mainly to one fact: they fought and checked the Romans. The Seleucids, too, had engaged the Romans, who defeated Antiochus IV at Magnesia in 189 BC. The shadow of Rome gradually superseded that of Greece. And as Roman interest in the east developed it was the Parthians, and not the Seleucids, who held the bastion of Babylonia. By 141 BC, Mithradates controlled much of Mesopotamia and Babylonia, driving the Seleucids back into Syria. But for a while the Parthians inherited the dangers as well as the land of the Seleucid empire, particularly the vulnerability to incursions by the tribes in the wild north-east.

Eight years after Mithradates died in 138 BC, his empire was seriously undermined by these raiders (one tribe of whom were the resilient Massagetae). On the verge of being overwhelmed by nomads in the east, and in the west by internal rebellions, the Parthians rebounded under Mithradates II, around 124 BC. Both the western and the eastern limits of the empire were regained, and with them Parthian confidence in their Persian inheritance. To celebrate it, Mithradates carved his own plaque at Bisitun, in the manner of Darius, with himself assigning powers to his nobles. And during his reign the old Achaemenian title 'King of Kings' reappears on Parthian coins (and with it the bogus Achaemenian genealogy).

Although the Parthians were established as a world power, Rome seemed arrogantly unaware of their weight. Around 95 BC the Roman general Sulla arrived on the banks of the Euphrates, assessing the lie of the land. He signed a form of 'non-aggression' treaty with the Parthians, but was dismissive of Parthian calibre. An uneasy co-existence persisted for a while. The west, rather than the east, still dominated Rome's ambitions: within the next century the legions would reach London, and the European colonization find its natural limits. What mattered in the east were the increasingly valuable trunk routes, and especially the new Silk Road established between China and Rome. The value of this to Parthian Persia was immense, the ancient equivalent of striking oil. The silk traffic provided an abundant source of customs revenues, as well as transmitting cultures and ideas. The Parthians were the brokers between east and west, ensuring the security of the caravans, and making sure that Rome had no direct contact with China.

By the middle of the last century BC, the aristocratic alliance which had run republican Rome was giving way to a fight for personal control, and one of the contenders saw personal gain in an eastern adventure. The ageing Crassus needed a military success to equal or surpass that of his rivals, Caesar and Pompey. From his base as the governor of Syria, Crassus – against the pronounced sentiment of Rome – decided to challenge the Parthians. In the spring of 53 BC he took an army of forty thousand men across the Euphrates. Two strikingly dissimilar traditions of warfare were on a collision course. By chance, the contrast was greater than it might have been.

A new weapon appears, and one that armies from Asia to northern Europe eventually had to adopt in order to survive: heavy cavalry, horse and rider armoured like tanks. Its genesis lay in the steppes. When nomads like the Parni settled for the first time, their best horses could be stall-fed from grain crops instead of living, winter and summer, in the open and on whatever food could be grazed. As a result, a new breed of horse was developed. It was larger, and had more stamina. It could outlast the fleeter nomadic horse and, given the armour, become devastating. This innovation was called the cataphract, meaning 'bulwarked'. In the eighth century, Europe was to be saved for Christendom by the timely adoption of the cataphract, to stem the Arab armies.

The Parthian army which Crassus faced had only a quarter the number of his Roman legions; the main Parthian force, under King

Orodes, had gone to wait for him in Armenia, and Crassus had been soundly advised to follow it there because the hills would favour his infantry. The Parthians had left a small covering force in Mesopotamia under a young general called Suren. This had very few infantry. But it had two complementary arms of cavalry – the light cavalry, who were expert archers, and the cataphracts. When Crassus was told that Suren's force was near by in the neighbouring desert, it was too much of a temptation. Rather than turn north into Armenia, and towards Orodes, he impulsively gave chase to Suren.

The Romans were given no chance to rest. They plunged into the desert, and below the town of Carrhae they found Suren. The cataphracts, lancers as encrusted with mail as their horses, attacked the Romans before they had time to complete their classic defensive square. After the first charge the Parthian lancers withdrew, and the archers moved in. Their bows were more powerful than those of the Romans, and the arrows pierced shields, breastplates and greaves. To the Romans' amazement, the Parthians fired arrows accurately over their shoulders as they retreated – 'the Parthian shot'. But even then Roman morale held, in the expectation that the arrows would soon be exhausted. But Suren had provided against such a contingency; baggage camels kept in the rear were laden with supplies of arrows. The Romans, hardened by experience, technique and discipline, were given no chance to engage this enemy as they were used to doing – at close quarters. The cataphracts could not be repulsed, and the archers stayed out of reach. In desperation, Crassus sent his son on a diversionary raid, but all that returned was his head, impaled on a lance, to be displayed before the beleaguered Romans. Under cover of night the survivors of Crassus's legions fell back to Carrhae. Rather than depend on the dubious loyalty of the town's Greek population, the Romans again fled by night, making for the Armenian hills. Two contingents, one led by Cassius, the future assassin of Caesar, reached safety. But Crassus, with the bulk of the survivors, was tricked into a parley with Suren, and killed in a scuffle. Ten thousand Romans had escaped: ten thousand were taken captive; twenty thousand died. Parthian casualties were light. Legend gives Crassus a grisly end: his head, substituted for a stage prop, delivered in the middle of a performance of Euripides's *Bacchae* before the Parthian king and his Armenian ally. Naturally, the victory acquired the aura of giant-killing. In fact, it intimated two flaws in the Parthian regime. The first was – at least with a man of Orodes's temperament on the throne – that conspicuous personal success was dangerous. A little later, Suren was murdered on the king's orders. Secondly, the full potential of Parthian military technique was seldom realized, because the armies were (as had been Suren's) more the creatures of the nobles than of the king. This lack of concerted and central control plagued Parthian affairs.

None the less, Rome continued to suffer at the hands of Parthia's partisan armies. In 36 BC Mark Antony lost thirty-five thousand men out of a force of around one hundred thousand during an abortive campaign into Azerbaijan. Augustus had urged restraint in dealing with Parthia; six years after Mark Antony's retreat he visited Syria to direct the border policy at first hand. Armenia and western Mesopotamia became buffer zones between the two powers, and were recurrently overrun by each side, as is often the fate of buffer zones. During the remaining two and a half centuries of Parthian rule the Romans were never able to establish themselves east of the Tigris.

Inevitably, the classical accounts of the Parthians are dominated by the east–west conflict. But this distorts both Parthian achievements and Parthian priorities. Strategically, the eastern frontier was much more demanding and difficult to hold. Battles there were frequent and bloody, though little documented. Internally, the nation was as weak or as strong as its king, and in nearly four centuries the quality of those was uneven. As the early Achaemenians had borrowed from proximate sources, so the early Parthians followed Seleucid practices. But gradually the ancient order of the plateau reappeared through kingship and the social structure, with a marked Median influence. Aristocratic families, the Surens among them, deferred only to the king, and then with some equivocation.

The Parthian achievement was, in part, to hold such a competitive alliance together. The king had nothing like the omnipotence of an Achaemenian monarch. In the further reaches of the plateau his authority was distant and nominal. Perhaps what glued things together was the constant danger from outside. It was the warrior nobles, each served by lifelong companions, riding superbly into battle on their armoured horses, who provided the dynamics, and the style. At Carrhae Suren had a bodyguard of a thousand knights *and* a well-endowed harem. These were not men of the Persian heartland, but northern buccaneers risen to worldly airs. No matter: they refurbished the Persian heart, they subsumed the Greek conqueror, and they made possible the ultimate Persian resurrection. Many centuries later, when the Persian laureate Firdausi compiled his version of the national epic, his cursory treatment of the Parthians was followed by the apology: 'Since their roots and branches were short one cannot say that their past was illustrious. I have heard'nought but their names and have not seen them in the chronicle of kings.'

As scholars bend more diligently to recover Parthian works we find more than military inspiration, and more than the incubation of past glories. We find evidence, tangibly, of an architectural idea without which Persian and Islamic building would lack its classic form. The exact roots are still obscure, but Parthian buildings reveal the development of the *iwan*, a great hall with its front open to the sky and, usually, a barrel-vaulted roof. The Parthian *iwans* open on to court-yards, as the nomadic tents might once have opened on to the camp fire (the similarity is emotive but unscientific!). In at least one instance, at Assur on the Tigris, a palace has been traced with *iwans* opening from each of the *four* sides of a courtyard, precisely anticipating the plan of Persian mosques eight centuries later. Structurally, the striking feat is the arching barrel-vault stemming directly from the walls, a great canopy of brick holding itself up and containing its own stresses. This created the three-sided hall, the first structure really to embrace and control the climate: full of light, yet airy and cool.

In giving flight to brick, the Parthians left behind the Greek depen-dence on columns. During the first century AD, the column in Parthian buildings becomes an adornment, ingested by walls, instead of func-tioning as a support. How were these vaults possible? Not by using scaffold (wood was scarce and expensive) but by a new technology: quick-drying gypsum mortar. Gypsum cement was made by heating the parget stone, indigenous to Mesopotamia, and mixing the deposit of powder with water. The mortar set so rapidly that the bricks were secure almost as soon as they were put in place. Thus was rectangular architecture 'liberated' into a new plastic phase; a watershed of ancient and medieval building. The same gypsum, perhaps mixed in varying formulas to control the speed of drying, produced the stucco plaster which enabled a new virtuosity in surface decoration, the designs shaped *in situ*, and then brilliantly coloured, another hallmark of first-century Parthian cities. This love of colour, the legacy of the nomadic eye, explodes in a controlled miniature scale on the rhytons, horn-shaped vessels carved from elephant tusks, which have been reconstructed from fragments found at Nisa, in the tribe's old pasture grounds (now in Russia). The rhytons are studded with polychromatic glass, silver and bronze. On a different scale, the bronze cast of an oversize Parthian warrior-lord, unearthed at Shami in southwest Persia, is art used to portray the full, physical *charisma* of the empire.

So Parthian society had developed depth enough to leave its own considerable seam of Persian art, only now being adequately explored and valued. The rude aspect of the Parthians emphasized by the classical writers will, perhaps, begin to mellow. Ironically, the heights of Parthian architecture seem to have coincided with the military and political degeneration of the empire. The plateau itself became so prone to anarchy that the east–west trade was diverted through India and the southern sea–land route to Rome. The fragile consensus of monarch and nobles had, apparently, ruptured. A great plague (suffered alike by Chinese, Parthians and Romans and carried into Europe) afflicted the western borders, and in the east, from both north and south, tribal risings exploited the collapse of central authority. This debility determined far more than the end of Parthian rule in Persia; by its nature it shaped the future. One style of kingship was discredited; another, heedful of the dangers, took its place. In the early third century, world history was redirected by a dynasty whose traditions had been protected for centuries by geographical remoteness.

Not long after Alexander's death, southern Persia found itself distant from the attentions of the Seleucids – and the world. Control of such distant parts was, at best, arm's length, invested in a satrap working with the local aristocratic families. The province of Fars, with its illustrious associations, was not long in exploiting the looseness of Seleucid rule. As early as 280 BC there was an uprising in the province (confirmed by evidence found at Pasargadae). It became, in effect, an independent principality, where the local dynasts issued their own coins, bearing atavistic names like Darius and Artaxerxes. The social order in Fars may well have reverted to something similar to the tribal monarchies from which Cyrus sprang. Unmolested by the conflicts to the north, this society preserved its stability and traditions for a very long while. Curiously enough, local identification with the Achaemenians became tenuous and shaped more by legend than fact, perhaps the enduring cost of the trauma inflicted by Alexander. Between the ruins of Persepolis and Pasargadae a new provincial capital rose, called

Istakhr. Exactly how conscious its citizens were of being the guardians of Persia's first golden age we cannot know; but a flame *was* kept burning in Istakhr, at the temple of Anahita, the Zoroastrian provider of water.

At the turn of the second and third centuries, the provincial king of Fars was one Papak, erstwhile keeper of the Anahita shrine. In AD 208, Papak's son Ardashir succeeded to the throne. The court was ritualistic, without a bureaucratic tradition, and modest in keeping with its relatively small dominion. But Ardashir's horizons were far wider. He had watched the debasement of Parthian rule: all over the plateau villagers and nobles alike were withdrawing into fortified enclaves to gain protection from either the caprice of an addled court or from the ravages of freely roaming brigands. In this chaos, Ardashir did not follow the pattern of retrenchment. He saw, instead, an opportunity. The order and security of Fars could be served better by a broadening of authority. His policy was to absorb, either by force or alliance, the adjacent kingdoms and thereby to forge a new kind of power-sharing regime, with himself at the head of it. His dynasty took its name from his grandfather, Sasan.

Treading the delicate line between conquest and conciliation, Ardashir began reassembling the Persian state. By 224 he had narrowed his opponents to one: Ardewan, the last of the Parthian kings. Ardewan accused Ardashir of usurping his power, to which Ardashir replied in a tone typical of his nature: 'This throne and this crown were given me by God. He has given me victory over these kings. I hope that I will also be victorious over you, to take your head and use your treasures for adorning fire temples.' There are almost echoes of 'Ahuramazdá bore me aid'. The threat was made good in the most personal way: after smashing Ardewan's army ('I shall attack you on the plain of Hormizdjan at the end of the month – prepare') Ardashir and Ardewan resolved the future of Persia by fighting in single combat, two mailed figures circling each other in the vast desert arena in the heroic style of a medieval joust, with an empire hanging on the result. Ardewan was bludgeoned to death with a club. That day, Ardashir took the title King of Kings, knowing full well what it meant. The Sasanian dynasty lasted four centuries. In that time the art of kingship was elaborated and refined into a cosmic force.

It was Ardashir's particular genius that he made grandiloquence practical rather than offensive. The mystique that he invoked may now seem extravagant, but he realized that for one man to be unequal *above* all others he must acquire the aura of divinity. Or, as Professor Peter Brown puts it:

You aren't a king just by being a god, you are a king by acting like a god. In a society of sub-kings, where every one of them thinks he is the equal of everyone else, they have to agree that one person is top dog – 'majesty' is an agreement to cut down competition, to allow one man to be the King of Kings.

In realizing this, Ardashir was curing the Parthian failing of unresolved leadership. Other power structures had grappled with the same problem. Roman autocracy had supplanted Roman republicanism. At the time Ardashir came to power, the dispersion of Roman power and the Greek currents running strongly within the empire were slowly dividing Rome into two cells, each capable of taking on a life of its own, east breaking from west in substance and style. What *was* the eastern style of rule? When the Parthians improvised their dynasty they had not only reached hazily for an Achaemenian connection, they had also imbibed enough of the Greek surroundings to style themselves the 'Phil-hellenes'. This intermingling of traditions went further back: the later Seleucids are suspected of divine aspiration; their court included the Achaemenian concept of the 'house of the king', a privileged family caucus. The confluence of royal, bureaucratic and religious claims to authority created rivalries which were hard to reconcile, and which created a threat to secular kingship. And then there was the theological authority; until the Sasanians appeared, the Magi of Persia kept the 'Good Religion' of Zoroastrianism alive independently of kings. It was the salient innovation of the Sasanians to incorporate religion and state. We can see in this the shrewd self-interest of the king: if god and king were indivisible, the divinity of the king was beyond challenge. Across the variegated empire two – and only two – forces could focus loyalty: god, and a god-like king. The sacred flame of the temple at Istakhr became the king's flame as well as Ahuramazda's.

But the personal embodiment of 'majesty' was not enough. It needed an arena, it had to be displayed – or, in terms we understand, it had to be *broadcast*. How was this to be done? When a Persian king considered his image, he turned to architecture, the most evident extension of the man and his style. Ardashir's architecture, like that of Cyrus and Darius, was a personal statement. But it shows a different kind of mind, responding to different problems. Ardashir's sense of theatre was superb, and the theatre he chose was Fars itself, a landscape combining harmony and dissonance. His first palace, the Qaleh–i–Dokhtar, was built like an eyrie atop the sheer face of a gorge, a gorge through which his subjects had to pass on journeys from north to south, and as they did so they would look up in awe at the symbol of royal power.

And there the palace still remains, ruptured by earthquakes but still holding together the core not only of Ardashir's *hubris*, but also of a new architectural form: the *iwan* – and the dome. For here is the oldest surviving dome of real size, the forerunner of every dome in the Islamic world. It was fashioned from rough-hewn rock and the remarkable gypsum plaster. And already it had solved the problem of mounting a dome on a square base: Qaleh–i–Dokhtar's dome resolves the geometry of plane and bowl with the 'squinch', in which the surfaces fuse.

A true moment of genesis, or not? The technique is Parthian, not Sasanian. But we have no Parthian domes, not one. We can only tell what the Parthians must have achieved by knowing what the Sasanians *already* knew. It is very doubtful that the Sasanian dome was a single leap, without antecedents (in the same way that we cannot tell if the *iwan* was, *sui generis*, Parthian or, possibly, Median). The probability must be that there were Parthian domes before Qaleh–i–Dokhtar, and that by achieving the forms of Ardashir's palace the Sasanians show what a fine culture they superseded.

Though important, this quibble does not diminish Ardashir's performance: the great vaulted hall of the palace opened on to the skyline and demonstrated that the king was truly master of all he surveyed. To reach his presence, visitors had first to climb a steep side track, tether their horses, pass through a large courtyard and the intervening protocol until, going from stark light into the shade of the hall they caught the flash of gold, felt under them the opulence of carpets and prostrated themselves before the King of Kings. Here was the living focus of the Persian resurrection, having won by arms and force of personality the consent of the powerful to direct their power himself. In little more than a decade, Ardashir received the homage of all the sub-kings of the plateau – at least, all but one.

In the mountain province of Tabaristan, far on the plateau's

The oldest surviving dome in Persia is poised on top of a gorge, split by earthquakes. This is the palace of Qaleh-i-Dokhtar, built by Ardashir I at the inauguration of the Sasanian dynasty. The dome is combined with a square base, the two fused by means of the squinch, an architectural innovation that anticipated by centuries the form of the Persian mosques.

northern rim, Gusnap the king sent a message to Ardashir complaining of ruthless imperialism, and especially of the destruction of rival fire temples. Gusnap made it clear that he would never submit to the King of Kings. And because of Gusnap's audacity, we have a rare and instructive insight into the philosophy of Sasanian kingship. The missive from the north provoked a detailed reply, and this was written by a man who held a significant new office in Ardashir's court, a combination of priest and mandarin. The Letter of Tansar, named after its author, has tantalized scholars since it was luckily recovered in a thirteenth-century translation by a Persian muslim. Modern opinion on its true origin is still divided; the most likely explanation is that the bulk of the letter dates from Ardashir's time, but that it was supplemented and re-promulgated much later in the Dynasty, when the mainsprings of Sasanian rule were felt in need of reinforcement. In essence, the letter is a manifesto naked in the arrogance (and assurance) of Sasanian power.

The directive to Gusnap is explicit: 'My counsel to you is to take horse and come with crown and throne to the king's court. Know and understand that a crown is what *he* sets upon your head and a realm is that which *he* entrusts to you ... if any man come submissively before us, seeking to walk upright on the highway of obedience, we shall not deprive him of the title of king.' The new anatomy of Sasanian power is spelled out: 'Church and State were born of the one womb, joined together and never to be sundered.' And under that regime, the dual divinity, the social order is stratified exactly into four estates:

The first estate is that of the clergy; and this estate is further divided among judges and priests, ascetics, temple-guardians and teachers. The second estate is military, the fighting men, of whom there are two groups, cavalry and foot-soldiers. Within them are differences of rank and function. The third estate is that of the scribes, and they too are divided into groups, such as writers of official communications, accountants, recorders of verdicts and writers of chronicles; physicians, poets and astronomers are numbered among their ranks. The fourth estate is that of the artisans, tillers of land and herders of cattle and merchants and others who earn their living by trade. It is through these four estates that humanity will prosper as long as it endures.

Carefully regulated stations in society were a Sasanian obsession: they held things in place against the ever-threatening virus of anarchy. And the cost of that was clear within living memory. The collapse of good order followed the displacement of social stations, and Tansar

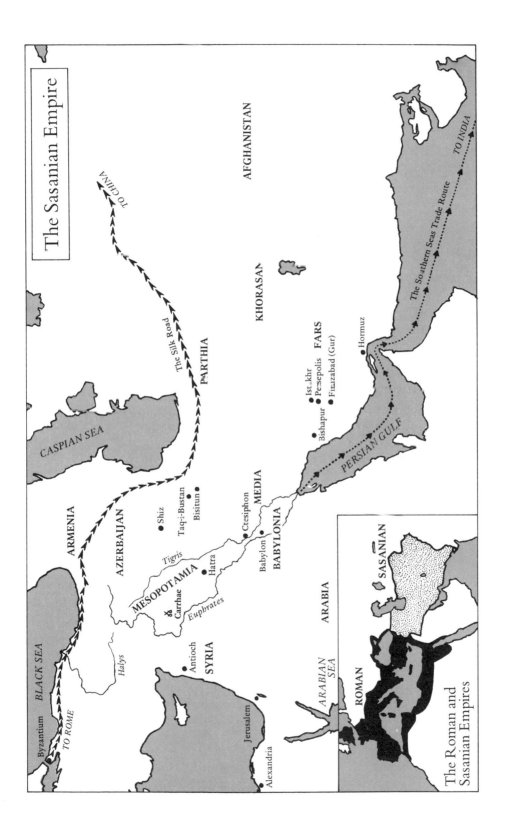

The Sasanian Empire

TO CHINA

AFGHANISTAN

The Silk Road

PARTHIA

KHORASAN

CASPIAN SEA

FARS
Ist-khr
Persepolis
Bishapur
Firuzabad (Gur)

Hormuz

The Southern Seas Trade Route

TO INDIA

ARMENIA

AZERBAIJAN

• Shiz
Taq-i-Bustan
• Bisitun

MEDIA

Ctesiphon

PERSIAN GULF

Tigris

MESOPOTAMIA
• Hatra

Babylon

BABYLONIA

Carrhae

Euphrates

BLACK SEA

Byzantium

TO ROME

Halys

• Antioch

SYRIA

• Jerusalem

ARABIA

ARABIAN SEA

• Alexandria

SASANIAN

ROMAN

The Roman and
Sasanian Empires

left no doubt of the king's sanctions: 'The more punishment he inflicts to make each estate return to its own sphere, the more praise he will receive.' But even-handed *predictable* justice was too lenient. Like Machiavelli later, Ardashir had discovered the terror of calculated caprice: 'Sometimes one should exact death for a transgression which merits and deserves pardon, and sometimes pardon a transgression which demands death.' We may well bridle at this, but the fact is that it could be advanced as a *principle* of 'strong government'. For only a god-like figure could choose between mercy and severity.

Harsh realities dictated harsh measures. Any Persian empire faced a problem of basic stability. The Achaemenians and the Parthians had suffered it, so now did the Sasanians. The empire had two parts, its ethnic heartland and its volatile, polyglot satellites. Unless the centre held, the rest would be lost. To leave the heartland the king had first to make sure of his authority there. The king's 'eyes and ears' returned. Gusnap had complained: 'The King of Kings has set informers and spies over the people of the land, and this has filled all men with fear and stupefaction.' Tansar replied: 'Innocent and upright men have nothing to dread.' Gusnap was unpersuaded; Tabaristan did not submit to Ardashir. Perhaps the truculent manifesto had an element of bluff. Faced with implacable resistance, Ardashir preferred the pen to the sword.

To the west the collapse of Parthian power gave Ardashir swift possession of the Fertile Crescent. Ctesiphon, the new city on the Tigris that had superseded Babylon, fell to the Sasanians in 226. Economically, Mesopotamia remained the Persian milch-cow. Strategically, the east, both in Central Asia and the Indian subcontinent, was the real danger. As with the Parthians, western histories of the Sasanians are coloured by the Roman wars. Although Sasanian kings appreciated the kudos to be gained by deflating the Romans, they knew the high cost of neglecting their eastern borders. Dreadful things happened there. The Persians might have been barbarians to the Greeks and Romans, but in Persia the real barbarians were the rude tribes of the steppes who seemed always to be unravelling the marches of the empire.

To see the world through Ardashir's eyes we need to understand geography in a way made difficult in our own age. Those stoical nineteenth-century adventurers who began reconstructing the fabric of the ancient world were far closer than we to its reality. Like the

The irrigation techniques of the Persians, which had drawn on many sources,
found further inspiration from the Roman prisoners brought back by the
victorious Sasanian armies. The extensive water-works at the city of Shushtar, in
south-west Iran, still show some of the bridge-dams and water-ducts built by the
Romans which greatly improved agriculture.

ancients, they were earthbound and constrained to the same horizons and same immutability of distance and time. Their perspective was far humbler than ours, as we shape our judgements by the living relief map unrolling thirty thousand feet below. They had to share with their subject many of the physical dangers now removed by the immunized cultural capsules in which we 'travel' across the epic landscapes. We need to come back to earth, and our feet, to see how the plateau imposed a recurrent course on events, on how men lived, moved, fought and survived.

The nineteenth-century historian Sir Percy Sykes caught sensibly the vulnerability of the Sasanian north-east, simply by climbing to the top of a ridge in Khorasan and writing: 'From the west I looked across the yellow plain, stretching westward in level monotony, and was struck by its immensity; for I realized that it extended as far as the tundra and the distant Arctic Ocean, with no intervening hill.' The Silk Road, as fragile as a gossamer thread, travelled through this migrational corridor. The prestige and wealth of Persia depended on being able to ensure the safety of the caravans, and in having monopoly control of the route. The trade had been lost once when the Romans by-passed the Parthians by using the monsoon route in the Indian Ocean. The Sasanians were determined to sustain both the new southern sea routes, to the profit of the Persian Gulf, and the land routes across the north and into the catchment of Ctesiphon.

Overland travel was arduous. Professor Brown says: 'A world so large was oppressed by the sense of distance. The huge horizons opened out by the geographical position of the Sasanian empire were enough to dispirit any traveller within the empire itself. The edges of the kingdom were immeasurably far away by modern standards: it took a party two months and eight days to travel from the mountains of Armenia in the north to the court of Ctesiphon.'

Fars, which had hibernated for five hundred years as a cul-de-sac, was suddenly well placed for the new combination of northern land routes and southern sea traffic. Two miles to the south of the gorge where Ardashir built his first palace, a new Sasanian city arose at Firuzabad. Its circular shape symbolized the spirit of being at the centre of the world: at each of the four points of the compass a gate led out to a trade route – to China, to India, to Arabia and to Rome. A society as dependent as this one on open connections with the world could not help but be catholic in its tastes; the consolidation of church and state in

Sasanian Persia did not preclude tolerance of alien religions. 'It was', says Professor Brown, 'a pluralistic society, made up of a shimmering mosaic of differing cultures and religions. Subjects of the Sasanian empire felt they could go anywhere and do anything.' Perhaps it was that kind of confidence (when things went well) that enabled the society to be so tolerant.

But there were less tolerant periods of conflict and bloodletting. For example, there were two eruptions of heresy. The first came in the reign of Ardashir's son, Shapur. A religious visionary called Mani appeared from a village near Ctesiphon with a pessimistic new creed, that the world was the dominion of evil rather than of good forces, and that redemption could come only from a severe, celibate existence. It was the antithesis of Zoroastrianism (hence, possibly, its appeal) but it was also a sign that in Mesopotamia, in contrast to the plateau, there was a strong sense of rival theologies, western and Oriental. For a while, Mani was accepted at Shapur's court, and became a threat to the established priests. But they regained their influence and put Mani to a slow and diabolic death, confirming, no doubt, his expectation. Manichaeism was not snuffed out so easily. It gained converts as far as Europe and China. After passing through Byzantium, Armenia and Bulgaria it surfaced in twelfth-century Europe as the great Albigensian heresy, only extinguished by the Inquisition: 'If the blood of martyrs were really the seed of the Church,' wrote one scholar, 'Manichaeism would now be the dominant religion of Europe.'

The second heresy, Mazdakism, was very different, a kind of positive radicalism which bred on a period of unrest at the end of the fifth century, when Sasanian Persia was ravaged by famine, drought and military defeat. Mazdak was, in effect, a communist and, in the context of his time, a full-blooded revolutionary. 'The rich and the powerful', he preached, 'are the same as the empty-handed poor'; the granaries of the nobles should be opened and the contents given to the community. In a direct assault on Zoroastrian orthodoxy, Mazdak insisted on breaking the custom of inter-marriage among the aristocracy and he wanted the wives forcibly re-married into the peasantry. Astoundingly, this doctrine was approved by the idiosyncratic King Kavadh, though possibly more from a cynical and expedient wish to gain popular support against the nobility than from conviction. At any rate, the indulgence ended in 524 with Mazdak's murder and a purge of his followers.

These were stresses within an empire that carried the weight of world power. As Cyrus had been followed in Darius by a consolidator, so was Ardashir followed in Shapur by a similar talent. He inherited the throne in 242 with a campaign against Rome in progress. For three more centuries the buffer zones of Armenia and the Euphrates were to be disputed in war with Rome. In a success culture like Persia, Roman defeats were, though possibly less taxing than the border wars of the east, invaluable as trophies to embellish the aura of the king. Roman pride was no less at stake. But the attrition of these wars served neither side in the long run; indeed, it weakened them like a drawn-out and terminal infection.

The Roman chronicles leave a mixture of awe and abhorrence. Ammianus Marcellinus, on Shapur II: 'The power of heaven had given the king an enormous self-confidence that all the besieged would be paralysed with fear at the mere sight of him.' On the Emperor Julian's speech to his army before he died at Persian hands: 'We must wipe out a most troublesome nation, on whose swords the blood of our kinsmen is not yet dry.'

Shapur's first campaign concluded with the death of the Roman commander Gordian and his succession as Emperor by Philip the Arab, who ceded Armenia to Persia. In a second campaign, probably in 256, the Romans lost an army of sixty thousand men and Shapur swept Syria and Cappadocia. In 259 he crushed another army and captured the Emperor Valerian, who died from his wounds in captivity. Here was the stuff of a propaganda carnival: Shapur ordered a relief to be carved at Naqsh–i–Rustam under the tombs of the Achaemenian kings, showing Valerian cowering before the King of Kings, with a truculent inscription: 'Valerian Caesar came against us with seventy thousand men ... we fought a great battle ... we took Valerian the Caesar with our own hands, and the provinces of Syria, Cilicia and Cappadocia. We burned with fire, we ravaged and conquered them, taking their peoples captive.' Like the Persians at Marathon and Plataea, the Romans seem not to have adapted their tactics to deal with the Persian order of battle. The Sasanians had made the cataphract even more terrifying: 'And when the first gleam of dawn appeared, everything so far as the eye could reach shone with glittering arms, and mail-clad cavalry filled hill and dale,' wrote Marcellinus.

This could not go on. There was a military revolution in Rome.

ABOVE A rare, possibly unique portrayal of a Sasanian trinity: Ardashir II being invested as king by the god Ahuramazda in a carving by the grotto at Taq-i-Bustan. To the left of the king is the god Mithra, with a halo of the sun, offering the sabre of justice, the barsom. At the feet of king and god is the body of a fallen enemy – a recurrent Sasanian motif.

RIGHT Something of the sheer extravagance that flawed the last Sasanian courts is captured in this detail from a scene of a boar-hunt carved at Taq-i-Bustan at the time of Chosroes II. The hunt included a water-borne group of harpists, 300 horses, scores of elephants as mobile grandstands, 700 hounds and attendants who sprinkled rose-water ahead of the king's party.

Soldiers risen from the ranks replaced the aristocratic commanders of the army (with profound consequences on the empire's future leadership). The legions were converted to smaller, more flexible units and heavy cavalry units were introduced into the front line. Imitation was an essential form of flattery.

Persia forced on Rome more than a military upheaval: there were social and economic repercussions. The army had been doubled to a size of about six hundred thousand men, unprecedented in the antique world. The cost of maintaining this, and its attendant bureaucracy, bore down heavily in taxes. But the breaking of the élitist army establishment refreshed the empire with new blood. The Emperor Galerius, one of the new wave, later regained the lands lost to Persia. But more disasters were in store. In 363 Julian was humbled by Shapur II.

Having enjoyed recurrent victories, the Sasanians showed no determination to emulate the Achaemenian hegemony in Anatolia. This would have required a total commitment to war with Rome, and this was unthinkable because of the menace remaining on the eastern frontiers. In the late fourth and the fifth century the eastern threat materialized in the shape of the Hepthalite empire, which had subsumed the empire of Kushan and now looked belligerently to Persia. The Persian raids in the west had helped to finance the defence of the east, and the King of Kings prepared a major onslaught. The whole Sasanian nobility rode out behind King Firuz, as confident as ever. The Hepthalites feigned retreat and lured the Persian cavalry into a concealed pit, its bottom lined with upturned spikes. The Sasanian élite fell into a mass grave.

Had a catastrophe of this scale happened in a western campaign it would have been the subject of detailed chronicles. Because it happened in the shrouded east, little detail survives, not even the exact location. Because it was enacted under a western-directed spotlight, Sasanian history forms a pattern of vivid triumphs interspersed by often extended lapses of memory, with vague suggestions of trouble. For several generations after Firuz's downfall, in 484, the Sasanian empire was enfeebled. The Hepthalites ruled from Chinese Turkestan to Persian Khorasan. After the Mazdak aberration the eccentric Kavadh was deposed and imprisoned, but then restored to the Persian throne with help from the Hepthalites.

In the west there had been a profound shift in world power. Since the defeat of Julian, Rome had fractured into the western and eastern halves. Byzantium was the focus of Christian development. Jerusalem was a Byzantine city, and Byzantium itself was independent of Europe. The enemy on Persia's western border was no longer 'western'. At issue was the control of western Asia, between two *Asian* powers.

Fortunately for Persia, sixth-century Byzantium was militarily at full stretch, with campaigns being waged all round the Mediterranean, from Spain to North Africa, and in Europe along the Danube. Her main forces could not be brought to bear on Persia, and when, in the last year of his life, Kavadh took the field against the Byzantine general Belisarius he beat him. The debilitating border wars had barely a century more to run. In the interval, Persia regained self-confidence under a man who took the indigenous style of kingship to its apogee: Chosroes I, the son of Kavadh. Chosroes *Anoshak-ruvan* ('he of the immortal soul') had reforming zeal. He moved in two contrasting directions. He re-emphasized the mystique of the throne, embellishing his court at Ctesiphon with such grandiose trappings that, by comparison, Ardashir's court pales into modesty. Simultaneously, he curbed the influence and power of the great aristocratic families. This he did by strengthening the bureaucracy, and by elevating the village lords into a new kind of loyal squirearchy, to rule by the king's decree the lands they owned.

The king won more grass roots support by standardizing the taxes on Roman principles, according to the size of land holdings rather than their yield. The general idea was greater equity, but the head taxes continued to discriminate in favour of Zoroastrians and against minority religions, such as the Jews and Christians. The army, which seems earlier to have lapsed into baronial control, was reorganized into four sections and with a clarified chain of command. It became a true field army, able to sustain longer campaigns than before, which was essential in an empire so extensive. The scope of Chosroes's reforms must reflect the hiatus reached under the preceding regime. The overall effect, no doubt calculated, was to polarize society more explicitly between the absolute and extravagantly displayed authority of the king, and the more integrated instruments of the state.

In a sense, Chosroes was paying his respect to what were, by then, ancient if neglected principles of Sasanian success. Order and insignia were lynch-pins; the parameters of each power group had to be set by the king and remain beyond question. Heraldic pride was all very well, but the nobility had been taking on too many airs. The consensus was restored, on the same terms spelled out in the Letter of Tansar (the second coming of this manifesto probably occurred during Chosroes's reign, when it acquired its contemporary additions). Though Chosroes carries the soubriquet of 'The Just' there are overtones of the Lord Protector in much that he did. We should sympathize, perhaps, with him, as with Cromwell, that the task of conciliating a neglected and divided society calls for an iron hand. Certainly, Chosroes was pragmatic: 'The monarchy depends on the army, the army on money; money comes from the land tax; the land tax comes from agriculture. Agriculture depends on justice, justice on the integrity of officials, and integrity and reliability on the ever-watchfulness of the king.'

These were the words of the son of a delinquent. We must imagine that Chosroes knew more than could have been learned at his father's feet. He had enough intellectual curiosity to send a physician, Burzoe, to India to bring back medical works and literature in Sanskrit. In an open world, notwithstanding the hostilities, he probably knew of Byzantium's intellectual powerhouse, and we know that Greek classics were translated and preserved for posterity in Persia as well as in Byzantium. Persia under Chosroes may have been more a repository than a laboratory, but it was no less valuable for that. Chosroes read and knew his history; for him the throne had to rest on a bedrock of the heroic legend. How intoxicating, how useful to the glands, were these oral and epic memories? Useful enough to legitimize his *style*, but not, it seems, enough to permit nostalgia to override reality.

For the riddle of Chosroes is this: he recovered order by looking backwards, but he modernized Persia at the same time. He anticipated history without knowing – as we can smugly know – that his was the last flourish of one era, and the beginning of another. His reign lasted forty-eight years, long enough to complete a transition. And nothing more symbolizes the way he pulled Persia from her past than the court at Ctesiphon. Once more, as with the last of the Achaemenian kings, the Fertile Crescent had drawn the king and the centre of his empire; a centre of the mind, rather than of geography.

There was a puzzling asymmetry in the choice of Ctesiphon as a place from which to survey the empire. It was inconveniently distant from the eastern borders, and yet that was still the military imperative: Chosroes's coins bore the legend 'Delivering the world from fear'; he meant the Huns, not the Romans. The Hepthalite Huns were destroyed between 558 and 560, with the help of the Turks who had now appeared on the landscape, to remain there. Chosroes seduced the Turks away from an alliance with the Huns by marrying the Turkish leader's daughter. In the west, Chosroes had captured Antioch, and to Byzantium this was a disaster to equal any previous Persian conquest.

Fars, the cradle of two great Persian empires, had again left the royal affections. Mesopotamia had always been more *worldly* than Fars, which was inclined to chauvinism. That had, after all, been its value, to breed those quintessential Persian strengths. But once emancipated, Persian dynasties were apt to dream of more, to enjoy the extravagant life sustainable only in the richness of the Fertile Crescent, in cities like Susa, Babylon, Seleucia, and now Ctesiphon, where Chosroes took the vaulted *iwan* to excess and required a crown so encrusted with gold that it had to be suspended on chains lest it broke his neck. There was a recrudescence of western voices at court: Mesopotamian Christians, Byzantine architects, and even philosophers from Athens, who went into exile to Ctesiphon after Justinian closed the Academy. Here was the *real* change, sophistication. Crude imagery was gone, and with it the need to perch the Zoroastrian deity on the royal brow. Had the Christian ethic percolated enough to shame such imagery? We cannot know. But it is clear that parts of the Zoroastrian tableaux came to be thought gauche, the *kitsch* of a past age. Ethics were being refurbished with help from Aristotle; no wonder that this new level of royal manners caused dyspepsia in the old guard, whose hearts and minds could not be moved west.

In this changed atmosphere of 'modern' thought the temporal power needed less to embrace the spiritual: Zoroastrianism was *politically* obsolescent, too. Here in Mesopotamia, where religious codification had evolved via Babylonia, Darius and the Judaic Torah, Christianity had absorbed all the currents and offered a new map of good and evil in which man himself played a virile role. Much of the simple, elemental appeal of the Zoroastrian rites must, in this atmosphere, have seemed *déclassé*. The conservative elements, those with their feet still firmly on the plateau, would have resisted such a drift of thought. But Chosroes? He had hit a winning streak, his new squirearchy were with him all the way, he could afford to clip Ahuramazda's wings. *He* had 'delivered the world from fear'. The tangible agent of goodness was mortal, and without need of supernatural assistance.

Success called for celebration. Chosroes's royal banquets were gargantuan displays in which the King of Kings emulated his Achaemenian forbears and 'showed the riches of his glorious kingdom and the honour of his excellent Majesty' (Esther 1:4). One feast for his warriors might take twelve days in the preparation, and each guest was assigned 'with great pomp the rank and position which he should occupy at table'. The *brio* of these occasions has been caught, as though by an ancient forerunner of the court photographer, in scenes embossed on silver dishes, which give us an intimate glimpse of late Sasanian style.

For three centuries the priesthood had been at the heart of Sasanian power. The Magi, in their white robes and conical caps, had with the rest of the hierarchy gone to the wars, to cleanse the land of demons after the conquests. They had dispensed the king's justice. Tansar was the prototype of a powerful holy figure, a kind of Zoroastrian Pope. The position was developed and established by a priest called Kartir, who, as a young man, succeeded Tansar, towards the end of Ardashir's reign and served five more kings. Such became his authority that he was even permitted to proclaim it in a detailed inscription, the closest anyone not of royal blood came to immortalizing their role. The inscription recounts, through the reigns of one king after another, his accumulating honours:

> Hormizd, son of Shapur, for me created the name Kartir, magupat of Orhmazd ... divine services increased and many fire temples were established and many Magi became prosperous ... Vahram, brother of Hormizd, succeeded and held me in pre-eminence and dignity ... Vahram, son of Vahram, made me superior in the empire in rank and dignity ... the demons received great blows and torments, idols were smashed and the demon's den was destroyed ... fires and Magi were there where the horses and men of the King of Kings penetrated the town of Antioch and the land of Syria, Tarsus and the land of Cilicia, and beyond that, Caesarea and the land of Cappadocia up to Galatia, Armenia, Georgia, Albania....

In this spirit of zealotry the priests and the army rolled over the lands together on a crusade. The sacred flame marked the conquests and supplanted the 'demon's den', no doubt in salutary fashion. Inside Persia, Kartir's regime was just as firm. It was he who engineered Mani's end; any whiff of heresy, any survival of paganism, was purged with the same vigour as, say, the later European Papacy. There may also have been sectarian tensions within Persian Zoroastrianism, but

Kartir ensured that nothing impeded the development of a monolithic orthodoxy, to reinforce the alliance of church and state. He must have been an intimidating figure, valued by kings and feared by the rest. The world of Kartir seems to have been muscular rather than cerebral and, as one scholar has written, the plateau 'rears up no monks or ascetics ... but men of action, who are inclined to see life as a perpetual struggle against evil forces. Vigilance and strenuousness were precepts enjoined by the nature of the land itself, long before they were set down in the Avesta.' (The Avesta was the Zoroastrian gospel as finally put down in the Sasanian era.)

This was the kind of topographical *essence* that was (as Cyrus had warned) diluted by the fashions of Mesopotamia. Chosroes had substituted bureaucratic power for the theological one, and the civil servants were more adaptable to his cast of mind. The 'Pope' gave way to the grand vizier, the professional mandarin.

Chosroes died in 579. By the end of his reign he had rebuilt the empire, and once more it impinged upon the west. He defined his own policy thus: 'To know the truth and knowledge, and to follow them, this is what honours a king above everything; what is most harmful to them is to be ashamed to learn, to abstain from seeking knowledge through embarrassment. He who will not learn cannot become wise.' For a Sasanian king, this is a new note of intellectual humility. Chosroes extolled the virtues of eclecticism: 'We examined the rules of conduct of the kings of Roum (Byzantium) and of the kings of Hind (India) and chose from them what was praiseworthy....' But the irony was that by reinvigorating Persia Chosroes made inevitable a renewed conflict with Byzantium, which he himself began. With more things than ever in common, the two powers were still sadly incapable of rapprochement.

That collaboration between them was fleetingly possible was proved in a fiasco which followed the death of Chosroes. He was succeeded by his son, Hormizd IV. After eleven years of indifferent rule, Hormizd was deposed in a coup organized by a general, Vahram. Vahram installed Hormizd's young son Chosroes on the throne as his puppet. But Chosroes boldly tried to constrain the king-maker, whereupon Vahram took the throne for himself. Chosroes turned for help to the Byzantine Emperor Maurice. Taking land concessions as a *quid pro quo*, Maurice helped Chosroes to regain the Persian throne (Chosroes married a Byzantine princess) and Vahram was killed while trying to escape. Chosroes II thus began his reign with western sympathies and connections, but after Maurice died, in 602, the old hostilities resumed. And there was now a crucial difference. Chosroes had more in mind than border raids. He dreamed of taking the Persian empire back to the Mediterranean.

For this, Chosroes has been accused of over-reaching himself, of killing the empire with ambition. But his reasoning could have seemed sound at the time: the eastern borders were quiescent and Byzantium seemed to be of uncertain resolve. Maurice had been murdered by his successor, Phocas, and there were internal stresses. But so were there in Persia. The old nobility of the plateau had been alienated by the western manners of Ctesiphon. Perhaps Chosroes saw a victory in the west as a way of proving himself to be still imbued with the warrior virtues.

Taking the avenging of Maurice as his pretext, Chosroes took his army westwards in 603. By 620 the Persians had pushed Byzantium all the way back to an enclave in Constantinople; after four centuries the Sasanians did, indeed, seem on the brink of restoring the limits of Darius's great empire. Antioch fell to them in 613, Jerusalem in 614, Sardis and Ephesus in 616 – and, with the fall of Alexandria, Egypt in 619. Easily overlooked, though, is an event in 611. Chosroes I had gone across Arabia and captured the Yemen. Chosroes II, attending to unfinished business, followed into Arabia, but the tribes had by then united in self-defence, and the Persians were trounced by the Bedouins. One year earlier, in 610, in the Hijaz on the south-western corner of the Arabian peninsula, a merchant troubled by failures in business had taken to wandering the hills outside his town, Mecca. He suddenly found himself experiencing visions of great spiritual power. He descended on the citizens of Mecca convinced that he was the prophet of a new deity, whom he called Allah. Mecca did not share his enthusiasm; Muhammad had to move to neighbouring Medina to find a more responsive audience.

The Sasanian encounter with the Arabs was no more than a hiccup in Chosroes's progress to a new world empire, and the west had cause again to look with trepidation on the designs of a Persian king. The court at Ctesiphon, enriched by the substantial plunder of the conquests, pullulated with the trappings of success. Even the great *iwan* could barely contain the gratification now due to the King of Kings. Chosroes became a magnetic figure in the glow of reflected glory; this is how he appeared to Bahram, a futile rebel at the gates of Ctesiphon:

> When Bahram now saw how Chosroes was in full regal state with the crown on his head, and how near him the greatest banner in the kingdom waved, and how the great noblemen of the kingdom stood beside him in the most splendid dress with magnificent horses, then he became quite sad and said to his companions, 'Look ye well, look at how that son of a whore has become fat, look at the way in which his beard, his moustaches, grow upon him. . . .'

Behind the king was a persuasive woman. The royal harem was a microcosm of essential alliances, a wife for each interest group. One of these was Shirin, a Christian noblewoman from the southern delta lands, who had been introduced to the court by Chosroes's Christian doctor. The marriage began as a political expedient: the Christians were important not simply as a constituency, but also as a means of contact with the west. But Shirin rapidly became a grand passion for Chosroes, and was his favourite wife for thirty years.

He seemed to be replete with blessings. But the edifice crumbled with surprising speed. It was brought down by a brilliant stroke of strategy: the new Byzantine Emperor, Heraclius, had conceived a classic flanking manoeuvre to outwit the Persians. While the élite of Chosroes's army were luxuriating in the conquered lands of Asia Minor and Egypt, the comparatively small Byzantine army was fashioned into a new kind of fast-moving striking force, and shipped across the Black Sea into the Caucusus to strike at, not the 'soft underbelly' of the empire but its 'soft shoulder'. Heraclius reinforced himself through an alliance with the Khazar tribe, and then, in 627, plunged south through Armenia and Azerbaijan, directly at the glittering totem of the King of Kings, Ctesiphon. The city was put under siege, and fell into panic. Chosroes left the palace and fled to the arms of Shirin. There he was murdered by his ministers, encouraged by his son Kavad. In a real sense, the empire was decapitated. The morale was broken. Chosroes's end bore the staple ingredients of legend – a romance and tragedy to recur later in classic ballads as the memory of the Sasanians shone with the brilliance of a freshly unearthed diamond. For although there were eleven more Sasanian kings (and possibly a queen or two) the dynasty had little more than a decade of life left.

In the Valhalla of Persian legend it is the Sasanians who most stir the national pride. Their most enduring quality, Professor Brown believes, was *style*:

> There is this sense of a style of rule, and a style of rule controlled by the general values of the society. This means that throughout the near east, even until today, if you want the idea of a just king you think of Chosroes *Anoshak-ruvan*. And then, on the more humble level, but the one that will really survive, there are the values summed up in the Zoroastrian faith; the values that lead to the preservation of the good things of life, the good things which the gods gave to the land – water, green, organization. And it is the dogged determination that these things should continue in a land where they can never be taken for granted.

As the empires of that time heaved and shifted like the plates in the earth had done when the continents settled, the eruption of the Sasanian empire fixed a part of the landscape of the post-antique world. After the fading of the Greek world which had been inserted into Asia by the Seleucids, the possession of that territory had been inherently unstable. It had always been at least *possible* that instead of reverting to Oriental character, western Asia might, as Alexander had dreamed, have been subsumed into the eastern Greco-Roman world. The power of Rome and then of Byzantium might easily have prevailed. With the late Roman world split between Europe and the near east, there *could* have developed a Christian *and* Oriental amalgam. Christianity was, after all, as much a religion of the east as Judaism and Zoroastrianism. That this did not happen must largely be credited to the Sasanians: in this sense, Ardashir's appearance on the world stage is decisive. Until then, the line between east and west was indistinct and fluid; after it, the Orient was once again a separate world – and would always remain so.

5

The Shadow of God
on Earth

640-1200

Where is Chosroes Anoshak-ruvan,
the best of kings?
Where is Shapur, gone before him?
Death has not respected him; his power is
shattered, the crowds no longer press at his gate.
Where are these kings, which the winds of
the east and the winds of the west
Have swept away like dry leaves?

Between 636 and 642 the Persian empire collapsed under a rapid military assault. The
invader had none of the drilled precision of Alexander, and no military
tradition to equal that of Rome. The Sasanians faced an enemy far
fewer in number than themselves, from a civilization that was as
rudimentary as Persia's was elaborate. Once established, this force
marked Persia more profoundly and more lastingly than any.

It seemed to be an unequal contest, the proficient royal Sasanian
armies facing bands of nomads from the desert. But the Persian army,
like Persian society, had grown ponderous. Its surface magnificence
was militarily encumbering. And, equally telling, its *élan*, that essential

aphrodisiac of war, had been drained in the futile campaigns against Byzantium. Persia and Byzantium had mutually wearied each other, and each was more vulnerable than it looked. The Persian cataphracts, supreme in set-piece battles, were not now in themselves enough: the Arab armies had far greater mobility. Theirs was the style of the raiding party, without long supply lines and moving swiftly on horses and camels. They lived off the land as they passed through it, in classic nomad style; if they encountered a stubborn fortress they would simply by-pass it, to starve it into submission.

But there was more to this spectacular success than tactics. The Arabs were no longer proudly isolated in their Bedouin culture. They had been galvanized by a force that the desert could not contain: the gospel of Muhammad. Islam, literally, means 'submission'. And submission came with disconcerting speed: all the great cities of Syria, Egypt, Mesopotamia and Persia fell to the Arab armies. Persia's humiliation was absolute. In 636 the Sasanian general Rustam (to appear later as a hero of Persian folk legend) was routed at the battle of Qadisiyya. Two years later the physical embodiment of late Sasanian art and ego, the vaulted palace at Ctesiphon, was in Arab hands. The last Sasanian king, Yazdagird III, fled to Media, to be pursued beyond into Khorasan where he was squalidly murdered for his jewels. Two more battles, the first at Jalula and the second decisive one at Nihavand in 642, opened for the Arabs, as Gaugamela had for Alexander, the way to the heart of the plateau, through the passes of the Zagros. The cities then fell like ninepins: Ecbatana, Rayy, Isfahan and the origin of Sasanian power, Istakhr.

Victory of this extent and speed brought serious problems: what were the Arabs, with a simple tribal distaste for the pretensions of monarchies, to do with the palaces and the temples? Even more pressing, how would they run the empire? By 670 the conquests were complete, and some means of government had to be devised. Despite the driving force of Muhammad's message the conquest had initially been military, not theological. The invasion imposed Arab rule – not Islam. Given such a vast new dominion, the Arabs inherited conflicting forms of government, depending on where they were. For example, the Persian poll tax was religiously based; the Byzantine one was not. At first, as a peaceable form of coercion, the Arabs granted tax advantages to those who became Muslims. Then there was a change of mind, and conversion was discouraged. At the heart of the admin-

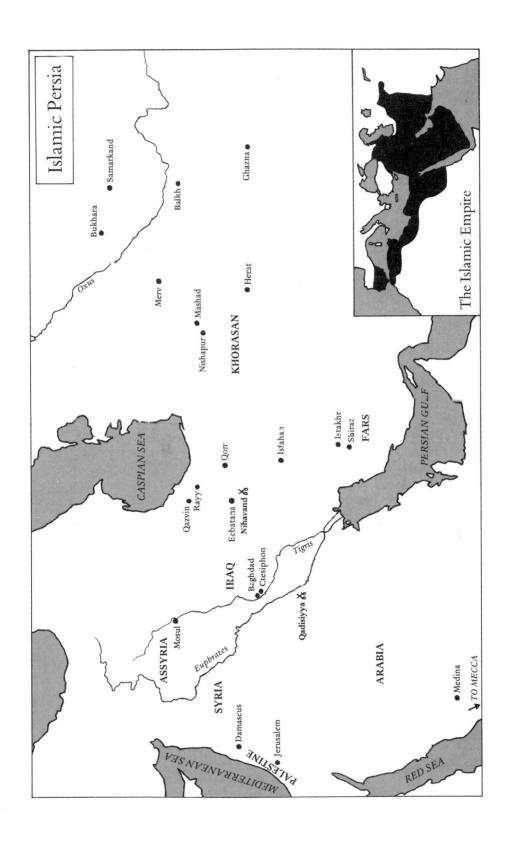

Islamic Persia

Samarkand
Bukhara
Balkh
Ghazna
Oxus
Merv
Mashad
Nishapur
Herat
KHORASAN
CASPIAN SEA
Qom
Qazvin
Rayy
Echatana
Nihavand ⚔
Isfahan
Istakhr
Shiraz
FARS
IRAQ
Baghdad
Ctesiphon
Tigris
PERSIAN GULF
Mosul
ASSYRIA
Qadisiyya ⚔
Euphrates
SYRIA
ARABIA
Damascus
Medina
TO MECCA
Jerusalem
PALESTINE
MEDITERRANEAN SEA
RED SEA

The Islamic Empire

istrative muddle was a religious one: was Islam a religion only for Arabs, or for all? The Arabs could not quite decide.

The size of their problem was daunting. Looked at from Damascus, which became the empire's first capital, the diversity of the subject peoples and of their lands seemed to beg coherence. Within a century, the lines of communication stretched from central France to deepest Asia. And the Arabs were themselves tribally diverse, subject to feuds. (Muhammad's early fame came from his success as a conciliator between the urban and desert factions.) Yet the empire, in spite of persistent schisms – theological, social and racial – held together *and* grew. How?

The religion had an infectious certitude. This was as true for non-Arabs as Arabs, and it was something which in the end resolved the dilemma over the policy of conversion: it simply could not be restricted. It was too appealing. Persia makes the point very well. Zoroastrianism had been extraordinarily well integrated with the country; it grew organically from the nature of the land and the ordeals of living in it. And it was peculiarly Iranian, having evolved there for more than one thousand five hundred years. Yet it quickly lost the contest with Islam, although Islam did not displace it overnight; it was at least a century before Islam got its roots down. In one important sense Islam demanded more: it asked that allegiance should go first to Allah, only secondly to nation. Zoroastrianism had never asked that. (How could it, with the king demanding so much?) Islam followed Zoroastrianism (and Judaism and Christianity) in one respect, by holding out the prospect of the Last Judgement. Muhammad had shattered the self-esteem of the Arab tribal society and replaced it with the humility of every being before his maker; that was what 'submission' was really all about, and there was no room in this for the intervention of state or king. So by converting to Islam, Persians had to elect to belong to something greater than Persia. That was novel. Nationality, for converts, was subordinated, though not, as it turned out, lost. But the process was not all one way: Arabs also became Persians, albeit by domicile. Arab soldiers and their families, confined at first to garrisons, were deliberately settled in towns and cities; fifty thousand alone in Khorasan, a significant percentage. Cross-fertilization progressively blurred the original distinction of conqueror and conquered.

While assimilation developed in the Arab colonies, stresses began to afflict the capital. The spiritual and governing apex of the empire was the caliphate of the Umayyad dynasty in Damascus. These princes of Islam had strayed far from the simple precepts of the prophet. Pleasures of the flesh, self-indulgent building and unashamed dissipation were soon an affront to the pious. One of the hedonists built himself a palace in the middle of the desert, filled his swimming pool with wine, and used the Koran for archery target practice. In a style reflecting his habits, he wrote:

> Come hand me the cup and pour us a drink!
> Hell-fire's my destiny – I don't think!
> To teach men the worship of booze is my mission:
> Let the paradise–seekers plod on to perdition!

More ominous for the unity of the caliphate was the massacre in 680 of the prophet's cousin and son–in–law, 'Ali, and his followers. Here began a sectarian fissure. The dispute, which rolled on for centuries and was eventually to give a name to Persian separatism, arose from one of the prophet's lacunae: the method of succession. Three different solutions were advanced. The earliest, prevailing until 660, was selection by consensus. The second, on which the Umayyads had been installed, was dynastic. But 'Ali and his followers believed in a bloodline – a divinely ordained heredity. The death of 'Ali gave his cause a new potency, that of martyrdom. Today, Islam's two sects reflect this ancient split. The Sunnis support electoral succession, the Shi'as believe that usurpers took over in the seventh century and that the prophet's true descendants, the *imams*, should lead the faith.

But the full cost of this schism came much later. What happened at first was that the cause of 'Ali was claimed by a faction who sought not independence, but the purging of the decadence which had tainted Damascus. The momentum for a change came from the peasants, bridling at the cost of sustaining the caliphate. Their unrest was directed into a rebellion by a Persian, Abu Muslim. He was the principal architect of the fall of the Umayyads in 750. A clean break was made in which a new capital was established. The focus of the empire moved from Syria eastwards to Mesopotamia, to Baghdad (the name means 'Gift of God') astride the Euphrates.

This change marks the transition of the empire from an Arab one to a Muslim one. It also marks the end of the convalescence of the Persian spirit and the beginning of its recovery. Islam moves into an eclectic, questing mood, refreshing itself from whatever sources it can tap. The most adjacent source was Persia. Already the Arabs had appropriated Persian skills in putting together the machinery to run the empire; they had been helped by the Persian nobles of the plateau who had been so disaffected by the airs of the court at Ctesiphon. These had collaborated with the Arabs, embracing what they considered clearly to be the lesser of two evils – and acknowledging the sheer necessity of keeping things going in the fragile ecology which they depended on. The Arabs were acquisitive conquerors, but they were not vengeful.

Now, with a new language and a new religion inexorably taking hold in Persia, the Persians had other talents to be harvested by the new Abbasid caliphate. To a capital and a religion open to the world for ideas, the Persians brought a distinctive gift – that of the catalyst. Since Cyrus's conquest of Lydia, the Persians had been a great cultural sponge, tolerant of diversity within their empires and quick to absorb whatever was of value to themselves, giving it in the process a singular Persian flavour. Persian experience, and Persian contacts, were far more universal than those of the Arabs. Persia was the great repository of Oriental ideas. Although it could never be said of Persia that Greece and Rome had made an impression on her sensibilities, she had always looked receptively to the east.

In contrast to Damascus, the desert city, Baghdad was clearly Oriental. The city was built to a circular plan, just like Firuzabad, the classic Sasanian city. The Abbasid court favoured Persian costume, adopted the Persian office of vizier, and even had a Persian-style executioner. The mentality of the caliphate had changed. Sasanian grandeur was reflected in the style of the caliph's palace; its dome, at the exact centre of the city, crowned a hall which was punctuated by four *iwans*. Like the later Sasanian kings, the caliph put a distance between himself and the people: the palace was encircled by a plaza accessible only through four guarded gates. The mortal who ruled from this fortress called himself 'The Shadow of God on Earth'.

Despite the symbolic remoteness of the caliph, the intellectual range of Islamic thinkers under the early Abbasids was far from being parochial. They were catholic in their tastes and vigorous in their curiosity. Islam was a multi-racial mélange in the process of enriching itself with all the knowledge and ideas available from lands that stretched from the Atlantic on one side to the borders of China on the other. For the Persian intelligentsia there was now the exhilaration of being an important part of a wider universe of thought than they had known, and part of an age which was to scale the heights of spiritual, intellectual and artistic experience. Theologically, Islam had not hardened; it was still malleable. Coming so long after Judaism and Christianity, Muslim theologians felt the urgency of refinement. They competed with the intellectual resources of, on the one side Christianity and Greek philosophy, and on the other Oriental creeds like Buddhism which had established itself in north-east Persia. A balance had to be struck between the desire to lay down the code of the faith, and the spirit, so pronounced in Islam, of anti-dogma. The prophecies and exhortations of the Koran allowed liberal interpretation; to circumscribe this interpretation opposed the principle of free will.

But what gave Islam its great popular appeal was its comprehensive (and comprehensible) code for living, which obviated the need for variable secular laws. This was a relief to the people, but what stimulated the polemic of the scholars was the spiritual voyage possible beyond this prosaic code. The licence for mysticism was there, and it was irresistible. In this debate and the more vicious dialectic about the line of succession from the prophet lay much future tribulation. But while the brew matured, Islam transcended the rest of the civilized world in a way that Europe was not able to achieve until its renaissance centuries later.

The Persian catalyst was crucial. It had absorbed the ideas of east and west: strands of Greek thought, Mediterranean architecture, astrology, Indian medicine and mathematics had mixed with the more martial and administrative talents of the plateau. But two elements of Persian life were now in question. One, the religion, was obsolescent. The other, the Persian language, had to survive if the culture in any meaningful sense was to avoid the fate of Coptic Egypt, which was expunged by Islam.

The language of the Sasanians (previous dynasties having used both cuneiform and Aramaic) was 'middle Persian' or *Pahlavi*. Scholars do not value this as either a rich language in itself, or, more significantly, an adaptable language that might have appealed more widely. The conjunction of Arabic and middle-Persian had a result which bears out such a judgement: Arabic prevailed, by choice. The Arabic script and nomenclature was easier to use and far more expressive. Persians adopted it, though their own vernacular survived. In the linguistic mutation which followed was the means for a literary renaissance.

Professor Frye likens Persian without Arabic to English without French and Latin. To see this as sublimation would be foolish: it liberated Persian thought and art, and meant directly that they could more readily permeate Islam. And it meant in the end that the whole of eastern Islam was effectively Persianized.

But old passions could reassert themselves. A strident argument, the Shy'ubiya movement, raged around the relative virtues of the Arab and non-Arab cultural traditions. Persians and Syrian Christians not only promoted their own traditions but translated into Arabic the major works of Greece and India (it was from India that what we perversely call 'Arabic' numerals, decimal units and the concept of zero, passed to the Middle East and then to Europe). Persians systemized Arabic grammar. All this carried the implication of Arab deficiency, as a Persian poet was later thus able to stigmatize:

> Retreat to the Hijaz and resume eating lizards
> and herd your cattle
> While I seat myself on the throne of kings
> supported by the sharpness of my blade and
> the point of my pen.

But the Shu'ubiya was not too much demeaned by partisan argument. Persians supported the Arabs; Arabs non-Arabs. It was all fuel for the cultural explosion. Before the chance transcription of the Greek classics by the monks of ninth-century Byzantium under the imposition of their lay patriach, Photius, the scholars of Baghdad were devouring (and preserving) them as part of an extraordinarily open-minded search for learning. One of these scholars, a Persian called al–Biruni, left important work on mathematics, natural science, medicine, astronomy, physics, chemistry and chronology. Academic life could flourish because it was a time of political and economic stability; indeed, the caliphate accumulated great wealth from a better taxation system and expanding trade. Money management, in what we would now regard as a sophisticated form, was already well advanced. The perils of banditry had brought the solution of credit notes ('cheque' and 'exchequer' are Persian-derived words and ideas), and capital investment and liquidity were accepted principles. The old Achaemenian vice of hoarding now looked very archaic indeed.

With this vigorous theological, cultural and commercial life the Islamic city became a phenomenon: Baghdad grew to a population of one million, Cordoba of seven hundred thousand and Damascus of five hundred thousand. In Egypt urban populations predominated. But these ninth-century cities were not divorced from the land around them; city and country were interdependent. The country needed the city as a market, the city needed produce from the country. The western stereotype of a city simply did not apply; agriculture went on inside as well as outside the city walls, and there were law schools in the villages. So the dichotomy of urban and rural cultures was avoided. Although much of the population of Asia remained either nomadic or semi-nomadic, settled and mobile life successfully co-existed. Monolithic central control was not imposed, and given this freedom some of the distant provinces began to test the climate for independence.

In Persia a refined family dynasty called the Taharids rose in Khorasan and created a provincial sub-kingdom, but continued to pay revenues to Baghdad and was tolerated. But Persia was beginning to revert to type: another breakaway kingdom appeared in south-eastern Persia, a buccaneer dynasty called the Saffarids, who displaced the Taharids and extended beyond Khorasan into Central Asia and what is now Afghanistan and Pakistan. The cities in the area around the Oxus river created a counter-balance to the Arabian cities of Mesopotamia and moved Persian culture farther east more noticeably than at any time in the pre-Islamic past. The legends of Tashkent, Bukhara and Samarkand were offsprings of this change.

The ninth century had been the apogee of Baghdad and the intellectual quest within Islam. The tenth century marks a Persian renaissance. The Saffarids (867–903) were, in their turn, supplanted by the Samanids, who plausibly claimed to be descendants of the Sasanians. The family converted from Zoroastrianism to Islam and provided the caliphs with a succession of regional governors. They came to exemplify at its best the Persian gift of assimilation, being both pious in their faith and devoted to the integrity of the Sasanian-style social hierarchy. All of the Sasanian love of panoply and martial graces was preserved, but combined with a greater sensibility: physicians, philosophers and, notably, poets prospered under Samanid patronage. Persian poetry, in the work of Rudaki and Daqiqi (still revered today), came of age. Bukhara and Samarkand soon rivalled Baghdad as cultural centres. The prosperous Samanids paid no revenue to the caliph but formally acknowledged his authority. That this was tolerated was a sign of new political realities, and of the stealthy and extraordinary penetration of court life in Baghdad by a rising power, the Turks.

It was not so much a case of the poacher turning gamekeeper as the gamekeeper turning master of the estate. At first the Turks of Central Asia came to Islam as domestic slaves, then as mercenary slave soldiers. Their bravery and martial skill, particularly as archers and cavalry, put their services at a premium. Young Turks were bought by Abbasid princes to be trained as bodyguards, and by the ninth century Turks were the real power behind the throne, forming a praetorian guard, running key offices of state, and even dispensing appointments. The caliphs became creatures of their protectors, and victims of their intrigues; in one decade, three were assassinated by their Turkish guards. As viziers and commanders of the army the Turks effectively emasculated the caliphs while carefully supporting their nominal authority. It was against this counterfeit rule in Baghdad that a nascent and indigenous Persian force moved.

In the Alborz mountains between the Caspian and the western half of the plateau, the successive invaders from west and south had never managed to subdue an elusive and indomitable people called the Dailamites. Even Alexander, who was normally provoked into his most punitive actions by such insolence, did not press home his attack in this barely accessible enclave. After the Arab conquest, pockets of Zoroastrianism persisted here, and where Islam did take a hold it did so in its aberrant form, Shi'ism – the belief in the legitimacy of 'Ali, his two martyred sons Husain and Hasan, and the direct line of their successors.

Like the Turks, the Dailamites were formidable soldiers and sought-after as mercenaries. One of these mercenaries, Abu Shuja Buya, usurped the authority of his employers, and left three equally proficient sons to transform the spoils into a dynasty, called the Buyids. The Buyids appropriated a large area of western Persia and Iraq and finally took their army and their Shi'a zeal to Baghdad. But they did not depose the Sunni caliphate; instead they gave Shi'ism increased and acknowledged status by creating their own theological colleges, and by formalizing the sect's beliefs so that it would endure. This was of historic importance for Islam, and for Persia – to be ranked with the early protestant division of Christian Europe.

The Buyids, once in Baghdad, displayed unmistakable Sasanian proclivities. The senior of the brothers, Mu'izz al–Daula ('Splendour of the State') installed himself as Commander-in-Chief, took over the treasury and appointed the vizier and the chief of police. He then devised and acquired the new title of Sultan. His brothers took other key offices and gave themselves grandiloquent titles, including Shahanshah. The trend continued in their successors, who fabricated a genealogy linking them improbably with the great kings of Fars. The most accomplished Buyid leader, 'Adud al–Daula, put his own inscriptions alongside those of the Achaemenians at Persepolis and claimed that he had had the cuneiform inscriptions translated by a Zoroastrian priest, surely *braggadacio*. Coins of the Buyid dynasty show the ruler wearing a bungled copy of a Sasanian crown, and some give him the title of Shahanshah.

The Buyids prevailed for a century; for a time Shi'ism annexed western Persia and Iraq, while Sunnism persisted to the east under the Samanids. But the Buyids were undermined by the Turks, internally by the Turkish faction in their army, the cavalry, and externally from the east as the Samanids were themselves supplanted by the Ghaznavids, a dynasty founded by an ambitious Turkish slave called Sebuktigin. Once more, the interlopers rapidly assumed the colours and manners of their surroundings. Even more than the Buyids had done, the Ghaznavids identified with Persia and followed the Sasanian pattern. Mahmud of Ghazna, who ruled from 994 to 1030, was invested as king with the title, 'Right Hand of the Dynasty, Fiduciary of the Islamic Community, Representative of the Prince of Believers'. This gesture to the caliphate was politically disingenuous. The proclaimed piety of the court was undermined, at least in hindsight, by Mahmud's preoccupation with money and how to raise it. He created a huge standing army which included cavalry, camel-borne infantry and armoured elephants deployed rather in the manner of tanks – a mark of how far India was drawn into his sphere of influence. Keeping this army going emptied the treasury as fast as the avarice of the court.

The language of the army was Turkish; the language of the chancery Arabic; the disposition of the culture Persian. Under Mahmud the term 'command performance' assumed a salutary meaning. Anxious to match the esteem of other cities, he called to his capital at Ghazna the learned and literary giants of the day – or rather, he summoned them. Some came, some fled. The most profound result of this capricious patronage was the work of Persia's celebrated laureate, Firdausi. The recovery of Persia's past had been helped by the adoption of Sasanian

107

traditions by the Arabs and by the new Muslim dynasties; Professor Frye suspects that, under Islam, Persians came to know more about the Achaemenians than had the Sasanians themselves; the scholars of the caliphate, including Arabs, assiduously studied pre-Islamic Persia. But Firdausi single-handedly became the most pervasive agent of Persian folk-memory (and, posthumously, of Persian nationalism). He spent thirty years writing the *Shahnameh*, the Book of Kings, a prolific reclamation of the ancient Persian epic. The work is a dynamic, fluid narrative of great emotional power.

Modern Persian, the language of the Samanid poets, was taken by Firdausi and pruned of Arabic excess into a 'pure' form. In so doing Firdausi gave his work maximum accessibility: the *Shahnameh* stirred the souls of an illiterate society and spread rapidly through the oral tradition. It greatly helped future assertions of nationalism, and verses of the *Shahnameh* are even today cited to curse the Arab invader, as here, in the forebodings of the luckless general Rustam before his defeat: 'There will be tyranny of soul and tongue. A mongrel race – Iranian, Turkoman, Arab – will come to be and talk in gibberish . . .'

Firdausi's Turkish patron, Mahmud, true to form, welched on the fee due to the poet for his lifetime's labours, and is reputed to have paid in silver instead of the gold which had been promised. He later repented, and sent some bales of indigo as a rather dubious compensation. The camels bearing the indigo passed into Firdausi's village of Tus just as a cortège bearing the poet's body passed out of it (so, at any rate, runs the tale).

Today's map severs from Persia the homeland of the Ghaznavids. To relate the plateau to Ghazna seems perplexing because it lies south of Kabul and not far from the Khyber Pass. It is as far east as a 'Persian' capital could possibly go. Mahmud raided India seventeen times and his empire ultimately reached Kashmir. In the west it touched the Zagros.

In the wake of Mahmud's armies great tracts of land became deserts. Rural security, vital for the maintenance of irrigation, was disrupted. There were years of famine and resort to cannibalism. Where it had been left unmolested, agriculture had adapted to the extremes of climate and landscape. More sophisticated irrigation extended the staple crop of rice; cotton replaced flax as the textile fibre. To the markets came wheat, barley, citrus fruits, pistachio nuts, figs, dates, olives, peaches, apricots, apples, cherries and grapes. Alongside the agrarian society a mercantile economy advanced. Textiles were its core: silk, gold and silver brocade, linen and carpets. And the range of crafts benefited from the wider world: the making of fine ceramics was learned from China, and the potters of Nishapur and Samarkand were inspired by Islam to produce a new element of decoration – calligraphy.

The Arabic script assumes a separate existence as a carefully inter-locked pattern; in ceramics, metalwork and architectural decoration Persian art found pious fulfilment through calligraphy. The western novice, at first stricken with illiteracy at the sight of Arabic script, has a barrier to cross before finding the genius of pattern, balance and colour. Once crossed, it may well be that the linguistic blindness heightens the appreciation. Certainly, we have no typographical resource to match it. Mahmud's tomb near Ghazna employs cal-ligraphy to ask of the Almighty 'a gracious reception' for the impecunious ruler. The art critic Robert Byron found that this inscrip-tion had 'a functional beauty; regarded as pure design, its extra-ordinary emphasis seems in itself a form of oratory, a transposition of speech from the audible to the visible'.

The Ghaznavids practised their Sunni orthodoxy with ferocity, and heretics were persecuted. Their westward displacement of the Buyids made fugitives of the Shi'ites and, as is the way with sectarian-ism, ensured that their dissent hardened in the hands of zealots. Under Mahmud's son Masud, the frenetic Ghaznavid adventure petered out as fast as it had arisen, and the dynasty ended up with an enclave in the Punjab which expired finally at the end of the twelfth century.

Like Persia before it, the Islamic empire was vulnerable to incur-sions from the north-east. Early in the eleventh century a prolific nomadic clan of Turkish origins, called the Seljuks, crossed the Oxus and filtered into northern Khorasan. It was not at first a systematic assault, more the movement of people led by the noses of their foraging flocks. But once they were massed, the Seljuks were a powerful war machine. Against the elephantine army of the Ghaz-navids, whom they now confronted, the Seljuks had (like the Arabs against the Sasanians) the advantage of greater agility. In 1040 they inflicted a decisive defeat on the Ghaznavids and began an ineluctable progress towards Baghdad. When they entered the capital city in 1055 the caliph received the Seljuk leader, Toghrul-beg, and appointed him

In the inner courtyard of the shrine at Mashad devout Muslims gather for the annual ceremonies of Moharram, including symbolic flagellation. The most holy tomb in Iran, that of Ali-ar-Riza, is reached through a gold-lined vaulted hall leading from this courtyard. Ali-ar-Riza died near Mashad in AD 818 while the guest of a caliph's son: victim, it is said, of an intrigue over the succession to the

caliphate. Mashad means 'the place of the martyr', and the sense of martyrdom infects the Shi'a faithful as they come here as pilgrims from Iran, the Gulf States, Iraq, Afghanistan and Malaysia. The custodians of the shrine collect money and valuables thrown into the tomb which provide generous sums.

Sultan with hereditary rights. For a century this marked a new disposition of power within Islam. The caliph relapsed into impotent
spiritual leadership and the Seljuks, the martial arm of Islam, expanded
the empire to include Anatolia in the west and northern India in the
east.

In themselves, the Seljuks were a phenomenon, a surge of aggressive creativity: fearsome, inventive, pious, brilliant. But they were
more. They epitomized something deep in human nature, the confluence (and conflict) of nomadic energy and the desire for per-
manence. The Seljuk dynasty has left behind it, more than any earlier
regime, tangible examples of what nomadic energy can achieve when
transmuted into a rooted culture. It seems that in the first adaptive
moments of settlement, in the desertion of the open horizon, the
nomad came to terms with his spirit by channelling it into a soaring
affirmation of settlement. Sometimes, as we have yet to see, the
nomad could vent a terrible fury on rooted society; even then, as
though through catharsis, he repented and built.

The Seljuks built to express piety. Their greatest legacy is the
definitive Persian mosque: an arcaded courtyard and, on the 'holy axis'
of the courtyard aligned with Mecca, the domed sanctuary opened
through an *iwan* to the sky. Structural daring, informed by a sophisticated command of the physical stresses, fused with a finesse of
proportion and shape, and produced an astonishing felicity of merging
surfaces – walls, pillars, squinches, piers, vaulted roofs and domes
overrode the geometrical laws to assume serene harmony. Here is the
consummation of the architectural vocabulary discovered by the
Parthians, and amplified by the Sasanians. It is the true transmission of
artistic genius from one wave to another, and the Seljuks set a standard
frequently pursued but never surpassed.

The genius lay in knowing how far to go – and then stopping; a
containment of the craftsmanship before it became over-confident.
The restraint is shown in the basic medium of Seljuk building, baked
brick. The surface texture of pillars, arches, walls and domes is an
organic part of the brickwork; the pale sand-coloured bricks are laid
and manipulated into geometric patterns and make a plastic theatre of
light and shade. The light either pierces the vaults in focused beams, or
filters through grilles. In the course of a day the shadows move across
the subtle patterns to conceal and to reveal; the effect is not hard but
liquid. It is a pubescent moment in Persian decoration: sometimes a

few pale blue glazed tiles punctuate the monochrome patterns, like a new instrument being introduced nervously into a fragile quartet. The harmony survives, the integrity is unbroken.

This selfsame control marks the calligraphy. Copies of the Koran made by Seljuk scribes show them taking greater liberties with the script than with the first austere pages of the original Kufic style of earlier centuries, but stopping well short of the polychromatic embellishments which were to follow (as they did also in the medieval European illuminations). A question hangs in the air, never to be answered: are we seeing artistic self-denial, a disciplined and calculated constraint, or is it that rare moment, found elsewhere in art, when the optimum balance is struck between technique and form?

Lest this hymn to Seljuk taste should give the dynasty an effete and benign aura (the craftsmen of their time are, alas, anonymous and, like many others, had a calculated propagandist function) it is as well to remember their martial side. They imposed their Sunni faith ruthlessly, and invoked the principle of the *jihad*, holy war, to channel the bloodlust of their Turkomen tribesmen. In the course of the drive to Baghdad they overran the remnants of the Buyid empire in south-west Persia and later they used an iron fist against the Shi'ites, pillaging their mosques, theological colleges and libraries.

The result of this repression was bizarre and far-reaching. The hard core of the Shi'ite movement in Persia withdrew to the mountainous enclave from whence the Buyids had first surfaced. They sought out an eyrie of devilish impregnability at Alamut, between the city of Qazvin and the Caspian. This fortress, known inevitably as the Eagle's Nest, accounts for the legend of the Old Man of the Mountain in Marco Polo – the old man being a sectarian leader of great age. Here was the headquarters of the extremist Shi'ite sect known as the Ismailis, who became not only an isolated state within a state, but the source of an underground movement which penetrated the intelligentsia of the Seljuks and attempted to foment peasant revolt. The contemporary echo of this faction is heightened by the method they pioneered to inflict political reprisals. The Ismailis gave us the word, and the modern sense of assassination. The word came from hashishin – the eater of hashish – which the Ismailis were said to have used for indoctrination. A single, anonymous killer was assigned a target and could, using patience and intelligence, reach and destroy some of the highest-placed officers of the Seljuk court – one of the assassins even killed a Sultan. The Ismaili redoubt became known as the Valley of the Assassins.

The historical reputation of the Ismailis tended, therefore, to suggest a psychopathic fanaticism. Recent scholars, with new evidence, have sought to rehabilitate them. Within the prevailing ethic of the medieval east the Assassins were possibly unexceptionable, a highly selective tyranny to counter a far less discriminating one. The substance of Ismaili appeal was theological, the promise of a 'worldly redemption' and – hence its communist strain – the hope of relief at last for that mass of peasants on the plateau for whom the developing refinements of court and city were merely a burden marked by more and more taxation.

Even without the harassment from the Ismailis, the Seljuk regime created its own built-in dissolution. Control of the state was racially specialized: military power was in the hands of the Turks, the administrators were Persian viziers (including the vizier Nizam al–Mulk who wrote a primer of political theory, *The Book of Government*), and the spiritual guidance reposed in the care of Arabs, as well as Persians. The abusive potential of the Sasanian tradition began to infect Seljuk government, which became over-endowed and corrupt. Nizam al–Mulk, despite his treatise, was notorious for nepotism. The hold of the state was progressively loosened by a dispersal of wealth and power – soldiers given land, or tax benefits from land, lost an interest in fighting. The tax-farming eventually wiped out many of the professional land owners, especially in Fars. And, as had the Cleitus faction in Alexander's army, the unreformed nomads of the clans resented the new urban Persian manners of their chiefs. They preferred marauding at will and plundering what was left of the countryside. Neglect of agriculture was a serious fault of the Seljuks, and was undoubtedly a symptom of the surviving conflict between the pastoral and nomadic temperaments. Thus the ambivalence of the dynasty: extensive conquest, consolidation of Sunnism, superb buildings and artifacts, but all the while an incomplete control of events.

They left enough for posterity to relish, particularly in the cities. In this period the classic shape of the medieval eastern city emerged: the spiritual apex of the mosque, the social and mercantile organism of the bazaar, abutting and umbilically linked to the mosque, and the embryonic form of the city square, or *maidan*, surrounded by the residential quarters. Damascus and Baghdad were rivalled and in some ways

Easily overlooked in a distant corner of the Friday Mosque at Isfahan is the Gunbad-i-Khaki, or Brown Dome. A chamber built at the end of the eleventh century by a Seljuk vizier, art critics acclaim it a masterpiece of sacred architecture. Though only sixty-five feet high, its structure fuses brickwork and decoration into a harmony of complex shapes and motifs.

eclipsed by the growing cities of Persia: Isfahan, Shiraz, Rayy, Nishapur. Islamic scholarship flourished in the east as much as in the west: two centuries before the first European university was founded at Bologna, Nizam al–Mulk founded universities at Nishapur, Balkh, Mosul, Herat and Merv, as well as one named after him at Baghdad. Orthodox Islam had been greatly reinforced by the transient unity of the Seljuk empire; when their temporal power declined the caliph was able to move into the vacuum and reassert a degree of political authority.

After the centuries of debate, the *schema* of Islam was beginning to harden. At the same time (and possibly as a reaction) Muslim thinkers turned more to mysticism. Under the Seljuks, al–Ghazali, an intellectual and theologian, proposed a synthesis of orthodox Sunnism, as it was then ordained, and Sufism – a mystical strain which ironically today thrives also within Shi'ism. At this fertile moment, Nizam al–Mulk, a relentless scourge of the Shi'ites, was struck down by an Ismaili assassin.

Historians dispute whether the Seljuks mark the beginning of a new social, political and theological order or the end of the old one. For Persia what mattered was that she regained not a national identity in any meaningful sense, but a *regional independence*. Persia was no longer subsumed within the Islamic whole, but a cultural and political powerhouse in her own right (and, without then knowing it, she already harboured the seed of theological independence). But there was no ethnic consolidation, or reversion. Two Turkish waves, the Ghaznavids and the Seljuks, were instrumental in pulling the centre of gravity of the Muslim world farther east. So by talking of 'Persia' we now mean a new racial admixture of Turkoman, Arab and Persian, what Firdausi disparaged as 'a mongrel race'. The ability to fuse and reconcile racial strains had been a gift of Persia from the beginning; just as well, because it was to be needed again. Nothing and nobody who passed through Persia failed to be marked by it. The nomads poured off the steppes and could not (except possibly the most inveterate of them) help but marvel at what they found. Arrested, seduced, inspired. And then transformed.

What, other than the land itself, kept the character of Persia together? Not just the regard of Persians for themselves, but the regard of others, especially the Arabs, for Persia and Persians. A ninth-

The Sasanian city of Shiz was built around a lake (said to be bottomless) at Takht-i-Sulaiman in the highlands of north-west Persia. The site had a great religious significance through many dynasties; the Sasanians built a fire temple there. When the Mongols first settled in Persia they were attracted to the striking highland setting and built there too.

century Arab poet, al–Buhturi, evokes the spell as he stands in awe of
the great arch at Ctesiphon:

> ... grieving for the decayed abode of the house of Sasan,
> high endeavours which, but for partiality on my part,
> the endeavours of 'Ans and 'Abs could not match.

And through five centuries it had been the *Sasanians*, time and again,
who symbolized not just what had decayed but also what remained
and could be passed on for practical use – and who generated the more
amorphous tonic of the historical legend. The folk history gathered by
Firdausi in the *Shahnameh* makes the Arthurian legend paltry by
comparison; Firdausi's Camelot, after all, had to evoke not merely a
fugitive kingdom but a great dynastic gallery extending far further
back in time than any upstart Anglo-Saxon heritage. The Persian
memory, without any tradition of chroniclers to bring the actors and
the events even remotely into authentic order, was peopled with
heroes part distinct and part garbled. Superstition and the hyperbole of
Greek mythology set off a merry dance, even co-opting Alexander as
'Iskhander' into the Persian gallery. Never mind credence, or the lack
of it. The voice was authentic enough, the voice of Persian *bravura*
mixed not inconsiderably with the Persian resource of melancholy.
Heroes had a fatalism about them. What use was heroism without
tragedy?

It has to be said for the Sasanians that they were as large in life as they
were in legend. And in the Sasanian superstructure, with its sense of
station and heraldic order, the nomads would have recognized a
solution to their urgent problem: the mechanics of a settled society in a
form they could follow. Professor Jerome Clinton, who has closely
studied the cultural marriage of Persia and Islam, says: 'Even before
the *Shahnameh* was translated back into modern Persian from the
Arabic to which it had been translated shortly after the invasion, the
Islamic rulers had been so much schooled in Sasanian monarchs and
Sasanian history – to discover how they might run their empire – that
there was never really any risk that Iran's historic and cultural heritage
would be lost.'

Persian administrators, employed from the first, kept alive the
profession of the vizier and, more, sustained the Persian style in
bureaucracy; a mixed blessing. Other professional and scholarly talents, harvested by the caliphate and later by the temporal courts, gave

Islam its polymath range and gradually produced a new class. By the end of the Seljuk period we can see, in the image of men like Nizam al–Mulk, what might be called a medieval technocracy. Nominally servants, they were becoming indispensable repositories of knowledge. The state in its advancing form could not function without them and there was an extra reason for their survival: they bridged the secular and theological worlds. With the new mercantile class which came to prominence in the bazaar, they formed a new strata of society, not lessening its hierarchical form but usefully broadening it.

In return for what Persia had given Islam, her own gain was considerable, as Professor Clinton evaluates it:

Iranian scholars who accepted Islam had been able to participate in a developing world civilization that extended far wider, and was deeper and more extensive – in many ways far richer – than the unitary Iranian civilization that they had belonged to beforehand. Iranian genius found greater scope. By the tenth century it was an age of extraordinary creativity – the creation of modern Persian literature, one of the most extraordinary examples being the *Shahnameh*. This literature caused for the first time in Islam, a rift between what had been a wholly Arab civilization and the new Perso-Islamic culture.

The truly fixed component in this volatile landscape was the religion. Despite the sectarian rift, despite the infusion of new races, despite the unstable power of the caliphate, Islam had taken root and gave its own order to life. As it superseded Zoroastrianism it quickly proved to be what Zoroastrianism had never been: one of the universal religions. None of the usurpers who came to build dynasties made the mistake of casting out the religion; the nomads of the steppes felt its appeal and embraced it readily. It clearly met a need. That need was as apparent in Africa as it was in Mesopotamia, in Iberia as it was in Persia. When Muhammad appeared with his vision the people of Medina had said 'Allah has sent us a prophet who will make peace between us.' But this went well beyond the reconciliation of the Arabs: it gave a drive to its adherents to save the world from the infidels.

The vigour of Islam directly determined the vigour of each state in the empire; intellect and faith were indivisible. If Islam remained dynamic, so too would the Muslim states. In this sense, Islam's limits were Persia's limits.

6

The Descent of the Hordes

1206-1450

On a bare alluvial plain in what is now the north-east corner of Mongolia, near the Russian and Chinese borders, a river called the Onon assembles from tributaries and threads northwards. In 1206, the Mongolian Year of the Tiger, the nomadic tribes of Central Asia gathered at the source of the Onon and raised a white standard edged with nine yaks' tails, the *tuq*. Under this banner they elected a certain Temujin as Chingis Khan, leader of the Mongols, supreme emperor of all the tribes of the steppes. The word 'Chingis' meant 'oceanic'; the title implied a universal ruler. It was not a vain boast. The newly unified tribes, under their invincible commander, were to sweep like an ocean across the length of Asia and deep into Europe, creating an empire which stretched from Korea to Germany. Although it proved perishable, the Mongol empire became a hinge of world history, with permanent consequences. Islam was transformed by it; Persia shattered.

Why did civilized society collapse so easily at the touch of the pagan hordes? It is tempting – and many have been so tempted – to see this catastrophe as a kind of ordained purgatory: the insensible force rendering the service of smashing cities on behalf of the purer counter-culture of the nomad. But this is, surely, the black romanticism of the twentieth century, rather than the reality of Asia in the thirteenth century. There were in that world no watertight barriers between the sedentary and nomadic societies – they co-existed and interacted (as in places they still do). Pastoral tribal life flowed around the cities often without conflict; agrarian and pastoral life were potentially competitive but, in normal times, there was space for both. Because of their unremitting carnage the Mongols have understandably been stigmatized into a caricature of the pastoral life, as though they were fit for nothing better.

In fact, pastoral nomadism was not an incongruous hangover from the ancient world, like a dinosaur suddenly risen and trampling through the gardens of Paradise, but a developed and highly specialized condition *followed from preference* – or necessity. Agriculture quite possibly preceded pastoralism, not the other way round. The rationale lay in the land itself, in the nature of the steppes, the great treeless expanse, part plain and part low hills, where by alternating the grazing according to the extremes of climate the horses, cattle, sheep and goats could be maintained. Organizing a society around seasonal migration meant making it durable and highly mobile. Underlying the physical nature of nomadism was (and is) the spiritual appeal of a life without confinement. It was from this life that there developed those qualities of character which gave Chingis Khan's armies their unusual obduracy.

Once the Mongols achieved mass, as they did under Chingis Khan's deliberate policy, they were a novelty not in nature *but in scale*. Before unification the separate tribes were aggressive but not, individually, overwhelming. They did not remain unified on this scale for very long, but while they did they possessed terrifying potential – and fulfilled it. The misfortune of Central Asia, Persia, Mesopotamia, Russia, Hungary, Poland and Germany was to be weak when the Mongols were at flood.

If their capacity as conquerors is beyond question, the motive for conquest is much more disputed. It was put at its most absurd by nineteenth-century historians who said the campaigns were carried out to satisfy the appetites of the Mongol horses – which, in that case, must truly have been insatiable. Modern scholarship suggests that Chingis Khan had, from the beginning, three carefully reasoned objectives: to secure the unity of the tribes and their allegiance to him, within Mongolia; to secure his flank in the neighbouring regions of China; and then to defeat the force he most feared – the Turkish tribes who ranged Central Asia to the west of his pastures. This theory reverses the traditional view that his priority was to smash the settled empires, and it shows how formidable the Turkish presence had become. Only when *they* were removed could Chingis pick off the vulnerable empires, like Persia. With the success of his first campaign outside Mongolia, the humbling of the Hsi Hsia state in north-west China, and the dispersion of the Turks under way, Chingis's baleful interest was drawn to Persia by an incident which must rank in its cost of human lives as the most disastrous provocation in history.

It happened at Utrar (now in Russian Central Asia) in 1218. This was a frontier post of the empire of the Khwarazm Shahs, who supplanted parts of the dissolving Seljuk empire at the end of the twelfth century. The Khwarazm Shahs had expanded from the rich pastures between the Caspian and the Oxus into the plateau, and eastwards as far as Samarkand. In doing so, they had over-extended themselves; and they had also antagonized their subjects in their new colonies on both racial and religious grounds. The second Shah, Muhammad, was a Turkish supremacist – and a Shi'ite, opposed to the Baghdad caliphate. His army was mercenary, of dubious loyalty. Heavy taxation compounded the public unrest.

The Shah's *folie de grandeur* was careless, and fatal. As well as beginning a march on Baghdad he entertained notions of expanding eastwards towards the rapidly rising power of Chingis Khan. Each power knew of the other, but Shah Muhammad was impulsive and ill-informed, whereas Chingis was always careful to think and plan well ahead. He placed great reliance on a stealthy intelligence network, often using travelling merchants as cover. A Mongol mission was sent west, ostensibly to explore trade with the Shah, but when it reached Utrar the local governor decided that it was a clandestine spying operation and massacred all one hundred members of the mission, including a Mongol diplomat and, perhaps more materially, seized all the goods. When a second Mongol embassy was sent to inquire of the fate of the first it too, was massacred, this time on the direct orders of the Shah. No more was needed to provoke the Great Khan. Quite conceivably, the mission *had* been a covert essay in espionage, but the truth became academic. A holocaust was unleashed.

'Who would find it easy to describe the ruin of Islam and Muslims?'

wrote the chronicler Ibn al–Athir ... 'If anyone were to say that at no time since the creation of man by the great God had the world experienced anything like it, he would only be telling the truth.' It took just three years for the Mongols, in their first assault, to devastate the whole of northern Persia as well as annihilating the empire of the Khwarazm Shahs, vast tracts of Russia and Transoxiana. The impact on Islam was traumatic. Bukhara, the eastern jewel of Islam, fell early. A story gathered by the Persian historian Juvaini conveys the abjection of Bukhara's holy men as they met the pagan conqueror. Chingis Khan and his son Toluy rode into the city's Friday Mosque, dismounted and ascended the pulpit. They asked if this was the palace of the Sultan, and were told that it was the house of God. Unmoved, Chingis said: 'The countryside is empty of fodder, fill our horses' bellies.' Cases containing the mosque's Korans were emptied at random and taken into the courtyard to be converted to mangers for the horses. As Chingis led his cavalry from the mosque a few hours later, the pages of the Koran were trampled into the dirt. A watching *savant*, trying to calm an outraged *imam*, said: 'Be silent: it is the wind of God's omnipotence that bloweth, and we have no power to speak.' A refugee from Bukhara put it less piously: 'They came, they sapped, they burnt, they slew, they plundered and they departed.'

Two years later a slightly mellowed Chingis returned to Bukhara. He asked the *imams* to explain the tenets of Islam. He listened patiently, approved everything he was told bar one thing: the annual pilgrimage to Mecca. The whole world, he said, was the house of God, not a single building – perhaps a clue to the universality of his own horizons, which by then seemed limitless. Bukhara had wisely opened its gates to the horde, and survived. Nishapur, the great university city of Khorasan, was not so prudent. It resisted the first wave, and one of its archers slew Chingis's son-in-law Tokuchar. The following year the Mongols returned for revenge. Tokuchar's widow presided over total butchery: even the cats and the dogs were killed in the streets. The entire human population was beheaded and the skulls of men, women and children carefully separated and constructed into pyramids. It was customary for all victims to be disembowelled; once a fugitive had been caught swallowing a pearl, and no potential hiding place was thereafter spared the sword.

So great was the momentum of the second swathe through Persia, completed in 1222, that twenty states fell as the Mongols completed a circuit of the Caspian. Chingis himself never led an army on to the plateau; his son Toluy and his generals Jebei and Subodei were the spearheads. At their worst, these commanders were punitive beyond reason. Resistance inevitably brought a bloodbath. The only survivors were those selected for certain skills who were taken back to Mongolia, or those used as cannon-fodder to go ahead of the army for the next siege. The land itself was poisoned by deliberate salting. Irrigation works were devastated and the cities dependent upon them left for dead. But the most lasting depletion was of human life. Even today the population of modern Iran has only recently passed its pre-Mongol level. The worst twentieth-century genocide never reached the appalling record of the Mongol invasions. The indifference to life and suffering was repeated over and over again, at the slenderest provocation.

But this was not random and wild butchery committed by an army out of control; it was quite systematic and organized, done to exact command. When they hunted animals the Mongols used a technique of encirclement: they surrounded the area containing game and then gradually closed in, herding the prey until it was tightly packed and then unleashing a precisely aimed barrage of arrows, leaving nothing alive. With people they were just as methodical, rounding them up, sorting them into groups, and then hacking them down.

Time does little to dull the horror. And yet there are apparent anomalies. The Mongols followed a form of Shamanism, a superstitious faith directed at a sky-god, Tengri, which incorporated sacrifices and elaborate burial rituals. It also placed great store in reading the signs; invasion campaigns were, on occasion, postponed indefinitely on a bad prediction. As strict as they were in their observances, the Mongols never made any attempt to convert others and Chingis encouraged the continuance of all the faiths he overran: Muslims, Jews, Christians, Buddhists. He gave immunity to the clergy, even in the midst of carnage.

The remorseless organization of slaughter was part of a total discipline governing all Mongol conduct, on the battlefield and away from it. To our modern sensibilities all this seems simply to multiply the horror, as though it was performed by robots whose efficiency is beyond doubt but whose purpose seems unforgivable. Apologists will point out that mindless butchery was a common aberration of those times, and for centuries later. It will also be argued that the pastoral nomad was not just uncomprehending when he found a carefully husbanded agriculture in his path, but that he actively despised the settled peasantry no less than he found towns and cities an impediment to the natural unrooted life. Others will see this as feeble pleading, as though to dignify the locust as an immanent arm of nature. Probably, the fury is truly inexplicable; all we can do is to reach further into the mystery and follow it to its resolution, the changing of the world.

Of the architect, it is hard to get any true picture: the portrait style of the period is decorative but innocuous. And a typical word picture is no better: 'A man of tall stature, of vigorous build, robust in body, the hair on his face scanty and turned white, with cat's eyes, possessed of great energy, discernment, genius and understanding, awe-inspiring, a butcher, just, resolute, an overthrower of enemies, intrepid, sanguinary and cruel.' But there is a remarkable record of Chingis Khan and his works, *The Secret History of the Monguls*. From this we see not just a clever and brave military commander consolidating this power-base, but a boyhood of almost mythical prowess; descent from a noble family; the selection of an appropriate bride only then to be torn from her and be banished as the victim of a plot; a precarious existence as a fugitive; gradual reappearance amongst the mighty and then a second mishap; recovery of the first love but then her abduction by hostile forces; recovery of bride only to find that she is blemished by a pregnancy of uncertain origin; final acceptance as ruler of own tribe and then the rapid rise to supreme and unchallenged power. As a character-building ordeal it could hardly be bettered.

Whether or not this is *post-hoc* embroidery – and the setting is, at least, credible – what equipped Chingis Khan for his destiny were gifts in some ways reminiscent of Alexander: the ability to organize on a large scale, a calculated strategy and, novel to the Mongols, a concept of law-making. His first practical step was to provide something which until then had been superfluous to Mongol needs, a written language. Chingis was not interested in literacy as a mark of culture; he simply wanted a *lingua franca* in order to be able to administrate. He ordered a Turkish prisoner of the Uighur tribe to transcribe the Mongol tongue into Uighur script. All his edicts were henceforth issued in this form. Aware of his own people's poverty of learning, Chingis took the tools he needed from wherever they were available. A Chinese mandarin organized his civil service. Financial management, international trade, policing, post-houses and courier routes, and taxation systems, were all progressively adopted. But two concepts, above others, marked the style of Chingis's empire: the legal code and the army's prescribed form and discipline.

The legal code was not, in fact, a formalized body of law, but the *Yasas*, an accumulation of Mongol custom, preserved orally. These customs were dominated by applications of the death penalty, directed at offences which in manners large and small might have jeopardized nomadic life: deliberately pouring milk or drink on the ground; urinating inside a tent, into a river or a well; adultery and fornication outside wedlock (although the Mongol princes enjoyed generous sexual licence). Women, who had to do a great deal of the physical work involved in maintaining and transporting a whole society as it moved, enjoyed a high measure of equality. Far more than under Islam, the women (who like the men wore trousers) were an arm of Mongol power; they rode straddling the saddle and were expert archers. At their most superstitious, the *Yasas* enshrined the qualities of fire. Fire was the great purifier. Outsiders like visiting envoys were made to pass between two fires as they joined a Mongol camp. Putting a knife or sword into a fire was forbidden – it was thought to drain the force from the flame. Water also had sacred qualities. Streams and rivers were thought to be 'alive' and hence not to be polluted, even by washing in them. The *Yasas* were intended to provide a universal system of law, but their application tended to be haphazard. All that was certain was the ultimate authority of the Great Khan: 'One son in heaven, *one* lord on earth.'

Estimates of the size of Chingis Khan's armies vary from seventy thousand to eight hundred thousand men depending on the source and the campaign. As ever, the figures were notoriously prone to exaggeration, and perhaps swollen by a Mongol trick of assembling dummies to appear more numerous than they really were. Whatever the numbers, the Mongols were able to deploy great masses, including many mercenaries, with a fine precision and unbroken discipline. The framework was decimal. A chronicler records: 'When he set up units of a thousand, he appointed leaders of the thousands, of each hundred and each ten.' Ten 'sections' of ten made a company (or a century); ten centuries a battalion and the largest unit was a division of ten thousand. The armies had the classic formation of wings and a centre. No single Mongol soldier had any doubt of his position in battle, or his duty. Desertion, cowardice and retreat were instantly punishable by death.

Although Chingis provided the cover of cannon-fodder for his men (the prisoners were also used as pathfinders in treacherous swamps) the Mongols were as brave as they were savage. Thousands of years of horsemanship were in their blood and they were, until the advent of gunpowder towards the end of their period, the supreme mounted war machine, fast, deadly accurate with their bows, and expertly commanded. Throughout his campaigns, Chingis retained the bulk of his people in their grazing lands, to breed horses to replenish the army's stocks and to train new horsemen on the steppes before they joined the army. At this stage he was not interested in setting up princes as kings in distant lands; that came later. The army's techniques gained from men drafted from conquered lands: sappers from Persia, and the Chinese who developed Mongol siege tactics. Fire floats, flaming missiles from catapults, and battering rams were backed up by psychological terror provided by the carpet of cannon-fodder left by the city walls.

This machine of total war was unlike anything Persia or Islam had faced for centuries. In Persia's case it was less like the Arab invasion, which had found sympathy from an oppressed people, and more like the systematic and often callous thrusts of Alexander. Persia was, in any case, in no way as formidable as she had been under earlier kings. The 'empire' of the Khwarazm Shahs was tenuous and not even really Persian. Its army *seemed* large, but it was disorganized. Before the Mongols appeared on the horizon the earlier conflicts on the plateau had been local, tribal and dynastic, not global. Here the invader was of a new kind, not sectarian, not messianic, but pagan and yet seemingly united and organized by a force greater than divinity – a sense of conquest that could run to the limits of the earth.

Six centuries of refinement had made of Persia an elegant synthesis of Islam and native sensibility; six months of subjection to the Mongol war machine was enough to reduce civilization to ceramic dust. The epitome of the Persian achievement was Seljuk culture. By the magnificence of what survived the Mongols we can get only a measure of how fine the whole must have been, and therefore some sense of the outrage beyond the smashing of bones. Like the Mongols, the Seljuks had been nomads. Unlike the Mongols, they came quickly to rest and to imbibe urban manners, to organize and cultivate and to add another layer of achievement to Persian history; the Mongols had a harsher and grander design and only became Persianized as an afterthought. In the beginning their aim seems to have been, in the words of the historian Dr Robert Hillenbrand, 'to eradicate the means of recovery'. Unthinking nihilism? 'You would have thought that if the Mongols knew they were going to stay they wouldn't have destroyed the country to that extent.'

The relative ease with which the settled empires were overrun led the Mongols to a growing sense of world conquest, which assumed the status of a manifest destiny. The successors to Chingis Khan (he died in 1227 at the age of sixty) carried this conviction to its conclusion. In 1245 the Christian hierarchy of western Europe was forced to react. Pope Innocent IV assigned a mission to treat with 'the King and People of the Tartars'. It was led intrepidly by an erstwhile companion of St Francis, the friar John of Plano Carpini (near Perugia) then in his sixties. It took Carpini over a year to reach the Mongol heartland, at a time when a new Khan, Kuyuk, was being enthroned. The Khan kept the Christians waiting for months, and finally gave a dusty answer in response to the Pope's invitation to accept baptism and his strictures on Mongol massacres in Poland and Hungary. The treatment was a consequence, said Kuyuk Khan's reply, of ignoring God's command as delivered by the Mongol armies. As for accepting baptism, the Pope had better personally explain the idea and then 'I shall make known all the commands of the *Yasas*'. Finally: 'If you ignore my command, I shall know you as my enemy. Likewise I shall make you understand. If you do otherwise, God knows what I know.' This 'God knows what will happen' tone was repeated to other missions. Diplomacy was irrelevant to these first Mongol Khans; subjection was the only relationship they offered. Later Khans were to learn more subtlety.

One of the Mongols' earliest subject peoples were the Persians, but the conquest came in two phases: the first invasion ran due west out of Khorasan, expunging Nishapur, Rayy (a suburb of modern Tehran), Hamadan, and then turned north to pass through Azerbaijan into Russia. The Persian provinces to the south escaped; Isfahan, Shiraz and Kirman had an interval of circumspect independence under local dynasties, quaking in their shoes. Provocation was clearly unwise. As an entity, Persia was once again in suspense, but one consistent irritant aroused the interest of the great Khan: the Assassins of Alamut. The legend of the Assassins had reached even western Europe, and when the French envoy William of Rubruck visited the Mongol court at Karakorum, deep in Mongolia, he found security measures of an almost paranoid desperation. The explanation was that more than forty Assassins, in various disguises, had been despatched to eliminate the Great Khan. It was more than a danger, it was an intolerable insult. The fourth Great Khan, Mongke (1251–9), gave his brother Hulegu charge of an army to renew the conquest of Persia and specifically to wipe out the Assassins. Hulegu was also instructed to humble the Baghdad caliphate, still functioning as the beacon of Islam.

The Mongol invasion launched under Hulegu in 1255 ended the tenuous independence of Persia. The entire plateau was incorporated into a Mongol sub-kingdom, the Ilkhanate. It was a part of the devolution of the Mongol empire itself. Although its first effect on Persia was vassaldom, the Ilkhanate re-established the geography of the old Persian state and therefore helped its ultimate survival. Some kind of natural law of survival seems to operate at times when the country all but disappears; perhaps the logic of the ancient administrative machine was too persuasive to be ignored, perhaps an optimum balance of land, climate and economy imposed itself. With the appearance of Hulegu the familiar process of assimilation begins slowly and rather painfully to emerge. A shrewd Persian astrologer, Nasir al–Din Tusi, was soon giving advice to Hulegu, partial to his own Shi'ite interests. As ever, the self-serving and indestructible Persian bureaucracy readily filled the wide gaps in their conquerors' ability to govern.

The extinction of the Assassins, a plague on one and a half centuries of Persian government, encouraged the idea of collaboration. The Assassins, or Ismailis, had continued their Shi'ite vendettas, which gained a kind of sacramental quality. Any established order was vulnerable to an Ismaili 'contract', the killing of the unrighteous, as the Seljuks found to their cost. Hulegu could (mistakenly) be celebrated as a saviour of orthodox Islam for ending the myth of Ismaili impregnability. It took all the Mongol tenacity and skill to breach the mountain redoubt and, naturally, when they did they left nothing alive. Afterwards the Persian historian Juvaini was allowed to comb the Ismaili library at Alamut. He gave his account of the victory a moralizing climax: 'And in truth that act was the balm of Muslim wounds and the cure to the disorders of the Faith.'

But any hopes of Mongol patience with Muslim orthodoxy were dispelled by the assault on Baghdad. Caliph Musta'sim represented a low ebb of Abbasid qualities. He was over-confident and incompetent. He warned Hulegu that his Muslim army 'would dry up the waves of the sea'. Three separate Mongol armies converged on Baghdad in January 1258. They were briefly repulsed, which inevitably worsened the city's fate. 'Both seed and stem perished,' wailed the Muslim chroniclers, echoing a phrase from the Koran.

The moving quill of events wrote on the leaves of the walls, and on the roofs reaching to the sky ... beds and cushions made of gold and encrusted with jewels were cut to pieces with knives and torn to shreds; those hidden behind the veils of the great harem were dragged like the hair of the idols through the streets and alleys; each of them became a plaything in the hands of a Tartar monster; and the brightness of the day became darkened for these mothers of virtues...

The caliph's palace, the grand mosque and the repositories of Abbasid culture were all destroyed. Hulegu observed a Mongol superstition which warned against the spilling of noble and sacred blood; Musta'sim was smothered in blankets. Baghdad's reign as the spiritual and intellectual powerhouse of Islam was over, and it was never regained. The physical scars were permanent. In 1933 Robert Byron noted testily that, 'the prime fact of Mesopotamian history is that Hulegu destroyed the irrigation system, and from that day to this Mesopotamia has remained a land of mud'. The description is accurate, but to be fair to Hulegu the Seljuks had already allowed the irrigation works to fall into decay, but the Mongols hadn't helped, either.

After pausing for breath, Hulegu pressed westwards, confident now of rolling up the map of Islam. Aleppo fell in 1260, and Damascus capitulated soon afterwards. The Mongols had grown used to victory; they overran a succession of poorly ruled and led people. But on 3 September 1260, at Ain Jalut ('Goliath's Well') near Nazareth they met a well-led and determined Muslim army which knew that the survival of Islam depended on it. The Mongols were beaten decisively; their general, Kitbugha, was captured and killed. Hulegu had himself been compelled to return to Karakorum for the election of a new Great Khan (on Mongke's death the lyrically celebrated Kubilai Khan succeeded). Hulegu's absence from the field may well have been fatal.

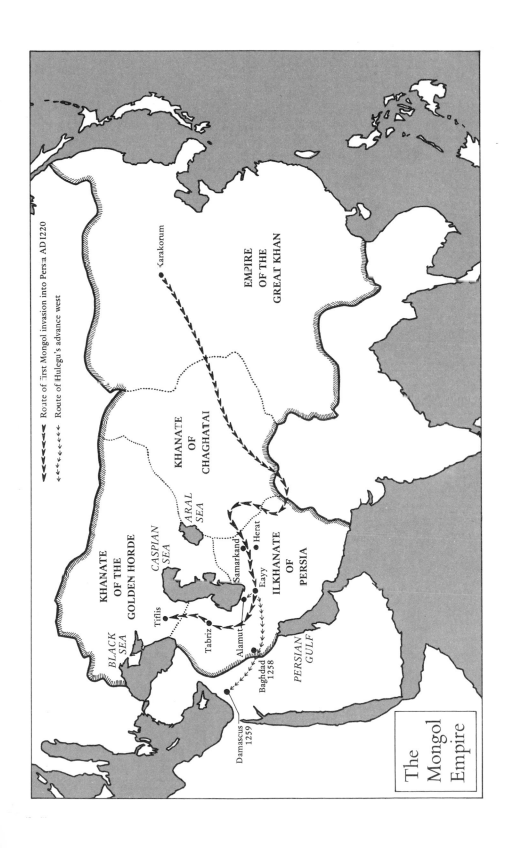

Route of first Mongol invasion into Persa AD 1220

Route of Hulegu's advance west

Karakorum

EMPIRE
OF THE
GREAT KHAN

KHANATE
OF
CHAGHATAI

KHANATE
OF THE
GOLDEN HORDE

ARAL
SEA

CASPIAN
SEA

BLACK
SEA

Tiflis

Tabriz

Samarkand

Herat

Eayy

Alamut

ILKHANATE
OF
PERSIA

Baghdad
1258

PERSIAN
GULF

Damascus
1259

The
Mongol
Empire

Sultan Qutuz of the Mamluks had humiliated the Mongol army and Ain Jalut proved to be – as he had told his army – the saving of the faith. The prestige of Baghdad passed to Cairo. Mongol dreams of limitless conquest dissolved. The Mamluks regained Aleppo and Damascus.

Hulegu had run to a halt. His power was contained by Mesopotamia and Persia. Accepting the reality, the Mongols underwent the change from transient imperialists to resident rulers. The Ilkhanate maintained a nominal allegiance to the Great Khan, but in effect Hulegu and his successors were independent monarchs – although a High Commissioner represented Kubilai Khan in Tabriz and his name remained for a while on the coinage. Hulegu's chief wife Doquz was a Christian, and kept a portable chapel where bells were rung. This, and the Christian sympathies of Hulegu's son and grandson, kindled hopes in the west that the Mongols might reinvigorate eastern Christianity and at least contain Islam. But it was not to be. The Mongol princes never made convincing converts to any faith, even though they were, at their best, tolerant of other religions and not fanatical about their own rituals.

The focus of Persia in this new flux moved to the north-west, to Azerbaijan where Hulegu preferred the climate. Tabriz, soon adopted as capital, was well placed to become a nexus for all the currents passing between east and west. Persians, Arabs, Turks, Uighurs, Byzantines, Italians and Chinese came to the Mongol Ilkhanate and for Persia the connection with China, reinforced by the security of the Mongol highways to the east, was particularly important. Chinese knowledge of astronomy, medicine and engineering enhanced the intellectual climate. Hulegu, for better and for worse, delegated to Persian administrators. Juvaini paid his master sycophantic tribute: 'That which exclusively occupies the Emperor's mind is that the scented breezes of justice and equity should perfume the corners of the world.' Not surprisingly, Juvaini's family prospered greatly in the service of the court.

Hulegu died in 1265, to be succeeded by his son Abaka. Like his father, Abaka was pragmatic about religion. He did not directly distress the Muslims, but indirectly he antagonized them by accommodating both the Buddhists (regarded as pagans by the Muslims) and the Nestorian Christians. The Nestorians were established compatriots of the Mongols; their faith had been implanted in the Uighurs as early as the seventh century, and through marriage Uighur women influenced the Mongols; Hulegu's own wife had come from such a tribe. In 1241 a Nestorian patriarch successfully pleaded for Mongol protection for all Christians who had not opposed them, and this led to unimpeded Christian activity throughout the Mongol empire. By the end of the thirteenth century there were twenty metropolitan sees in Persia alone. But the Nestorians were regarded by western Christians as deviates who excluded the Roman orthodoxy.

However, latent devotion to Islam in the Ilkhanate's royal family emerged in a curious way. Abaka died, addled with drink, in 1282 and was followed not by the chosen son, Arghun, but by Teguder, an uncle. Teguder's mother was a Nestorian and he had been baptized Nicholas, after the reigning Pope. It counted for little. As a youth he leaned openly towards Islam and, once installed as Ilkhan, took the Muslim name of Ahmad and the title of Sultan and endeared himself to his Muslim subjects as the first declared convert. But his army did not approve. In 1284 Teguder was, according to custom, bloodlessly beaten to death, and Arghun installed in his place. The aberration was over; Buddhists and Christians breathed again, and the Muslims were vigorously discouraged. The Juvaini family, waxing fat on their prolonged role in the government, fell from favour as part of a general purge of Persian Muslims. Arghun installed as his vizier an able and ambitious Jew, Sa'd al–Daula, who repaired a treasury sorely depleted by years of corruption and incompetence. His fate was to be too successful. So many Jews arrived during his regime that there were riots. He flattered Arghun with the idea that the Ilkhan should found a new religion, but it was not enough to save his skin. Angered by their exclusion from the commanding (and lucrative) heights of government, the Muslim bureaucrats allied with the Mongol aristocrats to assassinate the character of Sa'd al–Daula. With Arghun enfeebled, the Jew was executed and his family sold into slavery.

The longer the Mongols grappled with the government of Persia, the more difficult it was to resist the sheer force of the Muslims. Again after Arghun's death the succession was disputed. His son Ghazan was a Buddhist, and only twenty. The generals elevated another uncle instead, Gaikhatu. His short and dissolute rule was followed by an even shorter one under Baidu, who was hostile to Islam. Ghazan had bided his time as governor of Khorasan. He was advised that if he abandoned Buddhism for Islam he could win the throne. In Baidu's wake, Ghazan became the first secure Muslim Ilkhan, in 1295. Varying degrees of piety continued, but there were to be no more non-Muslim rulers of Persia.

Kubilai Khan had just died. He was the last of the Great Khans in the mould of Chingis, and the unitary Mongol empire was at an end. In Persia the Mongol aristocracy were becoming a settled and separate branch of the great tribe. Ghazan's conversion to Islam was serious: Buddhism in Persia was extinguished and the Jews and Christians, more deeply rooted, were hounded and humiliated. Churches were burned and the bishops thrown into jail. The Nestorians, after half a century in favour, retreated to an enclave on the upper Tigris, where they still survive.

Persia had languished for nearly a century. Once again the most hard-pressed victims of the occupation were the peasants. Taxes which should have been levied twice a year were levied as much as thirty times a year; embezzlement of the tax revenues was widespread, much of the money was siphoned off without ever reaching the Treasury. The state messengers who collected taxes were feared and reviled. Many towns and villages were deliberately allowed by their residents to fall into decay to discourage the demands of the rapacious civil servants. Even then the messengers would put their horses to graze in gardens and pursue the women. So burdensome were the taxes for the peasants that by the last decades of the thirteenth century only a tenth of the cultivatable land was in use.

In the towns the craftsmen and artisans were equally oppressed. Slavery, a rare condition in Persia, was introduced through state 'workshops' where not only destitute Persians were put to work, but also Greeks, Georgians, Abyssinians and Africans. Usury, banished under Islamic law, appeared and flourished.

When Ghazan took the throne at the age of twenty-four Persian life was at its nadir. He acted with celerity and purpose. The *Yasas* were superseded by the Islamic *shari'a* as the legal code, an immediate token of the state's new commitment to one religion. Tax reforms were implemented with an impartial ruthlessness: in one month five Mongol princes and thirty-eight emirs were executed for corruption. State revenues increased by twenty per cent. And as the bureaucratic tyranny lifted and economic life recovered the Mongol commitment to Persia, until then fitful and tentative, grew much firmer. The Great Khan's title disappeared from the coinage, and his representative left Tabriz. The Mongols and the Turks became perceptibly one race, especially in Azerbaijan, so creating a basis for the ruling class which would in future dominate Persia. Ghazan's own commitment to Islam moved from the pragmatic to the authentic. He freed insolvent debtors from all their liabilities, and introduced new systems of coinage and weights and measures.

For eighty years there had been no new Islamic architecture in Persia; on the contrary, much had been levelled. A renaissance began under Ghazan. Tabriz lacked distinction as a capital, and he remedied this with the help of Rashid ad–Din, one of those resourceful polymaths who recur in Persian culture. Here was a physician, philosopher, law-maker and historian to rebuild the culture. Spiritual and intellectual life was renewed in Tabriz by building a new theological school, mosque, observatory and hospital and a new suburb with, as its focus, a great mausoleum 250 feet high. Rashid ad–Din built a new quarter said to have contained 30,000 homes, 24 caravanserai, 1500 shops, factories and workshops. He also endowed a hospital which brought physicians from India, China, Egypt and Syria, and a library stocked with 60,000 books and a seminary for 6000 students.

Tabriz was able fully to exploit its geographical advantages as a cosmopolitan city, and rivalled Genoa as an international centre of trade. Venice maintained a consul in Tabriz, and the Genoese and Venetians were given special diplomatic privileges. Religiously, Ghazan could still be something of a dissembler. Despite the persecution of Jews and Christians, he managed to cultivate a reputation in Europe as an enlightened ecumenist. The English king, Edward I, was encouraged enough to send his country's first ambassador to Persia, Geoffrey de Langley, who donated a gold crucifix to a monastery near Tabriz without realizing how far the Persian Christians were being persecuted.

For Islam, the renewal of state patronage in Persia without the diversion of allegiance to Baghdad marked a step towards a more indigenous, more eastern frame of mind. The desecration of the Mongol conquests and their repeated repressions had produced a subtle, almost chemical reaction in Islamic philosophy. The mysticism of the Sufis, launched under the Seljuks, proved an apt spiritual resource with which to face the terrible years. Sufism went 'underground' and Persian society of a certain kind developed a taste for communing through arcane channels, in orders and brotherhoods. Poetry also expressed the mood of melancholy and mysticism, through the work of thirteenth-century writers like Sa'di and Jalul al–Din Rumi, who epitomized the mood in his 'Spiritual Poem'. Some strains of the Ismaili precepts had possibly flowed into these new currents of Sufi thought.

When Ghazan died prematurely of drink, aged thirty-three, in 1304, he had achieved a great deal for Persia, but his foreign military adventures, attempting to follow the inspiration of his forbears, were futile. Egypt under the Mamluks continued to be intractable. The Mediterranean and the Nile stayed beyond the grasp of the Mongols. Instead Ghazan had to contend with a rival Mongol khanate, the Golden Horde in Russia, and this struggle helped to drain the treasury but left the borders between the two unresolved.

Once more architecture makes the most eloquent comment on the spirit and the temper of a period. By the early fourteenth century Mongol rule was losing its alien quality and its new character is caught definitively in one building, the mausoleum of Ghazan's brother and successor, Oljeitu. He moved his capital from Tabriz to Sultaniyeh, near the present city of Zanjan on a highland plain near the Alborz. The city had been created earlier by decree, and now Oljeitu set out to build it into a cosmopolis. As a magnet to draw people and trade, he planned his mausoleum on a scale to transcend all earlier Persian architecture – and particularly to excel his brother's mausoleum in Tabriz. This motivation could have led to a vulgar disaster; instead it produced a masterpiece.

Today nothing remains of Oljeitu's city, which at its zenith housed several hundred thousand people. A straggling mud-brick village occupies part of the site, but towering above it is the mausoleum, topped by an egg-shaped dome of perfect proportions. Of eight minarets which originally gave this dome a crown-like girdle, only stumps survive. Fortunately, just at the moment when pillage and earthquakes between them seemed likely to break the building its unique value was heeded, and a programme of diligent restoration begun under Italian guidance. The most inexperienced eye will spot something familiar at first glance: here is the building that inspired the Taj Mahal – but to make the comparison is to demean the original. The dome rests on a brick octagon, eighty feet wide at the base. The genius of the whole lies in a marriage of the structural engineering, which goes to calculated limits of aspiration, and the decoration which invests every surface with an artistic event.

Oljeitu was raised by his mother as a Christian, but was converted to Sunni Islam by his wife. Then, as the work on the mausoleum began, he opted for Shi'ism, hoping to bring from Iraq the remains of two Shi'a martyrs to give Sultaniyeh the lure of a sectarian shrine. Disappointed in that design, he became, again, an orthodox Sunni – he was 'everything by turns and nothing long'. Like his brother, Oljeitu misled the kings of Europe into thinking that he was a luke-warm Muslim. His spiritual vacillation caused great suffering: Jews, Christians, Sunnis and Shi'ites were all, in turn, persecuted. The Mongol weakness for drink ended the torment: Oljeitu died an alcoholic at the age of thirty-six, leaving his dynasty to his twelve-year-old son Abu Sa'id. From then onwards fourteenth-century Persia reverted to factionalism and a series of dynastic feuds. Central authority once more dissolved. Abu Sa'id left no heir; Mongol rule devolved into a number of autonomous and erratic provincial courts.

In this disunited and vulnerable condition, Persia found herself lying once more in the path of an invader from the east, and one who superficially might seem a reprise of Chingis Khan and the Mongols. Unlike Chingis, this invader has had a 'better press' in the west – Timur the Great, romanticized by Marlowe as Tamburlaine. In military style Timur did emulate Chingis Khan's war machine. But Timur's hordes were Muslims, not pagans. And although Timur's lineage was sometimes traced back to the Great Khans (though not by him) his roots were Turkish. He was a galvanic leader, but no conqueror of the world. He spent much of his life in the saddle, but this was not a man who despised cities or the life they offered; much of his time was spent plundering other cities to enrich the one he made his own, Samarkand.

Timur was a great builder, but also a relentless butcher. Marlowe's treatment of him echoes a futile western hope of the time, that by savaging the Ottomans and sparing Byzantium Timur would turn out to have rekindled Christendom's eastern advance. The Ottomans had decimated the Crusaders, and Timur was avenging them – or so the fancy ran. Nothing was further from his mind, or his nature. Timur was a tyrant – and a Muslim. Christian heroes are not made of this.

Like Chingis, Timur was invested with his sovereign power at a tribal assembly, having risen to dominate the aristocracy through battle. His territory was the south-western region of the old Mongol khanate of Chaghatai, which had been confederated under the name of

Mawarannahr ('The Land Beyond the River'). Here, prosperous towns arose alongside the life of the pastoral nomads. The Persian province of Khorasan lay immediately to the south-west of Timur's small kingdom, and it was at Khorasan that he directed his first attack, in 1384. He had little more in mind than a raid for booty to embellish Samarkand, and it was so easy that he actually pushed as far west as Sultaniyeh, which provided him with a sizeable haul.

The weakness of Persia was clearly an invitation to a grander design, and two years later Timur set out once more, this time determined to take the whole of the Persian territories once presided over by Hulegu. By 1387 Tabriz, Hamadan, Isfahan and Shiraz were his. In Shiraz, according to a charming story of dubious authenticity, he encountered the most celebrated Persian poet of the time, Hafez. In a passionate lament, Hafez had said he valued the mole on his lover's cheek as highly as Bukhara and Samarkand – Timur's two most-prized cities. Timur summoned Hafez and reprimanded him for a perversion of values, but Hafez pointed to his tattered robes and retorted: 'Sir, it is through such prodigality that I have fallen on such evil days!' Timur is said to have been so disarmed that he gave Hafez a generous reward.

In the aromatic bowers of Shiraz it is *just* possible that Timur could have been so humoured, though the normal fate of artists and crafts-men who caught his eye was to be shipped back without choice to his cities to assist in the numerous works in progress. Timur's patronage was as voracious as his war-making: the court's entourage always included scholars who debated with him on astronomy, mathematics, medicine, architecture and, especially, history. He spoke Turkic and Persian, but was illiterate in both; none the less his intellectual curiosity seems to have been insatiable. Western travellers to his court reported that he incessantly played chess and was the most agile brain in the court.

Whereas Chingis Khan has in substance eluded us, the picture of Timur, though still distant, develops a finer detail. His deformity, the lameness in the right leg from which comes the sobriquet of Timur the Lame (Tamburlaine) was confirmed in 1941 when the Russians opened his tomb at Samarkand and examined the skeleton. This also showed a right leg shorter than the left, a distortion extended to the thigh which twisted his whole frame so that the left shoulder rose higher than the right. The cause of this injury, sustained in youth, is disputed. The most malicious version ascribes it to a wound received

'The whole of later Islamic architecture in Iran stands in the shadow of this building,' says the art historian, Dr Robert Hillenbrand, of the great mausoleum of Oljeitu at Sultaniyeh, now being restored. Oljeitu was a Mongol king and his Persian craftsmen achieved, in this dome, a feat of structural engineering: it is double-skinned and entirely self-supporting.

while sheep rustling. Another legend, that he once seized an open sword blade in his right hand, is endorsed by damage to the bone of his right index finger, and bones of the arm knit at the elbow. Given his deformity, Timur's preference for the saddle is understandable. Having exhumed the bones, the Russians then reconstructed a likeness of the head. It is fierce enough, but in reaching for his psyche it is useless.

To pursue Timur's campaigns as they leave in their wake millions of dead is often as tiresome as it is nauseating; there are moments of brilliant generalship, there are spectacular collisions of cultures and races, but there is a feeling in the end of energy expended largely to no result. Timur represents, in its most perplexing form, the schizophrenia of medieval tyranny; the mindless destroyer and the ambitious builder.

We glimpse him at court: 'Timur was tall and lofty of stature, big in brow and head, with eyes like candles, without brilliance; powerful in voice.... He did not allow in his company any obscene talk or talk of bloodshed, captivity, rapine, plunder and violation of the harem.... A debater, who by one look comprehended the matter aright; he was not deceived by intricate fallacy....' Whenever Timur returned to Samarkand after a campaign he was ruthlessly impartial in punishing anyone who had exploited his absence: 'For those of his officers in all places who keep justice strictly there is no misery or fear, but for a mere nothing he kills the greatest as the meanest of his officers.'

He was less summary, but still decisive, with his own kin. Miranshah, his eldest surviving son, was left in charge of Sultaniyeh. He took to the bottle and, amongst other depravities, tried to dismantle Oljeitu's mausoleum, which, fortunately, was too well built to suffer much. Miranshah is said to have complained that living in his father's shadow the only way he could think of leaving his own mark was by destroying something significant. This profanity led to his banishment, although later he appeared on various battlefields with some distinction. Another son, Shahrukh, was excluded from Timur's favour because of a cultured, pacific nature. He was, as it turned out, seriously underrated.

Neither Timur nor his descendants had much patience with or aptitude for government, and they left no lasting political structure except the Mogul empire in India. For many of Timur's ablest captives the journey to his cities was one-way. Their forced enlistment in the glorification of Samarkand and Bukhara allowed no return, and

RIGHT Twenty-four
vaulted brick galleries
surround the base of the
dome of Oljeitu's
mausoleum at
Sultaniyeh, each
brilliantly decorated
with tilework using a
minimum of colour to
great effect, as in this
portion of a gallery roof.
BELOW Oljeitu also built
a *mihrab*, or personal
altar, in a chamber of
the Friday Mosque at
Isfahan, which is a
tour-de-force of
calligraphy rendered in
stucco.

in this way many of Persia's cultural accomplishments were transplanted further into the rump of Central Asia where their influence was permanent. The patron's irascibility bore down heavily and unstintingly. One palace had to be built in six weeks; another commemorative building for a grandson so displeased Timur on his first inspection of it that it had to be rebuilt in ten days (and nights) of continuous labour. The essence of the man, bile and vision fused, comes across clearly from this episode: he was, by then, not only lame but old and prone to sickness; nevertheless he was carried on a litter frequently to the site to drive on the builders, sometimes under the flares used for the night work. He was manic, repressive and unquenchable.

Out of this tyranny, none the less, grew an aesthetic legend: Timurid painting and architecture. As a patron Timur cannot be simply dismissed as a man who kidnapped his art. Behind his patronage was a guiding taste which drew from all the polyglot arts and skills a deliberate and enduring style. Its manifest achievement is the use of colour. The palette is more extensive, but colour is never used indiscriminately for its own sake. Whereas the Seljuks' genius was decoration as an organic part of the structure, Timurid architecture is an art of the surface, and again that delicate line between realizing the capacity of a technique and over-indulging it is observed. Timur was never ambiguous in any instruction, and presumably the restraint must have reflected his control, but he was drawing on a tradition – Persian conservatism. Even when given unbridled funds and grandiose assignments, the architects and decorators from Shiraz, Isfahan and Mashad were masters of containment. And in the use of colours it is the Persian environment, the dun of the desert and the peerless blue of the sky, which frames everything. Robert Byron felt that 'the Timurid genius was to invent an architecture to show off colour without being swamped by it'.

The best surviving essay in the Timurid style in Persia is the Gohar Shad mosque at Mashad, named after one of the most beguiling women in the country's history. She was the wife of Timur's 'effete' son, Shahrukh who, against his father's expectation, turned out to be tough enough to inherit the empire. The most pious and aesthetic currents seem to have issued in this family: unlike Timur, Shahrukh upheld the Muslim law of the *Shari'a*; Gohar Shad herself initiated some of the finest religious building; their son Baisunghur was a celebrated calligrapher and patron of the arts. The Gohar Shad mosque carries an inscription in Kufic reading: 'By Baisunghur, son of Shahrukh, son of Timur Gurkani, with hope in God, in the year 821 [AD 1418].'

As with most Timurid building, there is little really new in the structure of the mosque; the exceptional feature is the decoration, for which the surfaces of the building seem to have been arranged. Robert Byron called it 'the most beautiful example of colour in architecture ever devised by man to the glory of his God and himself'. The mosque is now a part of the complex of religious buildings forming the shrine at Mashad. Although it is the shrine's gold dome that in its meretricious way catches the eye from afar, it is Gohar Shad's dome which has real quality.

Gohar Shad was the daughter of an amir, one of whose ancestors had saved the life of Chingis Khan. Her marriage to Shahrukh was a good enough match to be celebrated in ballads. One of her first benefactions was a college in Herat; as she made an inspection tour on its completion with the two hundred ladies of her entourage the male students were herded out to avoid temptation. But one was overlooked. Disturbed by the commotion he looked from the window of his monastic cell and caught the eye of a 'ruby-lipped lady'. The lady disappeared without notice but was detected on her return because of the 'irregularity of her dress and manners'. Sympathizing with the frustrations her visit had aroused, Gohar Shad instructed all her attendants to marry the students, previously condemned to celibacy. She gave each student clothes, salary and a bed and decreed that the couples should meet once a week. 'She did all this', intones the chronicler, 'to arrest the progress of adultery.'

Timur died in 1405, caught in the punishing winter of Central Asia at the start of a campaign against China. Four years of family feuding followed. Shahrukh intrigued his way to the throne, taking Herat as his capital while his son Ulugh Beg governed from Samarkand. This division foreshadowed a rupture of the empire. Gohar Shad, approaching sixty, was drawn more and more into the feuds between the rival courts of Herat and Samarkand. Shahrukh died in 1447, but Gohar Shad continued to meddle and finally, in her eighties, was assassinated. She was buried in her own mausoleum in Herat under the inscription 'The Bilkis of the Time' ('Bilkis' meant Queen of Sheba). The only compensation as the empire fell apart was the work of Baisunghur, who kept a team of illuminators, painters, binders and calligraphers at work on masterpieces which give radiant proof of his taste – although he, too, died of drink, in 1433. The renaissance of which he and his mother had been such forces was spent. Further distinction was confined to Babur, descended from Miranshah, who founded the Mogul empire, and left an intimate and delightful personal history of this imaginative and remorseless clan.

In the course of two centuries Persia had been repeatedly overrun by nomads insatiable for conquest and booty. The Mongol Ilkhanate left some redeeming architecture and Timur, as a Muslim of mercurial devotion, had not crushed buildings – at least the sacred ones – as carelessly as he had people. His conquests followed one consistent strategy: the securing of the caravan route from Baghdad to China, via Hamadan, Rayy and, of course, Samarkand. All this speeded the passage of riches to his own capital, as well as greatly stimulating trade throughout Persia and the empire. The northern caravan route above the Caspian and across Russia was eliminated deliberately, and with it the remains of the empire of the Mongol Golden Horde. Timur was always lured towards China, but never towards Europe; compared with the Orient, it was barbaric. Once he saw the shores of the Aegean he turned for home.

As Timur disappears over the eastern horizon we see a world profoundly different from that which lay before Chingis Khan. The distribution of the world's religions is re-ordered and, with marginal exceptions, settled from that day to this. Christianity failed to take root in any significant form east of the Levant. Its universe was to become predominantly western. Buddhism in Central Asia was decimated. And, crucially, Islam's original homogeneity had gone. From the fourteenth century there were divergent Islamic regions: a variegated but Arabic one to the south and west of Persia, and a distinctly Persianized one from Persia eastwards. This is not to be confused with the schism between Sunni and Shi'a, as yet not consolidated. There was from this point a *cultural* difference, manifest in the texture of the religion and especially in the world of ideas and art.

The overall Arab domination had gone. The Persian and Turkish languages superseded Arabic as the tongues of the eastern bloc; albeit with the Persian language transformed by its Arabic content. A Persian–Islamic culture infused the faith as far east as Malaysia. As an agent of Islam, Persia was donning its own garb. But despite this refinement the sheer intellectual *élan* which characterized Abbasid Baghdad at its peak was not rekindled. In the eleventh century, well before Islam had to close its ranks against the repeated body-blows of the nomadic invasions, it had begun to retreat into self-sufficient orthodoxy. The Mongols and the Timurids intensified this kind of defensiveness, forcing Islam even more into its own corner. It became introspective and otiose. This might be judged the most lethal blow administered by the insensible nomads. But there is a kinder point of view.

Professor Sayyed Hossein Nasr, a modern equivalent of the old court polymaths, argues that the nomads gave their own kind of *living force* to sedentary life, and that an occasional blast from the nomads restores to urban man a true, organic sense of values. Without the spirit of the nomads, he argues, 'the city would suffocate by having its windows closed'. He concedes the trauma of the Mongol invasions, but adds:

Islamic art has always been rejuvenated by the nomadic spirit. Islam is based on a kind of spiritual nomadism, a disdain for the excessive consolidation of life, a refusal to imprison the spirit within tangible and material forms. The great moral evils of civilization always came out of the cities, and the moral evils were often eradicated by a new wave of migration which brought with it a simplicity and a purity. Chingis Khan felt that he had a divine mission, to protect virgin nature from the scum of sedentary life.

This powerful advocate of the nomadic virtues seems as wistful as he is romantic. But whatever the forgiving gloss applied by Professor Nasr to the Mongols and the Timurids, they assisted the forces of reaction in Persia. They left no means of stabilizing Persian society, or of correcting its centrifugal tendencies. The nomads could organize themselves but nobody else. They provided none of the reasons for ordinary people to favour unity of interest over vested interest, and they bore down ruthlessly on the poorest and weakest group, the agrarian peasantry. In this respect they fell far short of the civilizations of the Achaemenians, Parthians, Sasanians and Arabs – all owing a lot to their nomadic roots – who had, each in their way, made sense of the commonweal, in spite of the diversity of blood. The nomadic mentality as represented in the Mongols and Timurids was alien to Persian civilization as it had evolved.

Much earlier, Persia had struck an equilibrium which composed the urban, agrarian and pastoral nomadic lives; they swirled around each other and did not emulsify and were, therefore, the livelier. The Seljuks, who came as forerunners of the great hordes, proved far more able to assimilate and to give Persia genuinely advancing hopes and ideas, in spite of their neglect of agriculture. The Mongols and Timurids were an historical aberration, on the grand scale; for Persia they retarded civilization for three centuries.

7

Half the World

1450-1750

The river called the Zayandeh Rud ('Giver of Life') rises from the heart of the plateau, runs through plain and hills and then forms Persia's richest oasis, bordered by a crescent of sharp-peaked hills. Beyond the oasis, the river rapidly expires in marshes, without reaching any lake or sea. The landlocked river has given its life most of all to a city, Isfahan. For centuries Isfahan has been the Persian city that most seduced western travellers. 'It is a great city, very beautiful,' wrote Pietro della Valle, a Roman, in 1617. But seventeenth-century Isfahan was not only an Oriental showpiece to ravish the western eye. It was deliberately created as an emblem of power. Persia, once more, had joined the world in her own right, after having very nearly disappeared.

Isfahan's roots went back as far as the Achaemenians. Over the centuries the city gradually flowered into an urban masterpiece, culminating in 1598 with its selection as Persia's capital; a time when it came to be called 'Isfahan nisf-i-jahan' – Isfahan, Half the World.

Today another Isfahan seeps over the land like lava, forming satellite towns, a new highway, an international airport and leviathan industries which suck the life from the Zayandeh Rud. In the heart of this molten growth the old Isfahan survives, miraculously embalmed, though perilously eroded. It is still what it was intended to be – an advertisement, a beacon of one man's energy, imagination and ego. The eternal blue domes testify to his piety; the epic central square, the Maidan–i–Shah, shows the scale of his plan: twice the size of Red Square, seven times the size of St Mark's. This Isfahan, bridging the sixteenth and seventeenth centuries, was devised and built according to the personal directions of the patron king, Shah Abbas.

Under Abbas, Persia was steered through a precarious age, flanked by two hostile powers: the Ottoman Turks in the west, and the Uzbeqs in the east. Abbas provided a new military confidence and shrewd diplomacy in which Persia played *realpolitik* to hold the balance between European and Asian powers. Persia's position on the continental trading routes had never been more important, and Abbas vigorously exploited it. Internally, a long period of political, tribal and religious factionalism which might have pulled the country apart into rival, Balkanized kingdoms came to an end with fierce and skilful leadership from Abbas. Persia found a new political independence and a new, decisive religious separatism. The centre and symbol of this ascendant spirit was Isfahan.

Abbas's grand design for his capital encompassed four and a half miles and integrated the secular, religious, commercial and royal strands of Persian society. In the past, Persia's capital had been as mobile as her people. From Tabriz, favoured by the Mongols, the capital moved to Qazvin, farther east at the foot of the Alborz. But early in Abbas's reign Qazvin was still too vulnerable to Ottoman incursions and he moved the court to the greater security of Isfahan, which was close to the heart of Persia and, with its great oasis and equable climate, far more congenial. Isfahan already had some of the finest architecture in Persia, of which the focus was the Masjid–i–Jumeh, the Friday Mosque. Successive builders and dynasties devoted their ablest artists and craftsmen to this complex of sacred chambers and precincts, one generation often striving to surpass another. The Friday Mosque became the single most valuable *cumulative* statement of Persian–Islamic architecture. Excepting one or two deprivations, it survived both the Mongols and Timur.

When Abbas drew up his grand plan he did so very much in the shadow of the Friday Mosque and its adjoining *maidan*. They presented a stiff challenge – safely, perhaps, beyond emulation. But in

Two distinct ages of Isfahan are characterized by two buildings, the Friday Mosque
(ABOVE) and the Royal Mosque (p. 151). The Friday Mosque was an accumulation
of the sacred architecture of many dynasties – Buyids, Seljuks and Mongols among
them, inspiring the finest work under many patrons. The Royal Mosque, on the
other hand, is the mark of one era, one style and one man: Shah Abbas, most
powerful of the Safavid kings.

Abbas's estimation Isfahan was not yet grand enough; it lacked the imperial aura which he desired, to impress the foreign embassies which were now drawn to Persia.

From the beginning, the city had also drawn invaders. It fell to the Arabs early in their conquest. Under both the Umayyads and Abbasids it thrived as a trading post and was renowned for cottons and silks. The original settlement was on the Zayandeh Rud well to the east of the modern Isfahan, around the ancient bridge of Shahrestan which still stands, rather marooned, in near-stagnant water. Towards the end of the Sasanian era a Jewish quarter, Yahudiyyeh, was founded to the north-west of the first settlement. The conglomeration of villages was first consolidated into a city, within its own walls, by the Buyids. Then, in the eleventh century, Isfahan was besieged and captured by the Seljuks. They enriched the city and, most of all, the Friday Mosque. The mosque was founded far earlier, on the site of an old fire temple, and the Buyids had left their own mark on it which has recently been revealed by excavations.

In the thirteenth century Isfahan escaped the worst of the Mongol savagery because it lay to the south of the first and most violent invasion. When the Ilkhans later conquered the whole of Persia they added their own patronage to the Friday Mosque with a prayer chamber, and an intricate stucco *mihrab* made for the dipsomaniac Oljeitu. As Mongol rule broke down into regional regimes, Isfahan had an interval of relative independence, but then, at the end of the fourteenth century, Timur appeared at the gates, pursuing the prizes of Hulegu. The Isfahanis knew what Timur had done in the north. They admitted Timur's advance party into the city and negotiated a ransom for survival. But this levy proved too much for the inhabitants, who turned on Timur's men and slaughtered them. The city then prepared itself for siege. It was a futile provocation: Timur administered his standard reprisal, and seventy thousand Isfahani skulls were made into one of his grisly towers as the price of resistance. Nevertheless, at least the bulk of Isfahan's architectural heritage survived and was later embellished as the creative repentance of the Timurids, too, left its mark with that of the Mongols.

But the Timurid hand on Persia never went deeper than the magnificent surfaces of Baisunghur's craftsmen. On the plateau it was a transient influence, and as the Timurid presence faded new tribal alliances emerged which were to shape the future distribution of

The dome of the Royal Mosque in Isfahan, unlike that of the Friday Mosque
(p. 149), has a dazzling ceramic sheen. But under this veneer was a technical
short-cut: the half-million tiles used in the Royal Mosque were not of mosaic
segments but painted whole, in seven colours. Though quicker to install, the tiles
were apt to fall off.

power in Asia. These movements were essentially of the Turkish-speaking peoples, the Turkoman. They sprang initially from outside Persia, in eastern Anatolia. In effect, the Mongol invasions had so displaced the old national boundaries that all the territories of Anatolia, Mesopotamia and the plateau were in flux. Throughout the fifteenth and sixteenth centuries the contest to redraw the map of western Asia was dominated by these Turkoman tribes. It was also a time of fanatical sectarian movements, and of one egregious new sectarian figurehead in particular.

Three successive Turkoman migrations were originated in eastern Anatolia; one moved west and the other two east. The first established the Ottoman empire in western Anatolia, in the wake of the collapse of Byzantium. By the fourteenth century the Ottomans had settled into a distinctive urbanized culture, and could afford to disparage their still nomadic kin to the east as 'Turks without faith' and 'brigands'. To survive between the Ottomans and Timur's empire in Persia, the nomads were forced into a tribal federation, which took the name of the Black Sheep. Timur allowed them to hold a buffer zone to the west of the plateau. After Timur's death the Black Sheep steadily encroached eastwards. Under Jahan Shah ('Lord of the World') they took Tabriz as their capital, and by the mid-fifteenth century had swallowed much of the plateau, even briefly taking Herat.

The Black Sheep were, in turn, superseded by the third Turkoman efflux, the White Sheep, who had also begun as vassals of Timur. Under Uzan Hasan ('Long Hasan') they defeated Jahan Shah in 1467 and the last Timurid in Persia, Abu Sa'id, in 1469. With this the White Sheep exercised hegemony over most of Persia, but not over Khorasan, where a fugitive Timurid culture survived before passing to Babur's Mogul empire in India. Uzan Hasan set out to make Tabriz the cultural equal of Herat, but never achieved it, although his Black Sheep predecessor built the Blue Mosque in Tabriz, which many critics feel to be the height of glazed tilework in Persia. In Isfahan, Uzan Hasan adorned much of the courtyard façade of the Friday Mosque.

Ostensibly, Uzan Hasan was an orthodox Sunni, but politically flexible enough to give refuge at his court to an activist called Junayd, who had lost a power struggle in a small Sufi order centred on the town of Ardabil, in the western Caspian region. It was at Ardabil, early in the fourteenth century, that a devout and orthodox ascetic called Safi al–Din had formed a new order of the mystical Sufi movement and called it, after himself, the Safaviyyeh. Safi al–Din built on an already established and richly endowed base which attracted lively students of Islam. Although Safi al–Din was a Sunni, the movement was open to wide-ranging debate and became drawn to Shi'ism. Generations later came the succession dispute in which Junayd was the loser. Afterwards, Junayd fell under the influence of extreme Shi'ite factions and identified his own political future with their cause, gathering around him a small but fanatical Turkoman force. Taken into the White Sheep court, Junayd married Uzan Hasan's sister, but he was killed soon afterwards while leading his zealots on a *jihad* (holy war), in the province of Shirvan. A son, Haidar, was born posthumously.

At this time Shi'ism became resurgent, largely because the Turkoman were attracted by its more extreme fervour which echoed their own background and inclinations. And breakaway movements based on tribal society could see in it a useful combination of faith and separatism. This happened in Khorasan, where a dynasty of brigands called the Sarbadars invoked Shi'ism for their own ends.

In Ardabil the Safaviyyeh order was in the hands of wealthy Sheikhs. Haidar had successfully regained Ardabil, and to avenge his father on another *jihad*, but was himself killed, like his father, by the Shirvanshah. The inheritance of this vengeful sect then fell to one of Junayd's grandsons, Ismail, who was aged only nine. Five years later, in 1499, Ismail precociously led an assault on Ardabil, but failed (it fell to him later). This setback did not deter Ismail's supporters, and the sight of this fanatical adolescent had a galvanic effect on the Turkoman tribes, who began to venerate him as a kind of Saffaviyyeh saint. So great was Ismail's appeal that it seems to have provided one of those historic and spontaneous moments when a number of fears – economic, racial, religious find relief in the leadership of one charismatic figure. Certainly, after all these devious developments Ismail, despite his youth, began to impose a pattern on events which had permanent results.

The death in 1478 of Uzan Hasan had been followed by the usual dynastic struggles. The tribal federations were ruptured. Ismail came at a time when, once again, Persia was ripe for a new order. Many strains were mixed in his blood: Kurdish, Azerbaijani, Persian, Turkoman, even Greek. From Gilan, the sub-tropical province where pine-covered foothills decline into marshland surrounding the

Caspian, Ismail gathered up his Turkoman zealots and, driving into the plateau, made of them an army. The emblem of their unity was a turban, first seen on Haidar's raiding parties, divided into twelve red gashes, representing the twelve Shi'a *imams*. Ismail's shock troops were thus called the *qizilbash* ('red-heads'). They rode through the forests, out over the Alborz escarpment and towards a kingdom of their own.

In 1501 Ismail and the *qizilbash* destroyed the factionalized White Sheep and took Tabriz for their capital. 'He will come out of Gilan like a burning sun' ran the crusading litany, 'and with his sword sweep infidelity from the earth.' In this uncompromising spirit Ismail was crowned as the founder of the Safavid dynasty. 'I am God's mystery' he announced and, as the ruthless custodian of Shi'ism, claimed direct descent from the Prophet. Warned of a reaction in Tabriz, where two-thirds of the people were Sunni, Ismail was truculent: 'I fear no one; by God's help, if the people utter one word of protest I will draw the sword and leave not one of them alive.' He was as good as his word: during eight years subduing Persia, the redheads repeated the worst degradations of the Mongols and the Timurids, imposing their creed through massacre, pillage and torture. In Khorasan Ismail personally killed the Uzbeq king who had seized the city three years earlier, and had his skull made into a drinking cup which he then sent to the Ottoman Sultan.

It was a curious purgative that had swept from the north-west. Beginning in the peaceful and mystical setting of a Sufi order, passing through the hands of political opportunists, harnessing the crude energy of the Turkoman tribes, and ending with the carnage invoked by a teenage demi-god: 'On seeing him the outsiders would prefer to turn to stone' was the promise of the Safavid founder, and all too true. Ismail bound together the tribes by drilling into them his doctrine; Safavid agents lived with the tribes to ensure their complete dedication. The *qizilbash* were reinforced in their loyalty by readings from Ismail's poems, in a Turkish dialect, in which he was equated with 'Ali and the Shi'a *imams*. It was not a profound theological conversion – far from it. But it was certainly inflammatory.

At the beginning of the sixteenth century the hold of Shi'ism in Persia was superficial, implanted more by the military and political will than by anything, and the population was still predominantly Sunni. Ismail seems then to have perceived that the sheer physical momentum of the movement was not enough, and that he needed to acquire theological *gravitas*. He imported the learned men of Shi'ism, the *mujtahids*, from Bahrein and Syria to rectify the deficiency. They could impose themselves only at the expense of the saddle-borne zealots, which they did. But this planted into Safavid society (and Persia's distant political future) a bedevilling dualism. It began a contest for power between the temporal and spiritual custodians of the state, in which the king had always to appease both, or support one against the other.

For Persia the only compensation of the new tyranny was that it restored her old boundaries, and Ismail's successors made no attempt to extend them. But within these boundaries was a new, and still unstable amalgam of old and new – of races, tribes and languages, with the Turkish strains predominant. For sixty years after Ismail, under Tahmasp, Ismail II and, briefly, Muhammad Khudabandeh, the Turkoman alliance held precariously together, more from the need to repel external threats than from internal accord. Ismail had been decisively beaten in battle by the Ottomans, and for a week they regained Tabriz. They were always a force to be feared in Persia, although they seemed never to covet total conquest, probably because such an empire would have over-extended their lines of communication. This defeat suddenly rendered Ismail's legend mortal and vulnerable. His successors were never secure; immediately on coming to power, Tahmasp had to face the contesting factions of the spiritual and temporal establishments. He opted for the spiritual, and it took a long struggle to assert their (and his) authority over the *qizilbash* chieftains. Whenever a king showed signs of age or weakness the tribal disputes broke out all over again. Muhammad Khudabandeh fell to a conspiracy in which one of his young sons was advanced by the governor of Khorasan as a supposedly pliant substitute. This early and traumatic experience of court intrigue marked the mind of the young crown prince, who saw that his own survival depended on trusting no one, not even his closest kin. Ushered from Mashad to a bloody throne in 1587, at the age of sixteen, Abbas then cut down the king-makers. The Safavids, and Persia, were in the hands of a ruthless and brilliant leader.

Dangers within were as threatening as those from without, particularly from one group, the *qizilbash* amirs. The self-interest of the amirs was in conflict with the idea of central authority. Ismail had turned to the traditional Persian bureaucracy, centred in cities like Isfahan, to counter the power of the *qizilbash*, but as central authority weakened they, too, gathered more power to themselves. Now Abbas acted boldly against both groups: he dispersed the *qizilbash* cliques, and he de-tribalized the leadership of the army by bringing in Georgians, Circassians and Armenians who formed well trained and loyal auxiliaries. Until the army had completed this process of reform, Abbas knew he could not risk war in the west. Ottoman use of artillery against Ismail had shown Persian equipment and tactics to be obsolete. Abbas bought time by ceding vast areas to the Ottomans, and he secured his eastern flank by combining military success with diplomacy, regaining Herat from the Uzbeqs.

The era of Shah Abbas is one of those moments when one man imposes himself on events and holds together what otherwise might well have disintegrated. The Safavid dynasty was not on a sound foundation. The bloody legend of the Shi'a martyrs had been enough to fire the simple Turkoman tribes, but once the energy of their *jihads* was spent two basic problems remained: how to channel the ambitions of the *qizilbash*, who could (and did) regard themselves as the force which had created the dynasty; and how to reconcile them with all the other traditional factions competing for power in the new state. In reasserting royal power, Abbas significantly changed the style and aura of Safavid kingship. Ismail had claimed theological infallibility and to be a *sayyed*, one of those descended from the Prophet. Tahmasp had been a seriously devout man, but this had not been enough. Although Abbas remained the titular head of the Sufi order, his god-like status was personalized on a temporal as well as theological plane – reminiscent in some ways of Chosroes I, who similarly re-imposed the authority of the king at the expense of the clergy. But despite his stature (many of his subjects credited him with supernatural powers) Abbas was not able to ignore the *mujtahids*, however much he may have been tempted to do so. Throughout his reign, though pragmatic in his dealings with non-Muslims, he took care to keep his own piety above attack.

Thus, in the contest between the keepers of the faith and the political factions, Abbas played off each against the other, hoping to use both. And he knew that the political benefits of Shi'ism to Persia were considerable. The English adventurer Sir Anthony Sherley (who, with his brother Robert ingratiated himself with Abbas) noted perceptively, '. . . the king knows how potent a uniter of men's minds the religion is for the tranquillity of an estate. . . .' The ethnic, tribal and class divisions of sixteenth-century Persia left little in common for the people *except* religion; fortuitously it provided the focus not only for internal stability but also against the great external dangers, east and west. Shi'ism's utility (for that is what it was) must be seen in this rather symbolic light, for in truth the conversion of the mass of Persians to Shi'ism was still a long way off; it was not complete until the eighteenth century.

In the age of Abbas, Shi'ism was crucial as the *emblem* of Persian independence in a hostile world *and* of the Persian separateness within Islam. For the Islamic world was never the same again. How ironic, then, that this snatching of Persian identity from possible extinction came about through the agency not of native Persians, but of the Turkomans! And it had been an accident; they had no motivation other than their religiuoious fervour. Only when Ismail gave them grants of land were the tribal chiefs given a vested interest in Persian sovereignty. The new state had been very nearly conjured out of the air.

Although Abbas re-established the identity of the monolithic state, a sense of *nationality* was another thing. Persia under Abbas remained a precarious entity. Its morale had to be maintained by military success. Its economy was not buoyant. A Portuguese enclave in the Gulf siphoned off valuable trade from India to Europe, and the English East India Company later did the same through its Persian trading posts. Defensive wars did not produce the booty to replenish the treasury that the wars of conquest had traditionally given Persian kings. Again the country really depended on being a middle man in world trade, creaming off the revenue from the caravans and selling its silk products to east and west.

Abbas's greatest political gift was the way he conserved his resources, to be used only when he judged that they had a reasonable chance of success. Every military commitment was prudently weighed. If diplomacy, embracing both guile and deception, could buy time more cheaply than war, then he resorted to it with skill. Sherley has an account of Abbas taking conflicting views on whether to launch an offensive against the Ottomans; each party to the debate, including Sherley, has a partial interest in the outcome. The impression left is that Abbas was more than the equal of his 'advice' and kept his own counsel as the only truly disinterested party. How far the dialogue is restructured by Sherley can only be guessed, but certain tenets of Abbas's statecraft ring true: 'not to attempt two enterprises at one time' and 'leagues are usually of more appearance than effect', for example. The solitariness of decision-making was ingrained in him from the start, a part of the paranoid side of his nature, though many of the threats to his life were not at all imaginary, and the line between paranoia and a sound instinct for survival was hard to know.

The dark side of Abbas's nature ran deep, and leaves an appalling record. His own kin were not spared: his father, who had been forced to abdicate in his favour, was imprisoned. His eldest son was murdered; two other sons blinded – all on Abbas's orders. The killing of his heir, the able Prince Safi, shows the poison of suspicion robbing Abbas of all reason. A spy had reported that Safi was spending an unusual amount of time with a particular court official. Abbas had the official killed, which provoked other courtiers into seeking Safi's support for a coup to overthrow Abbas. Safi reported the plot to his father, but despite this act of loyalty Abbas convinced himself that Safi must himself have been implicated and ordered his assassination. Worse was to follow. The assassin, a minor court official, commented on the Shah's remorse and melancholy, whereupon he was ordered to kill his own son. Making sure that it had been done, Abbas then told him, 'now you are the equal of your Shah in this respect'.

To be a nonentity could be as dangerous as being in the court. Before a Shah went hunting it was ordained that only the royal party should be in the grounds. Alas, during one hunt a traveller dozing in the undergrowth was overlooked, and when Abbas detected him from his snoring, he fired an arrow into the man's heart, saying 'I did the man no wrong. I found him sleeping and asleep I left him.' Western chroniclers came often from courts as blood-stained as that of Abbas, but it is hard to agree with Sherley that Abbas, though 'esteemed by us barbarous', was 'yet indeed fit to be a pattern and mirror to some of ours who have Christ in their mouths'.

The tendency is to portray Abbas as an 'oriental' monarch in the pejorative sense, and not to consider whether he was an archetype, whether he was a particularly odious aberration, or whether he behaved much as the time demanded. Because his court attracted ambassadors and travellers we have detailed accounts, few of them as nakedly self-serving as Sherley's. The most copious account is by the

The focus of Shah Abbas's Isfahan was an extensive square, the *maidan*. Looking north from the minaret of the Royal Mosque, the entrance to the bazaar is at the far end of the *maidan*. On the left, the Ali Qapu, or 'Sublime Porte'. On the right, the dome of the Sheikh Lutfullah Mosque, finest of Abbas's works. On the far horizon, the Friday Mosque is visible.

Roman patrician Pietro della Valle, who had to pursue the progress of the court for nearly a year before he was finally admitted into the presence. Then, it was worth it. He saw Abbas first at his winter palace at Ashraf on the Caspian. From this and later encounters, della Valle gives much more than a surface impression. In this, one of his best passages, there seems a good deal of the essence of Abbas:

> He knew how to make it seem as if he was friend and enemy at one and the same time; he gives satisfaction and yet he does not; he listens but does not, or rather he doesn't want to listen; in short he plays with the whole world and never concludes anything against his own interests.

The painted royal portraits of the time are stylized and seem to filter out the character. The verbal portraits given by travellers over several decades do not always tally, but there is a good deal of detail. According to Sir Thomas Herbert, who saw Abbas at the end of his reign, his eyes were 'small and flaming, without any hair over them: he had a low forehead, but a high and hawked nose, sharp chin'. Della Valle, a decade earlier, found, 'The king is of medium height, perhaps a little shorter, but he does not seem meagrely built, rather delicate, with a slender body, tense and robust . . . his features are attractive rather than ugly.' The nose in this account is 'long and aquiline' and the eyes 'sparkling, laughing, and in them as in all the rest one sees great spirit in which he surpasses all the other princes of his realm'. A decade earlier, Sherley, bent on flattery, wrote: 'He is excellently well shaped, of a most well-proportioned stature, strong and active; his colour somewhat inclined to a man-like blackness, is also more black by the sun's burning. . . .' In della Valle's audience Abbas's hands 'rested on the bone handle of his sword, whose black scabbard pointed menacingly upwards'; Herbert noted 'the hilt of his sword was gold, the blade formed like a semicircle, and doubtless well tempered; the scabbard red'.

Swords were not merely decorative. Abbas could be impulsively murderous. He liked personally to geld slaves, and enjoyed performing castrations with great accuracy. He made his own scimitar, skinned and gutted game he caught, and cooked it himself. The virtues of nomadic self-sufficiency remained with him amid the ostentation of his courts; he made a point of dressing plainly. Herbert notes: 'Circled with such a world of wealth, he clothed himself in a plain red calico coat quilted with cotton.' Della Valle found him more colourful:

'Violet hose, orange shagreen shoes, a bright green cloth coat tied with orange laces, a turban which he had put on back to front was red striped with silver....'

In the restless Persian manner, the court moved constantly between Isfahan, the Caspian retreat at Ashraf, and the old capital of Qazvin, where Abbas was closest to the frontier with the Ottomans. In each place the palaces were of a style which survives now only at Isfahan, and then only partially, in two buildings: the Ali Qapu ('Sublime Porte'), which led from the *maidan* to the palace complex, and a garden pavilion, the Chehel Setun ('Hall of Forty Columns'), which had a Chinese-influenced high-columned porch. Although it post-dates Abbas, the Chehel Setun resembles the style of the palace at Ashraf, where Herbert described the scene:

> The chambers were large and square; the roof arched and richly gilded. The ground was spread with carpets of silk and gold ... we were conducted into another square large upper chamber, where the ground was covered with richer carpets ... so much gold, transformed into vessels for use and ornament, were set for us to look upon that some merchants then present made an estimate of incredible value [twenty million pounds]... round about the room were also seated several tacit Mirzaes, Chawns, Sultans and Beglerbegs [princes and courtiers] who, like so many inanimate statues, were placed cross-legged, joining their bums to the ground, their backs to the wall, and their eyes to a constant object [the king].

Sherley, for once, is more succinct: 'In this court there was not a Gentleman but the king: the rest were shadows which moved with his body.'

Abbas used these audiences with western visitors to pump them for information: he followed the sectarian divide of Christendom and startled della Valle by knowing of the Lutheran threat to Spain. Though barely literate, his knowledge was extensive and his curiosity tireless. As Sherley said, Abbas followed the sound precept that 'Princes ought to hear all, and elect the best; and for that election's sake, to animate all to speak freely.' The animation was generously lubricated: della Valle had trouble, as a virtual abstainer, trying not to cause offence by declining the frequently passed cups, sometimes of nondescript wine, sometimes of the fine vintages of Shiraz. Abbas drank with gusto, but kept his head. But in the midst of the bacchanal he could often retreat within himself, apparently melancholic. After della Valle's first encounter, as he at last gratefully stole away into the night, he noticed Abbas, 'Leaning against one of the pillars of the *divankhaneh* ... the musicians having approached closer to him ... continued playing, singing softly, to which the king listened intently, but in the posture of great melancholy.'

In such moods, Abbas sought relief in the harem. No Oriental institution is more beguiling to the western mind than this; the harem's lascivious reputation often trivializes its role. As the most private and intimate cell of the court, the harem had political significance, both good and bad. It could easily debilitate and drain the will, or it could, as it had for Chosroes II with Shirin, be a source of support, or it could be a kind of massage parlour for the ego as well as the body, as it seems to have been for Abbas. His sanctum was guarded by black eunuchs: white eunuchs were rarely admitted. At any one time there were twenty or thirty favourite wives and scores of others. Some were recruited during festivals in the capital; women, carefully selected by the eunuchs, were admitted to enclosures and some of them, spotted there by Abbas, were taken for the harem, whether or not they were married.

Della Valle has a vicarious account of Abbas being coaxed back into humour in the harem: '... they gathered all around him, talked to him, teased and distracted him, play, sing, eat and drink together, and in this way he passes the time very pleasantly with his women whose number is almost infinite, but all fair in complexion, attractive, and almost all Georgian or Circassian, and Christian in origin.' But a courtesan's existence could be precarious. When the mobile harem was at Ardabil, during a campaign against the Turks, there was a risk of it being overrun by the enemy, in which event the eunuchs were under orders to decapitate the women. Fortunately for them, the Turks failed to arrive.

Despite all the princely comforts, Abbas strove to keep in touch with the life of his people. A colony of Carmelite fathers in Isfahan, whose accounts give an invaluable picture of urban life under Abbas, were surprised to find him at large in the city with a minimal escort and trying, as best he could, to go incognito. It is hard to believe that he really went unrecognized as he slipped into the bazaar, wandered the *maidan*, or as here from a Carmelite account, toured the shops:

He will come to the greengrocers, fruiterers, and those who sell preserves and sweetmeats. Here he will take a mouthful of this, there another of that – in one place sample a preserve, in another taste some fruit. Or he will enter the

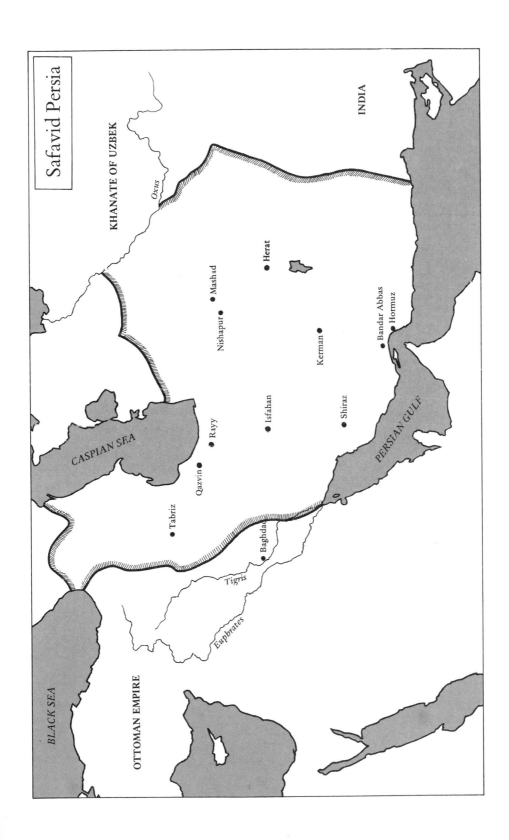

Safavid Persia

KHANATE OF UZBEK

Oxus

INDIA

Mashad

Herat

Nishapur

Bandar Abbas
Hormuz

Kerman

Isfahan

Shiraz

Rayy

CASPIAN SEA

PERSIAN GULF

Qazvin

Tabriz

Baghdad

Tigris

Euphrates

BLACK SEA

OTTOMAN EMPIRE

shop of a shoemaker, pick up a pair of shoes that takes his fancy, put them on at the door and then continue on his way.

On another occasion he rounded on the soldiers in his wake and complained that he could never go anywhere 'without everyone else wanting to come too'. Active, impulsive and curious, he asked the Augustinians: 'How do you feel about what I am doing? I am a king after my own will, and to go about in this way is to be a king – not like yours, who is always sitting indoors.'

There are, too, vivid cameos of Abbas in a proud, proprietorial flush, taking parties of ambassadors and travellers on a nocturnal spree during an Isfahan festival. They go through the gates of the Ali Qapu and push their way, with difficulty, through crowds in the *maidan*, making for the bazaar. The *maidan* was a congregation of Persian life: seamy, importunate, riotous, venal. Jugglers, wrestlers, story-tellers, puppeteers, acrobats, hucksters and whores vied for the passing trade. From the upper galleries of the arcades bordering the entrance to the bazaar came plangent music, played on copper trumpets eight feet long. Coffee houses, notorious for pederasty, were thick with babble. Approaching this rendezvous, della Valle saw one of the royal women, her bulk swathed in Turkish satins, eating while she rode. 'Her mouth was so full, and her cheeks so bulging, that in Italy you would never have taken her for a queen.'

Abbas, on foot, kept an eye on all his guests. A favourite victim was there: the courtly and unbending Spanish ambassador, Don Garcia da Figueros, and when Abbas embraced him he called him *Baba*, an endearment indicating age (Don Garcia was sixty-eight) but rather casual between a king and an ambassador. The Spaniard stood on his dignity, while Abbas led the party into one of the coffee houses. While they took refreshment two effeminate youths cavorted before them in a competition dance. Don Garcia was shocked; Abbas laughed. The Indian ambassador nearly choked the company with his large pipe. Abbas retaliated by tugging the ambassador by both ears and calling him an old cuckold, a treatment that seemed not to dismay anyone. The Turkish ambassador, unpopular with the crowds, was jostled, knocked over and lost his turban. One by one the party flagged, the carousing too much for them. Abbas, enjoying himself enormously, kept going until nearly dawn, leaving only a hard core of drinkers behind him.

As the sun came up and the crowds dispersed, the work resumed on the buildings which had changed the skyline of Abbas's Isfahan. On the east of the *maidan*, turning a subtle shade of creamy brown in the first light, was the squat dome of the Sheikh Lutfullah Mosque. This was very much a private place built for Abbas and named for one of his fathers-in-law. More modest in scale than the Royal Mosque, the Lutfullah has an enclosed and introverted feeling: a cranked passage leads to the dome chamber, and its gloom leaves the visitor unprepared for the sudden brilliance of the tilework lining the walls and inner surface of chamber and dome, perhaps the finest tilework of any Safavid mosque. There is no open courtyard – the chamber is divorced from the vibrancy of the life outside. Though pressed ahead with all its patron's impatience, the Lutfullah escaped the corner-cutting which afflicted the Royal Mosque.

On the other western side of the *maidan*, directly opposite the Lutfullah, was the odd, block-like Ali Qapu ('that brick boot-box' Robert Byron called it). But, like Abbas himself, the Ali Qapu has more depth than its appearance at first suggests. As well as being the link between the *maidan* and the palace complex, it was a grandstand from which the Shah and the court could survey the life and sports of the capital. In structure it is like a series of dolls' houses planted, one on top of the other, ending with a cleverly designed galleried music room. Under this there are a succession of low-ceilinged chambers and high-vaulted salons with fine decoration.

The Lutfullah and the Ali Qapu made the east–west axis of the *maidan*; the Royal Mosque is the southern focal point and the bazaar entrance the northern focus. The bazaar runs obliquely for more than a mile from the *maidan* to the Friday Mosque, thereby making the connection between the old Isfahan and the new. The new city extended south from the *maidan* to, and beyond, the Zayandeh Rud. The whole – old city and new – was bound together as one by building, on a north to south axis, the Chahar Bagh – a magnificent wide boulevard with four rows of plane trees and a central water channel. The Chahar Bagh ran for two and a half miles to the west of the *maidan* and crossed the river by the Allahverdi Khan bridge, not simply a way of crossing the river but a building in its own right with thirty-three arches. On each side of the Chahar Bagh there were gardens and pavilions, and small palaces, and the boulevard became the place where Safavid high society could preen and promenade and feel, with some justification, that this was the most luxuriant parade of any city in the world.

Abbas had given Isfahan more than a plan: his city, as great cities do, evoked an inimitable *spirit*, and one that can still be felt. As Robert Byron said: 'The beauty of Isfahan steals on the mind unawares ... before you know how, Isfahan has become indelible, has insinuated its image into that gallery of places which everyone privately treasures.' It is still true that given such sights the mind can be stilled by the eye, and yet there must be under this outward splendour some nagging questions. Something in the very resplendence of Isfahan is significant, not for what it is but for what it conceals. Byron went on to say that a few buildings 'illustrate the heights of art independently, and rank Isfahan among those rarer places, like Athens or Rome, which are the common refreshment of humanity'.

Yes, up to a point. But in at least one crucial respect Isfahan was never an Athens or a Rome. It had no intellectual engine as they once did. As the Persian craftsmen fulfilled the aspirations of their patron, the world outside was waking to disturbing new ideas. Some ancient schemes were falling: Copernicus had put the sun in its place, at the centre of the planets. Abbas might know the political implications of Luther, but he had no glimmering of how Galileo, confirming Copernicus, was unravelling the order of things which in the east was still holy writ – as, indeed, it also was in Rome. In persecuting Galileo the Papacy had locked southern Europe out of the future.

Persia's emergence as a new and independent eastern branch of Islam was not, like the rise of Protestant Europe, intellectually liberating. Shi'ism was no longer a revolutionary or even revisionary force: it became an intensively traditional one, bent on consecrating the fable of 'Ali and Husain, the martyred *imams*, through rituals like the *tazieh* passion plays which had overtones of genocide in their liturgy, and through the pilgrimages to the shrines of the Shi'a *imams*. And the secular climate was no more radical. Isfahan in the seventeenth century did foster a period of intellectual debate; it revolved around theological philosophy of great sophistication but there was little sign of the kind of intellectual questing that had distinguished Baghdad or Nishapur when Persian brilliance sharpened the dialectic of all of Islam. There was no equal of Avicenna, the great philosopher and 'universal genius' of the Saminid court, whose influence reached twelfth-century Europe, nor of the scientist al–Biruni. That calibre of secular exploration had been

Indulging another side of his complex nature, Shah Abbas takes wine on a picnic with a group of rather epicene young men. Wine was one of his milder vices, though offence enough to the sensibilities of the religious leaders. This mural is tucked away discreetly in a small salon of a pavilion in Isfahan, a city still replete with Abbas's works.

snuffed out in the petrification of Islamic thinking, just as it was in Europe by the reaction of the thirteenth-century Papacy.

Interestingly enough, Herbert noted that the *corpus* of the old classics still had currency in Safavid Persia: 'Many Arabic writers, learned both in natural philosophy and the mathematics, have flourished'; and he saw the works of Galen, Avicenna and Hunain ibn Ishaq (who translated Greek medical knowledge into Arabic). 'So well as I could appreciate,' he wrote, 'these are learned in the sciences, and few but are philosophers: nevertheless their libraries are small; their books usually in Arabic....' Herbert himself personifies very well a great irony of history – that the European travellers knew more of Persia's ancient past than the Persians themselves.

The fugitive Greek and Roman classics, gathered and translated in Baghdad and Byzantium, had, as those centres collapsed, been reclaimed by Europeans. Herbert, aged only twenty-three when he arrived in Persia, and who seems not to have graduated from his Oxford college, compares notes along his route with Xenophon, Tacitus, Plutarch, Strabo and Galen, amongst others. This was sounder equipment than the embroidery of Firdausi – if the tangible truth was preferred to the heroic legends; the truth would, in due course, at least equal the legend. The academic reclamation of the Achaemenians, Parthians and Sasanians begins really with these erudite amateurs of the seventeenth century. The unfairly mocked Don Garcia da Figueros made valuable researches at Persepolis; so, too, did della Valle, who made the first copy of a fragment of cuneiform, although decipherment was to take another two hundred years.

But the intellectual curiosity was very largely a one-way traffic. Merchants came and went, but no Safavid ambassadors were combing western civilization for its ideas, and no hint of the revolution in physical knowledge seems to have registered. Instead, Abbas worried about commerce, and about his deficiencies in weapons. Robert Sherley, kept as a kind of hostage while his brother Anthony went off to further Persian interests at the Christian courts, adapted to the life (he married a Circassian) and did what he could to create a royal ordinance factory and to overcome the innate Persian distaste for artillery, but the results were ephemeral.

Technology never took root. For some reason, things couldn't be kept working. The later Safavids developed a fascination for clocks, but no knowledge of how to maintain them. During Abbas's reign an

Englishman called Festy installed a public clock at the entrance to the bazaar, but it gradually ran down and nobody could be found to repair it. Eventually, after the Safavids themselves had run out of time, it disappeared, leaving just a hole in the façade.

Isfahan had scores of colleges, but education was in the charge of the Shi'a *ulema* who, as the custodians of the faith, eschewed all innovation. There might have been an understandable motive for this myopia: Shi'ism had still to win a broadly based conversion, and while the passions of the *tazieh* were a good recruiting agent amongst the uncritical mass the more sceptical and worldly classes (including those given to the pleasures of Isfahan's *demi-monde*) were less easily led to piety. Well into the seventeenth century much of Persia clung to its old beliefs and remained covertly Sunni.

We can also see in the severe conservatism of the religious hierarchy the beginnings of the sentiment, later very pronounced, that any hint of western manners should be rejected, which in turn sustained a blissful ignorance of western advance. The Parisian hats that appeared on ladies promenading the Chahar Bagh were viewed by the mullahs with the same hostility that was often brought to bear on western envoys to the court of Abbas; for many courtiers dealing with any Christian court came close to sacrilege. Conservatism may also have been an essential scaffolding for a state only just recovering stability and a sense of security – in this sense, reaction can be a refuge. The simple spiritual resources of Islam, accessible to the neediest and poorest, were a part of the integrity of the national morale. For a moment, Persia regarded herself as self-sufficient spiritually *and* materially, although this was to be proved a fearful delusion.

Whatever the forgiving arguments for the temper of religious life, Abbas made sure that Isfahan would not lack distinction in art – at least at face value. But he was far from being the most discerning Safavid patron of the arts. As a young prince in Herat he is said to have shown a quick and sure taste in the many works of that city, but the Safavid style had been planted at the very start of the dynasty by its savage messiah, Ismail. He was instrumental in the cultivation of a new level of Persian miniature painting. Two influences converged through his court: those from the White Sheep at Tabriz and from the Timurids, especially at Herat. From there the finest Timurid painter, Behzad, was called to Tabriz as Ismail's librarian, and his influence on Safavid art was seminal.

Ismail commissioned an edition of the *Shahnameh* which is now one of the most valued essays in miniature illustration. His motive may have included personal propaganda, but the quality of such a work vindicates the patronage. Like Timurid art, this early Safavid work drew on universal sources, and shows a particular Chinese strain. Under Ismail's successor Tahmasp, the strains fused into a new indigenous Persian school. This was an art of unabashed luxury, especially of the precious book – a taste beyond all but the princely purses. As a result, public interest was neglected to support private splendour, no new vice in itself. Later, as Tahmasp withdrew into his palace and to his women, the court team of artists and craftsmen was disbanded and other Safavid princes had to try to support the work, but continuing court intrigues disrupted it. With the stability that Abbas at last brought, there was another period of fine painting before the tradition atrophied into stilted repetition.

As those members of Persian society who could afford artistic patronage settled down to the new world of Isfahan, art acquired a wider audience and a more diverse inspiration. The results were mixed: on the one hand, a more popular art developed, where sketches of real life were in demand, which gave a refreshing documentary quality; on the other hand, churning out art by demand could produce mediocrity. Painting also became less chaste. Nudes appeared, as well as stylized groups of epicene young men in turbans. Abbas himself appears in murals of this genre, showing him on picnics – a clue to another side of his complex nature. Not content with his bountiful harem, he was an inveterate pederast and liked bathing in the company of lissom boys. In fact, the *fin de siècle* aroma which permeates illustrative art towards the end of Abbas's reign is probably an accurate mirror of what was happening at one level of Safavid society.

'He values more by weight than workmanship,' says Herbert, talking of Abbas's impecunious trawling of gifts. As an architectural patron, too, he was not always fussy. 'Shah Abbas did not pay much attention to perfection of detail,' writes the French authority on Persian art, André Godard: 'what interested him was to face whole monuments with brilliant glazed mosaics'. The *Haft Rangi* tile is the great compromise of its time: sufficient unto the day, but so poorly fixed that it fell off the walls within a few decades. So: façade architecture, dazzling *and* deceiving. It had *nearly* been the failing of the

Timurids, but Baisunghur's work at the Gohar Shad mosque in Mashed had depth, and did not fall off.

Behind the façade, what *was* life like for most of Abbas's subjects? Isfahan itself was insulated from the rigours of poverty and from climatic extremes which punished southern Persia with toxic fevers and northern Persia with paralysing cold. Jean Chardin, who saw Isfahan a generation after Abbas and who has become a primary source on social conditions, thought the peasants in the Isfahan oasis were more prosperous than their French contemporaries. But this proves little. The kind of life that travellers saw in cities like Isfahan, Qazvin and Shiraz, stimulated by their cosmopolitan trade and well-irrigated agriculture, was very localized and untypical. Away from the trunk routes, on the rims of the desert or in the isolated mountain areas, life was certainly far more marginal. It was a society of great extremes: 'The peasants here, as elsewhere in Asia, are slaves; they dare call nothing their own,' noted Herbert. The gulf between the noble homes carpeted with silk and gold, and the bare existence of the peasants was enormous

More than a third of the population still lived as pastoral nomads but the tribes, at least, had a kind of mobile sovereignty of their own, whereas the peasant farmers were vulnerable to rapine and extortion. Even though Abbas's reforms of government lessened the scope for local tyrannies, the idea of policing the whole country in an even-handed way was impossible: it was simply too diverse. To extend royal control, great trust was placed in a new élite, the *ghulams*. These were aliens, Circassians, Georgians and Armenians brought to Persia first as prisoners but then deliberately installed through the military reforms and into the bureaucracy to curb the power of the old establishment. At the end of Abbas's reign, *ghulams* held half the posts in provincial government and were said to be 'distinguished for justice, experience, valour and devotion to his Majesty'. Despite the resentment it might cause, Abbas was apt to reinvigorate Persian life with such alien transfusions, perhaps knowing that in return he would get unquestioned loyalty.

By such means the king's writ was strengthened, but there was and remained a dichotomy in the exercise of law, between the religious law of the *Shar'ia* and the arbitrary practice of secular authorities. And there was another order for the tribes, who tended to be a law unto themselves, with impromptu discipline decreed by the tribal *khans*.

But of all the competing hands for authority, it was the Shi'a theologians, the *mujtahids*, who most felt charged with the imposition of a national ethic. And with Abbas, they had to reckon with a style of kingship which was more assertive than the earlier Safavid style, and whose God-like aura was not sustained by impeccable personal behaviour. Though he wrote after Abbas's reign, Chardin well caught the dynastic style:

> The word of the King of Persia has ever been deemed a law; and he has probably never had any further restraint imposed upon the free exercise of his vast authority than what has arisen from his regard for religion, his respect for established usages, his desire for reputation, and his fear of exciting an opposition that might be dangerous to his power or to his life.

But Abbas was secure enough to be cynical about his 'regard for religion'. The gesture of building the Royal Mosque was as much to do with 'his desire for reputation'. If doubts arose, who, awed by that display, could accuse him of impiety? Abbas did seem to be quite serious about theological debate, which he carried out with the learned *ulema*, and he lavishly endowed the Shi'a shrines, including the gold plate made in Isfahan for the dome of the shrine of the *Imam* Riza at Mashed, a shrine he travelled to on an arduous personal pilgrimage. Hypocrisy? Pragmatism? But whom should he venerate, other than himself? His private thoughts remained private, buried in that volatile nature. One thing, at least, he was not – a man of dogma: 'in short he plays with the whole world and never concludes anything against his own interests'. Della Valle had the measure of Abbas.

By the end of his life Abbas's mind must have been well furnished with phantoms. He frequently had six or more beds made up and moved from one to another through the night. Astrological warnings were taken seriously. Given a prediction of assassination, he briefly abdicated and made sure that his proxy was killed to fulfil fate without sacrificing himself. Abbas was a mass of contradictions: gregarious and yet fugitive; sadistic and yet remorseful; impetuous and yet sagacious. He was a monster. What he gave Persia most of all was a charge of energy. He abhorred a vacuum, was unsparing with himself and demanding of everyone else. By leaving us Isfahan he can be superficially mistaken for a renaissance man. This he was not. Abbas was as firmly locked into the world of royal despotism as the Tudors. He anticipated no other world and no other condition.

Like the rest of the Muslim world, Persia was excluded from the reasoning which led to the industrial revolution – because such speculation was theologically disreputable. Ironically, the Safavids began as extreme heretics, and might have embraced profane philosophy as part of their separatism. But the Shi'a authorities (and the Safavid shahs) wanted to combine independence with respectability in the eyes of the whole Muslim world, and could do so only by becoming decorous in their theology. The theologians imported from Bahrein and Syria by Ismail to sanctify what had, until then, been a wild crusade of blood ended up by imposing an orthodoxy which upheld god's will and laws and did not permit of any others. The unchanging order of Muhammad was as firmly planted in Persia as in the Sunni nations, albeit through the individual focus of the martyred *imams*. The Ismailis, true heretics who *had* dabbled in philosophy, were snuffed out; the tolerance of Islam could only go so far. By today's western values this closing of the eastern mind to evident truths may seem deplorable, but – unlike the Christian world – Islam possessed a pervasive confidence in its eternal relevance and basic values, and a deep distrust of secular authority. Unfortunately, the faith deprived its adherents of what was, in the seventeenth century, an unimaginable leap in material well-being.

Persia was not, like Rome, fighting a rearguard action against the revolution of the intellect because, in Herbert's phrase, 'they continue their maimed calculations out of a blind conceit that antiquity commanded them'. The west could be equally obtuse. The Papal edict of 1616 had said: 'Propositions to be forbidden: that the sun is immovable at the centre of the heaven; that the earth is not at the centre of the heaven, and is not immovable, but moves by a double motion.'

Of all the sciences then dawning, Persia was to be doomed most directly by one: navigation. The Cape routes were sucking away the rapidly growing traffic between Europe and the east, making the caravans obsolescent. The ports of the Gulf were becoming important not so much for linking with overland routes, but for reasons of world strategy. The world was now far wider than the old arena of Asia and the Mediterranean; the Mediterranean was becoming a pond, northern Europe was about to industrialize, and in 1620, the last decade of Abbas's reign, the Pilgrim Fathers landed in America. Isfahan was half the world no more.

Abbas's disregard for the future had immediate results when he died, in 1629. His heirs had been given no preparation for leadership; they had been incarcerated in the harem and by adolescence were so addicted to its pleasures that statecraft was remote from their concerns. Here was the cost of absolutism in Persian monarchy: if a king put his authority so beyond challenge that it could not, as in the case of Abbas, be shared with his kin, then there was simply no way of passing from one generation to the next the acumen and skill needed to justify such power. The king held the country together, and he could also throw it away. When the Safavid crown passed from Abbas to the son of the murdered prince Safi he was already, at the age of eighteen, totally debauched. This Shah, Safi, died in 1642 and earned the comment: 'He meddled very little with affairs of the government; passing his whole life with his bottle, his wives, or in hunting.' Shah Abbas II, his successor, seems fortuitously to have been plucked from the harem just in time, at the age of ten, before the rot set in, and matured rapidly to give the dynasty something of a revival. The interval of neglect had not helped the king's position, and the *mujtahids* had greatly strengthened their influence. Abbas II none the less showed spirit. He followed Abbas I's policy of tolerance towards Christians, for the same pragmatic reasons – Abbas I forcibly transplanted thousands of Armenians from their homelands to his 'new Julfa', a community on the south bank of the Zayandeh Rud, where they built a cathedral, churches, a monastery and nunnery and brought valuable international trade to Isfahan. For endorsing the Christians, Abbas II was openly censured by the clerics (something unthinkable under his forbear): 'Our kings are impious and unjust, their rule is a tyranny to which God has subjected us as punishment after having withdrawn from the world the lawful successor of the Prophet. The supreme throne of the world belongs only to a *mujtahid*, a man possessed of sanctity and knowledge....'

Nothing could more arrogantly spell out the fatal divide between the temporal and theological competitors for power; Abbas II was not cowed, but the monarchy's authority was to be steadily undermined. Under Shah Sulaiman, who succeeded Abbas II in 1666, a new and insistent voice entered the court, that of a doctrinaire Shi'a theologian, Muhammad Baqir Majlisi. By the time Shah Sultan Husain succeeded Sulaiman in 1694 Muhammad Baqir had prepared the ground to become the real power behind the throne. He was not only fiercely opposed to the Sunnis, but also to the Sufis and denounced the classic philosophers as followers of 'infidel' Greeks. His worst fury was directed against the Zoroastrians and Jews who were persecuted and forced to embrace Islam. The Zoroastrian quarter of Isfahan was desecrated and the Jews were accused of practising magic. Although the Gregorian Christians of Julfa escaped the worst of these purges they, too, were subjected to an iniquitous decree enabling those who converted to Islam to claim the property of relatives who refused conversion.

This degree of religious intolerance was not only something new: it was self-defeating. Instead of unifying Persia it greatly accelerated disunity. The Christian Georgians who had risen through Abbas's reforms were disaffected and instead of continuing to be loyal to the Persian throne resumed the campaign for Georgian independence. The reassertion of regional feelings was intensified by the rapacity of the provincial government which took advantage of the court's distractions to pursue its own interests. Provinces which had been passive under the earlier Safavids were once more stirred into ideas of rebellion. Watching the state of Persia from Sultan Husain's court in 1721 the Ottoman ambassador wrote: 'The empire is threatened with a collapse into disorder and confusion ... sorrow is painted on everyone's face and they all say with one voice and openly – the Shah has ended his career, his empire is lost....'

Persia's two most powerful neighbours, Turkey and Russia, had been preoccupied by European adventures. But in 1718 Turkey had met a stalemate and made peace with Venice and Austria which left her free to look east again. Russia made a similar treaty with Sweden in 1721 and Peter the Great turned to designs he had long nurtured to seize part of the western Caspian provinces. His envoy in Isfahan contemptuously assessed the Safavid court: the Shah was 'not over his subjects, but is the subject of his subjects ... it is rare to find such a fool even amongst ordinary people, not to say crowned heads'. These threats from Turkey and Russia were serious, but the humiliation of Persia was not the work of either. An ill-sorted rabble of tribal brigands rode out of the east and stole the throne.

How a Shah as inept as Sultan Husain could remain in power can be explained only by seeing his court in the whole: a supine regime suited very well the eunuchs, the Shi'a hierarchy, the ministers, the commanders, the aristocrats and anyone else feathering their own nests. When the Shah was belatedly persuaded to raise an army for his western defences the court dragged itself ponderously as far as Qazvin but there came to rest; the Shah resumed his dissipations and the courtiers resumed the trade in bribes. No more was done about raising an army. There was an attempt to replace Sultan Husain with his more able brother Abbas, but this was discovered by the redoubtable court matriarch, Maryam Begum, and nipped in the bud. The court was heedless of its fate.

One of the factions provoked into rebellion by the extortions of the provincial government was the tribe of the Ghalzai Afghans on the eastern fringe of the empire. The Ghalzais claimed descent from Noah; in fact they were a part of the great Turkish migrations of the tenth century. By 1721 a new Ghalzai leader, barely in his twenties, had taken command in the provincial capital of Qandahar, and having watched one Persian attempt to crush the rebels fail he had something more in mind than simply gaining independence. He sensed that the whole dynasty might be brought down.

In February 1722 word reached the court in Isfahan that an army of Afghan rebels had passed two cities, Kirman and Yazd, and appeared to be making for the capital. A Persian army was hurriedly composed. It numbered forty-two thousand while the Afghans were no more than eighteen thousand, of whom only ten thousand were Ghalzais and the rest auxiliaries. There seemed no reason to doubt Persia's supremacy. In fact, her army was a rag-bag. Many of its number were hastily recruited and had no battle experience at all, and its commanders were disinclined to collaborate with each other.

On 8 March the two forces converged at Gulnabad, only ten miles south-east of Isfahan. On the evening before the Persians had been given a broth which, so a general assured the Shah, would render his men invisible on the field. The battle was a calamity. A whole wing of the Persian army, composed of Arabs whose loyalty was, at best, dubious, left the front to raid the Afghan camp for booty. The Shah's army snatched defeat from the jaws of victory and as it collapsed the young Afghan leader, Mahmud, could scarcely believe it himself.

The battle had been clearly audible in Isfahan; towards evening a dust cloud was visible beyond the ridge which separated the city and the battlefield. It was raised by the remnants of the Persian army as they fled back towards the capital. When the extent of the defeat became clear to them, the people of Isfahan broke into panic. The Zayandeh Rud was still swollen by spring floods; but for this

Mahmud's army might have crossed it and breached Isfahan's defences immediately. This would have been more merciful than what followed. The capital was besieged for six months, during which famine and pestilence reached appalling levels: 'The sword of hunger was sharpened so much that not only when a person died did two or three men at once cut off the warm flesh, eating it without pepper with great relish, but even young men and girls were enticed into houses and killed to appease hunger.' The Shah was reduced to eating camel and horse.

By the middle of October the misery was unendurable. Sultan Husain capitulated. As Mahmud's advance guard took possession of the Safavid palace complex, hysterical wailing from the harem could be heard all over Isfahan. Mahmud organized a coronation procession through the city, with the humiliated Shah riding at his side. The enormity of the disaster measures the true depth of Safavid decay. How *could* eighteen thousand tribesmen defeat and then hold in subjection a nation of between five and six million people? The answer is that they did not. *There was no nation left.* While the Afghans remained, they held the semblance of Persia – Isfahan and the cities. The amalgam called Persia which Abbas had reconstituted had, in reality, disintegrated. Turkey moved in to occupy large tracts of the western provinces, including the cities of Tabriz, Hamadan and Kirmanshah. Russia occupied the western Caspian coastal regions (Peter the Great wanted to block Turkish access to the Caspian). The Afghans had won the prestige of Isfahan, but it was only a toe-hold.

Had either Turkey or Russia shown the inclination, they might have carved up Persia between them. But the Russians never acclimatized to the fetid Caspian provinces and their soldiers died off like flies. Turkey, wary of prolonged war, was content with what she already had. Persia's survival rested, as fate would have it on a fugitive: Tahmasp, one of Sultan Husain's sons, who had fled the Afghans and pronounced himself the Safavid Shah-in-exile. He was pursued by the Afghans across the plateau, and nearly caught. His claim seems risible, totally without substance. But in September 1726, while reduced to a minimal retinue, Tahmasp appealed for help to a tribal Afshar leader called Nadr Qil Beg who was fighting the Ghalzais in their home territory. Nadr met Tahmasp at his refuge, the town of Khabushan near the north-eastern limits of Persia. From this meeting sprang the unlikely alliance which removed the Ghalzais from Isfahan and restored the Persian monarchy. Unlikely, because Nadr Qil Beg was as warlike and decisive as Tahmasp was pathetic. But none the less Tahmasp represented something which Nadr knew to be invaluable: the legitimate remnant of the Safavid monarchy. It says something for the mystique of the Persian throne that after the squalor of the late Safavid court the dynasty retained any appeal (or use) at all. Symbolically, as Nadr believed, it did.

The dynasty lost its nominal head a year after Tahmasp joined Nadr, when the imprisoned Sultan Husain was assassinated by the Afghans. Mahmud's mind had snapped, and he had been replaced by Ashraf. It was he who ordered the murder of Sultan Husain. The deprivations of the Afghan regime had reduced the capital, already decimated by the siege, to such an abject condition that Ashraf restricted the travel of visiting envoys in an effort to conceal the worst from them.

To be secure as Tahmasp's protector, Nadr Qil Beg had first to overcome the considerable influence of the powerful chief of the Qajar tribe, Fath 'Ali Khan. Fortuitously for Nadr, Fath 'Ali was caught planning treason, and executed. Nadr then built up a carefully drilled army around the figurehead of Tahmasp and in one great sweep to the west smashed the Ghalzais very few of whom survived to see their homeland. In December 1729 Tahmasp was installed as Shah by Nadr; Ashraf was hunted down and killed soon afterwards. The Afghan aberration was over.

Nadr Qil Beg was a master of military tactics. But he dreamed of being far more: he consciously reached for the mantle of Timur. The legend of Timur shaped Nadr's life, and world conquest was his dream. For a while Tahmasp served as the impotent agent of his designs. But by 1732 Nadr had swept the Ottomans out of Persia and felt able to get rid of Tahmasp. The contemporary view of the Shah was not flattering: 'He has forfeited the crown by his lazy, indolent management and his being a sot and a sodomite'; in that degree he was at least consistent with the dynasty's predilections. Nadr threw Tahmasp into jail and elevated his eight-month-old son Abbas, but only four years later the infant joined his father in prison and Nadr Qil Beg took the throne as Nadir Shah. By 1739 he had taken and sacked Delhi. The Mogul empire, with its court as dissipated as the Persian, dissolved at his touch. Amongst the vast treasures that Nadir took from India were the Peacock Throne and the Koh-i-Noor diamond.

Nadir Shah was not the kind of empire builder who could bring relief and exhilaration to Persia. He was an inveterate war lord, not a reconstructor. The Afghan brigands had merely been replaced by a home-grown variety, albeit better led. Nadir and his army were not, in a strict sense, even Persians. The Afshars were Turks who had been driven out of Central Asia by the Mongols and had then dispersed around the Caspian. They were bent on milking Persia to sustain their conquests. Nadir had no grasp of government, nor of economic affairs, and his campaigns brought continuous demands for money. The country was so stripped of supplies that in some districts there was famine for years. In eighteenth-century Persia there seemed no respite from medievalism.

For purely expedient reasons (he was not religiously serious) Nadir rejected Shi'ism and sought to restore a kind of Sunnism. Only his prolonged absence on campaigns prevented this policy from being severely enforced. The plan was to prepare the ground for Nadir's emergence as the secular leader of all Islam, but this was a mark of his *folie de grandeur*. He was becoming increasingly unstable and savage; Tahmasp and his children were massacred in 1740, and officials leaving Nadir's presence were apt to feel their heads to make sure that they were still in place. The Shah was treated for dropsy, and further physical problems brought more mental repercussions – the symptoms suggesting, perhaps, syphilis, which had been making an eastward advance. The bouts of madness became too much and in 1747 a small group of Nadir's commanders, at the end of their tether, slew him in his tent (though such was his awesome quality that they quaked with fear as they did it).

For three years rival tribes fought over the Persian throne. In 1750 the first non-Turkish dynasty to rule the country in nearly a thousand years was established in the old heartland of Fars, the Zands. Karim Khan Zand made his capital at Shiraz but declined to take the title of Shah, preferring to be called the *Vakil*, or viceroy. It was a lesser kingdom than before: the Zands did not rule over the extensive province of Khorasan. The dynasty provided Persia with an interval of much-needed peace. Shiraz itself flowered again as the arboreal paradise it had once been; the Zands were content with the horizons as they knew them. But as soon as Karim Khan died civil war erupted again and this time power passed to a northern tribe, the prolific Qajars whom Abbas had split into three groups because of their rising power, and who had had the ear of Tahmasp before Nadir arrived. It was the Qajars who moved Persia's capital to Tehran.

Isfahan's reign as the capital had lasted for a hundred and fifty years; like the Safavids she had passed from glory to decrepitude. In 1728 an Ottoman envoy saw people starving to death in the streets. In 1809 James Morier noted that the tiles were falling off the dome of the Royal Mosque, and returning a few years later the sights were even more distressing:

> One might suppose that God's curse had extended over parts of this city, as it did over Babylon. Houses, bazaars, mosques, palaces, whole streets, are in total abandonment; and I have rode for miles among its ruins, without meeting any living creature, except perhaps a jackal peeping over a wall, or a fox running to his hole.

In 1889 Curzon, the British Orientalist, found the Chahar Bagh 'pathetic in the utter and pitiless decay of its beauty'. Not until the 1930s was this process reversed and restoration begun. Isfahan's population when Abbas made it his capital was about 80,000; by the late seventeenth century it reached 250,000, including 30,000 in Julfa, the Armenian quarter. In the siege of the Afghans it is estimated that 80,000 died from starvation or disease and 20,000 were killed in action. The lifelessness and dereliction that Morier noted remained for a long while. Only relatively recently has Isfahan recovered its confidence and energy.

The last Safavid building of importance was Shah Sultan Husain's creation, the Madrasseh Madar–i–Shah in the Chahar Bagh, finished in 1715. This adjoined a large caravanserai which has been expertly restored and converted into the city's most graceful hotel, the Shah Abbas. With the Madrasseh, Sultan Husain provided the swan song of Safavid building and particularly of tilework: 'Nobody understood architecture or had a better taste in it than he,' wrote a contemporary, and as a single saving grace it serves him well. It is a beautiful building.

With the restorations the veneer of Isfahan is replete again, and casts its intended spell. Over it all hovers the *Zeitgeist* of Abbas, but the truth is that his was not really a golden age for Persia, merely an Indian summer. The culture beneath the show was flawed. Abbas was that paradox of history, the begetter both of recovery and of degeneration.

8

The Predators

1796-1941

The forces that early in the seventeenth century had restored Persia – her dominance of land trade routes, her military talent, her diplomatic cunning and her artistic flair – had been rapidly reversed or dissipated. No new resources, either of mind or material, were found to spare her from accelerating decline. Nadir Shah simply resorted to the ancient precept of refilling his treasury from plunder. It was but a fleeting palliative. All around Persia great tides were running.

The world's balance of power, held in a chance equilibrium during Abbas's reign, was now to change and in changing to transform the condition and aspirations of people in leaps; or, at least, those amongst them who lived in northern Europe and the new world. Persia had no part to play in this upheaval and was, in no real sense, to be touched by it or even to comprehend it. For two centuries the seat of the first world empire turned in on itself and withered, left with much of the Middle East and Asia as a part of what came to be called, rather patronizingly, the Third World.

Persia had gained the asset of religious unity at the cost of intellectual isolationism. But she was not totally sealed off. Since the sixteenth century intercourse with the west continued at a superficial level: travellers still came, drawn to the museum of Persia's past and the exoticism of her present, and fashionable Persia, that jewel in the dust, incongruously took to European finery, toyed with European devices and for the first time took up the European style of portraiture on the big scale, adding some singular Persian qualities, which gave to a culture rapidly becoming sterile in other ways a touch of lasting distinction.

The price of being petrified, like some exquisite anomaly in a lost seam of history, was severe for most of those assigned to live through these centuries in Persia. But they were, at least, spared any sense of comparison. And petrification had one compensation: it preserved as well as retarded. Persia's physical remains were not in any significant way defiled or disturbed; in fact, her oldest fabric was still silted up and lost. Had change come much earlier than it did, much might have been desecrated. As it was, the memory of distant greatness, the despair of sustained atrophy and the awakening of revolution were to collide, producing stresses which the west, through its evolution, had been able to minimize and which once more called for those gifts of assimilation and adaptation which Persia had so often discovered in herself.

It is hard now to comprehend how absolute was Persia's stagnation: even well into the twentieth century the social order was little changed from that of Safavid Persia. The population, roughly estimated at twelve million in 1920, remained predominantly rural. The settled peasantry were submissive by tradition. Only ten per cent of the whole land could support crops and only eighteen per cent provided forest and pastures. The substantial nomadic population hung on to bare subsistence and the tribal areas reverted to virtual autonomy under the khans. Brigandage flourished, travel was often extremely dangerous. The land, then, supported the majority. The towns and cities remained those of the middle ages. In their lives the most immediate power was religious. Education and the law remained for the most part in the hands of the clerics. Law and order was always the first casualty of the collapse of central authority, 'law' passed instead to the powerful and the armed. Possession of arms was more effective than dependency on the caprice of 'justice' and the tribes, at least, had their own arms. The 'army' as such consisted of provincial and tribal levies, palace guards and such protective bands as the diverse authorities could recruit.

There were, for example, the men called the *farrash*, masquerading as law-keepers, who were little better than vigilantes serving the regional governors without pay, who thrived on extortion. They wore red cloaks, had the symbol of the lion and the sun on their lambskin hats and carried whips. They hunted victims prosperous enough to be terrorized into paying their way out of false charges.

City life depended greatly on the social alliance within the bazaar, between the merchant bourgeoisie and the clerics. The bazaar provided the ballast of urban Persian society, a weathered organism which could hold itself together when all other forms of authority broke down. Equally durable were the land-owning aristocracy of whom the most powerful were the so-called Thousand Families, a purely figurative label for what was a more elusive but decisive alliance linking the royal family, the tribal nobility and religious and military élite. The 'professional' arm of this upper crust was the resilient Persian bureaucracy, who had absorbed the *ghulams* recruited originally by Abbas. The importance of this group lay in its vocational skills: in a society so encrusted in medieval ignorance and habits they were the ones most likely to know what was happening in the world outside, and the most likely to try to respond to it.

The civilization which had once illuminated the ancient world was now conducted in mean measure. Apart from the relatively small élite, illiteracy was, more or less, universal. But more pressing was the borderline subsistence of both the tribes and the peasants and the continued absence of sanitation and medicine. In the squalor, superstition flourished as a substitute for knowledge.

Politically the country had reverted once more to its old factionalism. The sense of 'nation' was fragile. In view of the racial mixtures which composed Persia a survival of any degree of cohesion was astonishing. Perhaps the faith was the only thing that most people had in common, and provided the glue. And there was still, however tenuous, the *character* of the Persian people. Despite all the ethnic, tribal and social rifts there was, and for long had been, a rooted Persian culture, and the culture expressed the character. The culture could be purely bravado, on the surface, as expressed through Abbas and his Royal Mosque, or much more personal and deep, expressed through the language in poetry which had the great resource of absorbing blows and salving the spirit. The Persian character could flex infinitely and not snap, it could dissemble or assimilate. Above all, it could survive.

While Persia suffered in her sleep, those around her were beginning their own processes of adjustment. Russia in particular, her European nose twitching in the scent of revolution while her Asian trunk remained inert, had to be watched carefully from Persia. Imperial Russia and Imperial Britain were the nineteenth-century predators most likely to exploit Persia's weakness. Britain came to regard and treat Persia as a convenient corridor to India, to ensure that the land was secure for the new telegraph and the Indian Ocean and Persian Gulf secure for the Royal Navy. Russia intended to consolidate her hold on the Caspian. Turkey, as yet somnolent to Persia's west, would herself awake and become an important influence.

Persia was taken into the nineteenth century under the prolonged and usually deplorable Qajar dynasty. Fath 'Ali Shah, who ruled until 1834, entertained delusions of grandeur which extended to a love of reflected glory: one wall of the Sasanian grotto at Taq–i–Bustan was freshly cut to depict Fath 'Ali's court, in crudely painted relief, sharing the arena with Chosroes II. It all went much too much to the head: Fath 'Ali sought glory by waging war on Russia, with risible results. As a settlement Armenia had to be ceded to the Russians, all claim to Georgia was renounced and substantial land on each side of the Caspian was given away. Impotent yet rash, the Qajars were caught in the competing tides of imperialism. The British acted with the kind of mentality which made 'spheres of influence' a euphemism for covert colonization.

In 1848 a Qajar monarch did appear who began with better intention – Nasiru'd–Din Shah. He seems genuinely to have tried to consider instruments for a more enlightened rule, but was unable to defuse what rapidly became a dangerous sectarian war between the Shi'a establishment and the followers of a new movement which sprang up in Shiraz, the Babis. The early success of this movement was a reflection, as Mazdakism had been in Sasanian Persia, of the frustrations caused by the reactionary nature of the prevailing orthodoxy. The Babis were martyred and finally, after an attempt on the Shah's life, brutally suppressed. Henceforth 'Babi' provided a convenient label for any dissident and sufficient cause for their elimination.

There had been no real grass roots movement for change; the subject masses remained fatalistic. What had been percolating through, at the privileged heights, was a combined sense of threat and obsolescence. The bureaucrats, especially diplomats aware of the outside world, realized Persia's paucity of constitutional machinery; which was not the same thing as speculating the merits of constitutional democracy. While power rested in too few hands, it was too easy for outside powers to corrupt it without there being any brake from below. The impunity with which Britain had moved in to Persia and installed its telegraph line to India, with an attendant military protection, showed how contemptible was the notion of Persian sovereignty.

The appalling backwardness of the country needs emphasizing: there was no meaningful Press until the 1840s, and then only a tentative one – those who could supplemented the meagre flow of information with foreign papers, which described ideas and a world beyond the glimmerings of most Persians, and as inaccessible as Mars. The tools of change were pathetically few, and the resistance to change implacable, from both the Shah and the theologians. The simmering restlessness of the bureaucrats was shared by some of the merchant class, who had begun to understand the prosperity that reforms might bring to them. But while Europe discovered how to harness multiplying capital and to concede to ineluctable social aspirations, Persia gained neither the material means nor the political institutions for advance.

There were, however, rich pickings for the predators. In 1872 the Shah gave the ubiquitous Baron Julius de Reuter a concession to create the infrastructure – railways, roads and irrigation – to tap Persia's newly discovered mineral resources. The concession, made on guileless terms for seventy years, had to be withdrawn after public outcry. Nasiru'd–Din Shah was tantalized by the pleasures of European travel and greedy for the income to finance it. He then granted an even more abject concession: a fifty-year monopoly on the buying, selling and manufacture of tobacco, in return for an annual sum of £15,000 and a quarter of the profits, the proposition of an importunate Major Talbot. The Persian tobacco interests rose in revolt and this concession too, had to be rescinded.

In 1896 Nasiru'd–Din Shah was assassinated by a supporter of a faction calling for a modified and liberalized Islam. The next Shah, Muzaffaru'd–Din, merely accelerated the dynasty's proclivities, granted more concessions and, as an invalid, toured European cities and spas in search of relief. The dynasty teetered miraculously on until 1925, though much of its twentieth-century existence was nominal.

The survival of Persia itself, at a time when whole European dynasties and kingdoms were wiped from the map, is either a marvel or an accident or a combination of both. The country came near to dismemberment several times, from both internal and external forces.

The misery awaiting Persian dissidents in the face of the unblinking orthodoxy was without limit. The social atmosphere is caught in the memory of the writer Mohammed 'Ali Jamalzadeh, whose father was a revolutionary at the turn of the century. The father, Jamal, was a religious orator living in Isfahan who turned to the cause of change after reading newspapers, in Persian and Arabic, imported from abroad. Isfahan was governed by a Qajar prince whose despotism was reinforced by a Shi'a zealot called The Wolf, and by the roaming *farrash*. The 'underground', composed of people like Jamal, civil servants, teachers, merchants and shopkeepers, held clandestine meetings in which the English language press, also, was translated and read. If dissidents were caught they were branded as Babis and treated summarily.

The young Jamalzadeh saw two merchants soaked in petrol, driven into the *maidan*, and ignited as torches by The Wolf. He saw the headmaster of his school, who had been caught using English books bought from the Christian Armenians in Julfa, hauled before the mullahs and beaten on the soles of his feet with whips and sticks. The use of English books qualified as both sacrilege and sedition. Eventually forced to flee Isfahan, Jamal became a mesmerizing leader of the movement for constitutional reform in Tehran. A crowd of ten thousand assembled in a mosque for one of his speeches, and ended by chanting the letters which spelt 'law' in Persian – 'qaf, alef, nun, vav, nun, qanun, qanun ... law ... LAW!' The cry echoed across the city and into the royal palace, where the enraged Shah rushed outside to a pond and systematically shot each of his goldfish, naming them after the revolutionary leaders. Law was not a Qajar strongpoint; Fath 'Ali Shah had asked a British ambassador how many wives he had. 'One wife,' said the ambassador. 'Why don't you take more?' asked the Shah. 'The law doesn't allow it.' 'Oh – what is law?'

Muzaffaru'd–Din Shah, the hedonistic invalid, had more on his mind than distant voices. He had not recovered his health and his European bills had to be underwritten in 1900 by a loan from the Russians, for which he gave as collateral most of Persia's customs revenue. In 1902 he raised another ten million roubles by granting

Russia the concession to build a road from south-western Russia to Tehran, virtually an open corridor for the Russian army to pass through the key cities of northern Persia. To the British, who had assiduously colonized southern Persia, this suggested that the Shah was preparing for his country to become a vassal state of the Czar. This fear turned British sympathies pragmatically towards the rising constitutional movement.

What kind of movement was it, in a country without any experience of political suffrage? Its target was easier to identify than its motives. The decadence of the monarchy, the corruption of officials, the overall sense of institutions failing and resources draining away – these made common cause for attack. But what was the alternative, and whom would it serve? Western labels of 'liberal', 'radical' and 'revolutionary' have little meaning. With the monarch discredited, the one remaining force embracing the majority was the religion. But the theologians were themselves divided. Many were implicated in the repressions. *Status quo*, for them, was understood far better than change. And because change came with ideas borne on a western wind, secular and materialistic, its effect on many mullahs was (and continued long after to be) to intensify conservatism and reaction. Those theologians who were in the 'reform' movement did not want a western-flavoured revolution but something quite different: a revised Islamic state in which the pure tenets of the faith and the religious laws would predominate.

What might now be superficially taken as the familiar cry of its time, of a people rising, was in truth an alliance of convenience between diverse interest groups who, in the smelting, would not prove to be reconcilable. Where the sentiment was genuinely popular, there was the impediment of a total lack of experience in the practice of adversary politics. Strong class allegiances remained unbroken and jealous of their privileges. There was no vestige of a galvanized proletariat. The 'revolution' that convulsed Persia from 1906 to 1925 was led and dominated by the élites; the articulate body politic was formed of merchants, civil servants, landowners, tribal chiefs, clerics, aristocrats and journalists – western words provided the banners, but ancient Persian instincts shaped the motives. In the end, the effective agency of lasting change was none of them, but the army.

First, Persia's fate lay not in Persian hands but those of the major powers, the most contiguous and menacing of whom was Russia. It was only the defeats of Czarist Russia, at first abroad and then internally, that spared Persia. The annihilation of the Russian fleet by the Japanese in 1905 raised great hope amongst the Persian dissidents, evidence, so they believed, that the bear could be slain by an impudent Asian upstart. The abortive Russian revolution of 1905 reinforced this hope. And for a while the Czar was so preoccupied that he failed to provide aid and sustenance to Muzaffaru'd–Din Shah, who was bent on smashing the constitutional movement.

In the summer of 1906 some of the movement's leaders were jailed, and many others were given sanctuary in the ample grounds of the British Legation in Tehran. The British had expediently decided to back the dissidents as a check to the Shah's Russian flirtations. Caught between these two powers, and with Britain for the moment in the ascendant, the Shah conceded a constitution which set up the first Persian parliament, the Majlis, in Tehran. The drafters of the constitution had little knowledge of such devices; in desperation they had adopted the first example they could lay their hands on, which happened to be Belgian. Even then, they were fearful that the Shah would die before signing it. During a meeting at the palace they had to call in the royal doctor, an Englishman. He told them: 'Your king is not as ill as he seems – it is the courtiers who are making him ill.' A few days later, after the signing, Muzaffaru'd–Din Shah died.

His son and successor, Muhammad 'Ali, was a recidivist. Hostile to the demands of the Majlis, he was reinforced in his position as a result of the first steps in the power game which led to world war. In August 1907 Britain and Russia reconciled their interests and carved up Persia in a joint treaty designed to contain Germany. Russia became custodian of all the major northern cities, and Britain was confirmed master of the Gulf and south-west Persia. A nominally independent central strip remained. Already devolving into rogue provinces under the Qajars' neglect, Persia was now annexed by two brands of imperialism. In some of the distant regions any lingering notion of statehood seemed ridiculous. In the south, the British dealt directly with the Bakhtiari tribal leaders and did much as they pleased without reference to Tehran. And in Khuzistan, at the head of the Persian Gulf, they had a keen new interest in holding a secure base. In the westernmost ridges of the Zagros, where they slipped suddenly towards the fertile delta, British prospectors were drilling for oil.

The British navy was considering plans to convert from coal

to oil-fired boilers. The Admiralty in London was concerned that the existing sources of oil were either distant from Britain (two-thirds came from the United States) or vulnerable. No oil had yet been found in the Middle East, but surveys pointed to the probability of a rich field on the western fringe of Persia, conveniently within reach of the head of the Gulf. A private consortium drilling in Khuzistan had so far come up with dry holes. The Australian entrepreneur behind the consortium, William Knox D'Arcy, was having trouble finding the money to sustain the exploration. The British government had given military protection and wanted the drilling to continue, but the backers got cold feet and early in 1908 wrote to the field manager, G. B. Reynolds, instructing him to sink wells to between fifteen hundred and sixteen hundred feet, and, if this failed, to 'close down'. Before the letter reached Reynolds he had struck oil at last, at a depth of 1180 feet, on 16 May. His rig was set up near a small mosque in a cleft of sand-coloured hills at Masjid–i–Sulemain. Once the drills went deep enough they found, as predicted, a prolific field. The Masjid–i–Sulemain strike was the first in the Middle East, and the proof of the most potent single resource in the future of Persia and the whole region. But Persia did not then know it.

On the morning of 23 June 1908, the Majlis was in session, moving haphazardly through an apprenticeship in the art of government by debate, something strange and alien to the whole Persian tradition. At the beginning, even the habit of standing while addressing the assembly had to be imported from the west. Now, without any warning, shells started raining down on the building. Under the Shah's orders the Persian Cossack Brigade was ending, by force, the constitutional experiment. The Brigade had been created in the nineteenth century, manned by Persians but commanded by Czarist Russians. Its involvement now in Persian politics was to have profound consequences. Those political leaders who escaped the bombardment were arrested and then, in many cases, executed. This act of Qajar lunacy was self-defeating. Outrage at the action led to a counter-coup and the Czar chose to switch his support to the parliamentarians. Muhammad 'Ali Shah fled into exile. His eleven-year-old son Ahmad, a pathetic caricature of Qajar obesity, took the throne, the last of the line.

Revolutions usually begin not with the mute oppressed but with the articulate. In Persia the alliance of vested interests which formed the first Majlis could not be called 'democratic' in any sense of that adaptable word. It was elected on a limited and élitist franchise, and had a heavy metropolitan bias. Reforms in 1909 went towards correcting this bias and extended the franchise to include as well as the mullahs some Christians, Zoroastrians and Jews, and gave each of the main tribes a representative. But the religious leaders could veto any legislation deemed 'contrary to the precepts of Islam'. To the peasant in the fields, if he comprehended it at all, the 'revolution' was remote, urban and irrelevant. His condition remained unaltered.

With a juvenile on the throne the only consistent priority of government was to try to preserve some semblance of nationhood, but the *de facto* control by Russia and Britain rendered this a fiction. Officials charged to carry out new programmes were unskilled and confused. Like the central European states obliterated in the First World War, Persia could easily have been ingested by one or other of the major powers. More likely, perhaps, was partition: the north ceded to Russia, the south to Britain. But the Russian revolution of 1917 forestalled this. And Britain, bent on hegemony over Egypt, Palestine, Arabia and the remnants of the Turkish empire was concerned not with swallowing Persia whole but with ensuring the security of her interests: the routes to India and especially the security of the Anglo–Persian Oil Company. By 1912 Britain was building the first oil-fired battleship. Within five years of Reynolds's strike the company had built one of the world's largest refineries at Abadan and was now under the control of the British government, which in 1914 paid £2·2 m for control of the Anglo–Persian Oil Company.

British plans for Persia were spelled out nakedly in a proposed Anglo–Persian Agreement drafted in 1919 as part of Britain's postwar Middle East strategy. Paying lip-service to Persian sovereignty, the British proposed technical, administrative and military 'assistance' involving British advisers and a British loan of £2 million. In effect, London viewed Persia as a protectorate. Because of the impending introduction of British personnel, the Agreement had to be ratified by the Majlis. But the Majlis rejected it (in spite of ministers being bribed to secure its passage). As diplomacy foundered, Persia was left to find her own salvation.

Amid the dissolution the most coherent secular force left in the country was the army, and in the army the most impressive unit was the fifteen hundred men of the Cossack Brigade. Its officers, trained and supervised by their White Russian superiors, had been kept apart from the rest of the Persian army since their formation in 1879 and were also insulated from Persian culture. But the anarchy of Persia in 1920 was clearly all around them. It was alarming to one of the Persian officers in particular, a man just promoted to the rank of general after a rise up from the ranks, Reza Khan. This was a man with a forceful presence: he was over six feet tall, unusual in a Persian, and had attentive unsmiling eyes. As Russian control of the Brigade broke up after the Russian revolution, Reza Khan emerged as its dominant personality.

In February 1921 a small cabal gathered in Tehran to organize a *coup d'état*. Reza Khan was given the role of chief of the armed forces. The conspirators swore oaths on the Koran to serve the Shah, to save Persia from Bolshevism and to restore order. The leader and principal architect of the coup was a journalist, Sayyed Ziya. Within a year Reza Khan had publicly re-written history to claim that it was he, not Sayyed Ziya, who had been the real mastermind of the coup. By then he was above challenge as the strong-man of a new regime pledged to restore Persia's sovereignty and to bring her, despite all her debilities, from the middle ages into the twentieth century.

Only ritual gestures were now made to Ahmad Shah, all but a cypher in the palace. But this showed only the fate of the Qajars, not a decision on the future of the monarchy as an institution. The symbolism of the monarchy was unresolved, and its capacity to represent temporal power as a check to the other great authority in the state, the religion, was not lost on the new regime. Whether the future temporal power emerged in monarchical or republican form it would still have to re-contest its primacy with the Shi'a authorities.

Reza Khan was not a pious man, although he observed the religion's formalities. His ethic was single-minded and military. He was not in any way reflective, but a man of action, as well as a passionate patriot. His goal was the restoration of Persian greatness *without* foreign support or foreign exploitation of Persia's resources. The means for that restoration had to be copied, he believed, from the west. But the ends, they must be Persian. On the anniversary of the coup, the day he pronounced himself officially as its author, Reza Khan revealed something of the temper of his mission: 'If you think a bit, you will realize that the land of Darius was on the verge of destruction because of the actions of his evil and illegitimate children … if hereafter anything contrary to the above [his version of the coup] appears in any news-paper I will suppress that paper and punish the writers . . . .'

In 1923, clearing his own path ruthlessly, Reza Khan gave title to his real substance by taking the position of Prime Minister. He had been closely following events in Turkey. The previous autumn the Sultan had been deposed; in October 1923 a republic was established under Kemal Ataturk. Ataturk was an inspiration to the Persian nationalists, and the Turkish example was not lost on Reza Khan. For six months the pressure to follow Turkey grew. Deposing Ahmad Shah was no problem, but the question of destiny was: could 2450 years of Persian kingship be jettisoned? Inexperienced in any form of modern government and not, by nature, inclined to Athenian democracy, the Persians hesitated. The appeal of a clean sweep was clear. Reza Khan appears to have been leaning heavily towards a republic – he urged the Majlis to vote through a bill establishing a republic before the Persian New Year in March 1924. If he was, in fact, still ambivalent it is understandable. A head of state stripped of the aura which had sup-ported the monarchy would be very uncertain of his survival, and would be overshadowed by the authority of the clerics. A man of little formal education, Reza Khan had none the less identified himself with Persia's pre-Islamic past and, in doing so, understood the mystique of kingship. There is also evidence that in 1921 he had promised General Ironside, the British commander in Persia, that he would not depose the Shah, and that four years later he asked to be released from this promise.

Against these influences can be weighed Reza Khan's despair with Persian institutions, not just the royal family but the whole of the court. His admiration for Ataturk cannot be discounted. It seems probable that for a moment he *was* sorely tempted to the prospect of being the first president of a Persian republic. What, without any doubt, killed the idea in the end was fanatical religious opposition. Unfortunately for the cause of republicanism in Persia, at the crucial moment the Turks abolished the Caliphate, in March 1924. The Shi'a authorities in Persia feared similar sacrilege and they summoned Reza Khan to Qum, the Shi'a shrine south of Tehran which was the core of religious orthodoxy in Persia. Their arguments must have been uncompromising, for within days Reza Khan publicly reverted to unalloyed support of a monarchy. He announced: 'A government must not oppose public opinion . . . I have always wanted to see the progress and promulgation of Islam ... we came to the conclusion that it would be better for the country if all efforts to promote a republic were halted.' From a man who was neither a great respecter of public opinion nor a devoted promulgator of Islam these were, at best, disingenuous words. The suspicion must be that a deal had been done; that if the Shi'a authorities were spared the fate of the Caliphate they would, in return, endorse a change of dynasty. They had won a battle, but not the war: by using their full power at that moment they had made very clear to Reza Khan, lest he doubted it, that the ancient contest between the temporal and religious arms of the state, endemic since Ismail established the Safavid hierarchy, had still to be settled. And he was not of a mind to leave things that way.

The aggressive reassertion of Persian nationalism after the coup and during Reza Khan's premiership might have been expected to dismay the foreign powers, especially the British. But the first British minister to see the new regime come together at first hand, Sir Percy Loraine, was quick to see the significance, and the qualities, of Reza Khan. This unusual breath of realism had infected even Lord Curzon, the arch imperialist, who reviewed events in Persia during a House of Lords debate in May 1924, and said: '... you cannot expect in the future any of that sort of natural, instinctive, automatic deference to western ideas and western opinion to which we were accustomed ... it is really a symptom of a world-wide movement. ...' But this balm came too late to disarm Anglophobia in Persia, and Curzon's spirit seemed not to instruct British diplomacy there for several more decades.

On 12 December 1925 the Qajar dynasty was formally dissolved and Reza Khan installed as Shah, and founder of the Pahlavi dynasty (a name with significant Sasanian associations). Ahmad Shah survived, and the Qajar royal family, with ample funds left in foreign vaults, suffered no discomfort. They had been supplanted by an outsider, a man without roots in any of the social network which had provided Persia's élite. Hagiographers delved desperately into his lineage; one version pronounced his father a sergeant of the cavalry, another raised him to colonel. Indisputable was the fact that Reza Shah came from northern military stock, from the village of Alasht in the Alborz mountains between Tehran and the Caspian. The hardiness and simplicities of his background are more relevant, and possibly more eloquent, than any imagined social gilding added later.

A classic example of the right man in the right place at the right time,

Reza Khan had imposed his will on events from the dawn of the coup. Sayyed Ziya was despatched into exile within the first year. None of Reza Khan's political colleagues endured; throughout his premiership and his reign, life within his gaze was hazardous. His only durable companions were a small clique outside the immediate court and political circles. He wore out or broke several devoted aides. Those suspected of less than devotion died or disappeared in mysterious circumstances. Like all driven and dominating men, he needed pliant associates but suffered from the lack of challenge, of counter advocacy. Reza Shah was an engine fixed firmly on a track and heading down it as fast as he could get the tracks to bear. Nothing could deviate him, and delay was intolerable. The metaphor is forgivable because throughout his reign one grand obsession became symbolic of his policy: the building of the Trans–Iranian railroad. At least fifteen minutes of every cabinet meeting was devoted to it. When the line was finished in 1938 it joined the Persian Gulf with the Caspian. As the first train moved off, Reza Shah slipped away from the official party and stood alone by the tracks, crying the tears of fulfilment.

The railroad also revealed the recurrent dichotomy of his policies: to appropriate western means *without* assimilating western attitudes. The railroad was built without foreign money and with foreign advisers chosen only from countries considered to be neutral: America, Germany and Scandinavia. Reza Shah sent Persian students to French military academies, to western universities and to work in western industries – but always with a caution about confused identity: 'I don't want to turn the Persian into a bad copy of a European.' But where did the line lie? A Persian composer who introduced western symphonic music to Tehran was ordered thereafter to 'westernize Persian music'. It was natural enough to avoid treating with the imperialist, their perfidy was proven. It was not a sudden burst of xenophobia that forced the finance for the railroad to be painfully found out of Persia's threadbare resources, it was intelligent self-preservation. But underlying the fifteen years of Reza Shah's fevered reconstruction of his country was a conflict of identity and values – a regard for Persia's original creators, a contempt for her latter day rulers, the inspiration of western material growth – but also a sound instinct that this could corrupt as well as rejuvenate. Persia's old ability to take, refine and adapt, to be the catalyst and to preserve at the same time her identity, could it be found again? Reza Shah committed his people to live with

RIGHT Before the first successful oil strike in the Middle East, at Masjid-i-Sulemain in south-west Persia in 1908, the British prospectors drilled many dry wells. Relics of their heavy equipment still lie rusting at the sites.

BELOW In 1936 Reza Shah freed women from the veil; the sudden adoption of western dress could have some bizarre results, shown when these tribal women paraded before the Shah.

this question well beyond his own lifetime, and they are still wrestling with it.

Reza Shah agonized over this, and as he did he brooded over something which he saw as a snare in the path of his grand design: the Persian character. A study of his reign leaves a picture of a man in revolt against the nature of his people. The anarchy and despotism of the past centuries had, he felt, taken the fibre out of the national character. Graft was not only endemic in the 'public' service, it was regarded as a vocational necessity. Nepotism was a matter of honour. Lawlessness an aristocratic privilege. Evasion of personal responsibility essential for survival. Delay, procrastination and the bearing of false witness all part of the craft of endurance in Persian government. Fecklessness, if not a virtue, was not a vice either. But perhaps the worm that really gnawed at Reza Shah's dynamic was Persian negativism. In Persia the urge to criticize rises more readily than the desire to praise – it was more important to see where something might go wrong than where it might go right; the danger of being implicated in failure overcame the appetite for a chance of tasting success.

To counter this deeply ingrained negativism the Persian system had only one drastic instrument, Persian autocracy. Perhaps we should recall how Herodotus had imagined the arguments for Darius's brand of monarchy: 'One ruler: it is impossible to improve upon that' – or the ancient divide between Greek debate, haggling for days as the invader nears, and Persian certitude, reposing faith in the absolute mortal power. Reza Shah's solution was the historical Persian one – he bore down on negativism with naked intemperance. His threat of suppressing newspapers which failed to credit him with the coup was not idle. The press, to him, was dismally prone to negativism. Altogether, there was a blitz on the Persian character. In 1930 he told a reporter from abroad: 'The Persian character has got to be hardened. For too long my countrymen have relied on others. I want to teach them their own value, so that they may be independent in mind and action.'

He knew their weaknesses as well as their values. 'I have tried to create in the Iranian mind', he declared on another occasion, 'the will to work, to put this idea in the mind of the common man so that he knows that when he gets up in the morning he has to go to work.' Later, as he groomed his son for power, he would cite examples to him of Persian traits, as a warning. And after he had surrendered power the only book found at his palace bedside was James Morier's *The Adventures of Hajji Baba of Isfahan*, the classic fable of picaresque Persian life, and a catalogue of some of those quirks of character that dogged Reza Shah.

Provoked or not by the perversity of his people, his actions were often savage. His political position during the years he moved towards the throne was greatly reinforced by the zeal of military actions he took against the nomadic tribes. The breakdown of central authority under the Qajars had left the tribes virtual masters of their own territories. Travel through many of these areas was dangerous. From the start Reza Khan saw restoration of central authority as the first plank in his new state. Using armoured cars and German planes – the beginnings of his air force – he decimated the most lawless tribes into submission.

For a man who was vocal in his respect for ancient Persian traditions, he was oddly out of sympathy with nomadic life. In 1925 he told some newly humbled tribal *khans*: 'It is not becoming that you, the sons of an ancient country with its illustrious historical civilization, should wander over desert and mountain like predatory animals. You must give up the nomadic and tent-dwelling life.' Did he understand how Cyrus had lived? Plainly he seemed not to grasp that without their migrations the tribes could not feed their herds. Agriculture and stock-raising were consistent blind spots in his policy. Perhaps his exclusively military background left him insensible to the realities of life on the plateau.

The tribes might be 'pacified' by force of arms, but achieving the submission of the Islamic establishment was altogether more difficult. His surrender to the Shi'a *ulama* at Qum over republicanism was not repeated once he was on the throne. The Shah and the clerics were on a collision course. Three of his intentions were particularly provocative to the conservative tradition: educational reform, a secular legal code, and the emancipation of women. Nothing would be a clearer (or more traumatic) sign of the new Persia than stripping the veil from women. In a sense, Reza Shah made women the cannon-fodder of his social revolution.

The intransigence of the mullahs hardened as the range of the reforms emerged. And the Shah's antipathy to them responded in kind. In 1934 he toured Turkey by train, as Ataturk's guest, a rare glimpse of the world outside Persia and one that impressed him. One night, while Reza Shah was sleeping, the train stopped and a crowd appeared to salute Ataturk, who was still up. He was furious to see that the crowd was led by a mufti. He leaped out, seized and shook the cleric, and hectored the crowd: 'You are still backward if you have a man like this in front of you.' Told of the incident in the morning, Reza Shah said, 'What a good thing!' It was another confirmation of the urgency which he felt should apply to loosening the grip of the religion. The experience in Turkey undoubtedly hastened change in Persia.

The conflict with Shi'a power became bloody. In 1935 an annual ceremony in the courtyard of the sacred shrine of the *Imam* Reza at Mashed was used as a platform to attack Reza Shah's reforms. Westernization, and particularly the unveiling of women, was bitterly opposed and the demonstration gathered such force that it lasted for days, without restraint. The governor general of Khorasan wired Tehran for advice. He was told to restore order, 'even if the shrine is levelled'. On the evening of the third day of the demonstration soldiers went into the shrine, up the iron staircases to the roof overlooking the courtyard, fixed machine guns to their mounts, took aim and sprayed the assembly with bullets. Between four and five hundred people died, many more were injured. The religious leaders were banished.

The fact that such a massacre, and such an outrage, could pass without provoking at least a local uprising in the devout province of Khorasan is a measure of the intimidating power that Reza Shah and his instrument of coercion, the army, now possessed. On 1 February 1936, the official regulations to banish the veil, or *chador*, took effect. It was not a total conversion, and never became so. Later attempts to complete the process have had to be content with only patchy acceptance. In some cities the majority of women gradually overcame the unnerving nakedness of appearing in western clothes, in others the full-length *chador* remains obligatory for many women. The most effective agency for removing it is the difference of generations; younger Iranian women do not share their mothers' inhibitions.

The revolution wrought by Reza Shah had little to do with ideology. It was, in that sense, perhaps a characteristically Persian experience. There was no Rousseau, Marx or Mao, nor a Mussolini. Persia's fearsome paternalist was not in the least cerebral. What mattered most to him was *physical* and *moral* change – explicit, and utilitarian. It was alleged later that he found aspects of Hitler's Germany appealing, that there was discovered a bond of some ancient Aryan memory. This idea was propagated by the Allies in the Second World War to justify the reappearance in Persia of British and Russian military forces. It doesn't bear examination.

The organic changes of Reza Shah's Persia were substantial. By the end of the 1930s central government had been given primacy and local officials were left with little initiative. Medical services had virtually to be built from scratch, since modern medicine had been largely in the hands of foreign missions. Law reform, something Reza Shah shaped according to his own concept of the state's power, was less straightforward. The confluence of secular and religious laws and the competing civil and military authorities, made any idea of judicial autonomy an impossible dream. And Islam's social codes were not at one with the ideals of a westernized state. Education, the final arbiter of the society's quality, had been used more to keep minds closed than to open them, to sustain reaction rather than to glimpse change. The great medieval Islamic universities had long since gone. Higher education was ignored, technical education non-existent. Students sent to Europe and America came back to staff new schools and universities. The change at first was not pervasive. It was urban-centred. While the religion's control of education was loosened in the towns and cities its overall hold on the illiterate mass was not really weakened.

In two ways the Persian class structure had to cope with new forces. Educational liberation brought into being an extension of the traditional middle class into a technological and professional corps. They came largely from the traditional élite, but they acquired a fresh western outlook. Secondly, Reza Shah's reliance on the army gave privileges, influence and wealth to favoured military families. The old power groups in society were not, though, displaced in any significant way, and bided their time. As an outsider, the Shah had to cultivate a personal constituency to make his dynasty, not just himself, secure. He needed to feel that its allegiance would extend to his son. He could not afford to disaffect the world of the 'Thousand Families'. This may well explain one of the glaring omissions of Reza Shah's reforms – any action significantly to end the old pattern of land ownership. In 1933 he made threatening noises to the landowners, but nothing came of it. The result was serious: despite all the tangible advances, agrarian society was left dwelling in the middle ages, while the towns and cities acquired at least a patina of modernity.

The changes might have become far more substantial had Reza Shah been able to harness the country's greatest potential resource: oil. In 1933 the concession granted to Britain to operate the Anglo–Iranian Oil company had been renegotiated. The original terms of D'Arcy's concession, their significance unseen at the time, had been risible. The pressure on Reza Shah was not simply to improve the terms; many Persians wanted a state take-over. Most of the wealth from oil was going elsewhere. Reza Shah took on the negotiations personally, and came away with so little that his cabinet was dismayed, not the least because his surrender seemed so out of character. There were hints of bribery, unsubstantiated. Perhaps the greatest mistake was psychological, too ready an acceptance of the idea that if the western technicians pulled out neither the wells nor the refineries could be worked.

Commercial imperialism was far more unbridled and imposing then than now; a state take-over by Persia might well have precipitated draconian measures by Britain – even in 1951 a British Socialist government, busy nationalizing major domestic industries, threatened military intervention and a trade blockade when Persia did nationalize the oil industry. Reza Shah might have got much tougher terms in 1933, but the *real politik* of the day precluded a take-over. The economic depression in the west had curtailed demand; Reza Shah's priority was to keep the wells in production. His mistake was to give the oil company the rights for another thirty-two years at 1933 prices. For another twenty years or more the oil wealth continued to be siphoned off. In 1950 the British company paid royalties of $45 million to Iran, and taxes of $142 million to its own government. Although the politics of oil were finally fought through the collective power of the producers, the first engagements were between individual states like Persia, relatively vulnerable, and the enormous power of the oil cartels. This contest prolonged Persia's poverty and left deep scars.

With limited resources, Reza Shah's revolution often seemed unsynchronized and fitful. The widening gulf between the urban and rural populations had lasting social consequences. Normal laws of evolution did not apply. Sometimes the twentieth century appeared overnight, sometimes it came in fragments, sometimes not at all. Persian life was like a madly eclectic time machine in which several centuries were juddering together. There may be no such thing as an immaculate revolution, and it would be churlish to diminish what one man's will had been able to build in so little time, but these convulsing time warps brought deep confusions to the Persian people. Strong antagonisms lay close to the surface as Persia caught up, piecemeal, with the modern world. The Shah's iron hand often exacerbated the tensions, but perhaps there was no time for subtlety.

Reza Shah was brought down by his ingrained antipathy towards Britain and Russia. As another world war approached he failed to see Persia's peril. His *idée fixe*, the Trans–Iranian Railroad, assumed a crucial strategic importance for both British and Russian military intelligence. As long as Russia's 'phony war' alliance with Germany lasted, it was the British who had the immediate need of a compliant Persia. In the first year of the war there was an uneasy pause. Britain fretted about German 'advisers' in Persia, but the imperial connection with India remained unmolested. Then, in June 1941, Hitler invaded Russia. Neutral Persia was once more sandwiched between an Anglo–Russian alliance. British military preparations in the Gulf area were speeded up, but Reza Shah's local commanders failed completely to see the implications. The railroad represented the lifeline for Allied supplies to Russia. Had Reza Shah at that point bowed to the inevitable and surrendered neutrality and pledged collaboration with the Allies he might (it is only speculation) have avoided a repetition of Persia's fate in the First World War. As it was, Britain and Russia once more turned Persia into their vassal. The British smeared Reza Shah as a self-seeking tyrant with Nazi sympathies. On 16 September 1941 he abdicated.

History was about to repeat itself. The royal autocracy collapsed. In the final years of his power Reza Shah had pondered the virtues of adversary politics, so alien to the Persian tradition. He told the cabinet: 'Some day there will be an opposition force in the Majlis. *Until that day I am His Majesty's loyal opposition.*' It may have been self-deluding, but he seems to have realized, rather late, the fallibility of uncontested rule and the need for strong advice. Tellingly, he confided to his son, the Crown Prince: 'I wonder what will happen after me, as I have not had time to establish the necessary institutions.' Muhammad Reza Pahlavi, precipitated on to the throne at the age of twenty-one at a time of national humiliation, soon knew the cost of that missing piece in his father's revolution. The young Shah found himself host to Stalin, Roosevelt and Churchill as they divided up the world. He, and Persia, were hostages to fortune.

9

Epilogue: A Timeless Land

T he best way to understand Iran is to take a relief map and strip it of all man-made markings; roads, towns and borders. Think of it as bare terrain, and then add climate. Only then can you see the immutable elements which have governed existence on the plateau from the beginning. These elements, mountains, plains, rivers, deserts, oases, valleys, swamps and the extremes of heat and cold, are often at odds with each other, so that man himself is caught not only in his own mortal conflicts but also between the protean struggles of opposing elements. He has been there for a long time: some of the earliest cave-dwellers settled around the Caspian. Later, when the Indo-European tribes migrated from the void of Central Asia, numbers of them laid down tracks across the plateau which were then followed by one wave after another, culminating with the appearance of Chingis Khan.

Civilization began with the first attempts at environmental control. In seeking to exercise choice and control of living space, man had first to find what was beyond his control, and then slowly what was within it. Irrigation and agriculture were the great innovations of control and adaptation. Tribes from the Iranian plateau joined the first

Straddling ploughed fields like a line of bomb craters, the shafts of a *qanat* mark the survival of an irrigation system going back at least as far as the Achaemenians. By tapping the underground water-table without needlessly exposing water to the sun, the *qanats* remain an efficient way of preserving and distributing water underground over long distances.

agriculturalists of the Fertile Crescent. As their techniques developed, the harvests of Babylonia became as productive as those of modern Canada. Mesopotamia was, for this reason, the key to affluence in the ancient world – and the richest source of taxes for empire builders. In contrast, the Iranian plateau made far greater demands on those trying to create the conditions for subsistence. Nothing better shows the ingenuity of the plateau farmer, then and now, than the *qanat*.

The invention of the *qanat* achieved two things vital to agriculture: it carried water anything up to sixty miles from its source, and it did so in such a way that evaporation was kept to a minimum. The idea of the *qanat*, an underground water canal, is basically simple; the feat lies in its execution. A *qanat* begins with a spring, usually some distance up the slopes of a hill or a mountain. The tell-tale sign of such a source is a clump of shrubs or trees suddenly breaking out of the bare rock. These springs can be 'gushers' with as much power behind them as an oil reservoir, powerful enough, in places, to provide wells at the summits of mountains, like the one which sustained the Assassins in their Eagle's Nest. A *qanat* taps the spring, but channels it through an underground course whose gradient is precisely calculated to carry the water as far as it is needed without any form of pumping. The canal is dug and maintained from a series of vertical shafts only a few yards apart. The line of a *qanat* is therefore easily spotted from the air: the holes for the shafts resemble bomb craters.

But the *qanat* is not only a symbol of clever irrigation – it has a political significance too. It is so arduous to build, and so precarious to maintain, that it becomes feasible only in a society given some hope of security and continuity. It is a commitment to good order. And the search for order in an environment which, in many ways more often delivered hardship and uncertainty, needed a growing sense of community. The rationalization of common interest and the stresses of the environment found expression in a religion.

The Good Religion

The rigours of the land and the climate were the *leitmotiv* of the religion that was born on the plateau, Zoroastrianism. Life had to survive by harnessing the competing forces of heat and water, forces which could destroy life and yet sustain it. What held the balance between drought and fertility, between food and famine, between good things and bad things? The prophet Zoroaster proposed an answer: man could himself choose between the Good Lord, Ahuramazda, and the Bad Lord, Ahriman. This idea of mortal choice was novel. It incorporated an ethic: follow the good and wise thoughts, and Ahuramazda would come to your aid. Follow evil thoughts or, in the Zoroastrian terms 'The Lie', and only ill could befall you. Zoroastrianism introduced a form of monotheism, the primacy of one God, *and* dualism, the choice between a heaven and a hell. But the heaven of Zoroaster was in this world, not the next. Paradise, that Persian haven, could be created on earth as the fruit of an alliance between man and Nature – the reward of hard work *and* sensibility.

Much of the appeal of Zoroastrianism in the ancient world lay in its clear relevance. Life *was* indeed a struggle, and as civilization developed the virtues of wise and good work were manifest: irrigation conserved and made the best use of precious water; the industry of agriculture brought well-being (and a political moral), loyalty brought security. So Zoroastrianism stood for the good order of society, with everything and everyone in their appointed place. For the world of the pastoral nomad, as well as that of the settled farmer, the prophet gave the tenets of good leadership which, in turn, enabled the consent to exist in the community for good order; keeping things in their place. Only when good order broke down did things go wrong. If a battle was lost, then it must be punishment for bad leadership or some other transgression. If there was a drought and famine, then the good order to Nature had been disturbed. All this may seem to us very naïve, but in its pristine form Zoroastrianism was a very accessible and essentially *elemental* religion.

It was a great advance on the pagan rites which it supplanted, although it made use of 'primitive' symbols, like the flame which symbolized the life force of the religion, and which remains the sacred focus of the Zoroastrian ceremonial today: 'These are the fires given to the land of Persia to protect us from disastrous and terrible events, to keep us safe from evil.' Describing Sasanian Persia, Professor Peter Brown says:

The fire temples were great fumigating plants. They sterilized the region of demonic infections. They were placed along the roads, facing out to the mountains and the deserts, and in all the towns which the King had settled in the outlying areas of the empire, to the considerable annoyance of their inhabitants. To the upholders of the Good Religion, they were a sign that civilization had come to stay in all the provinces of the empire.

There were also the sub-Gods, just as the Sasanians combined the almighty king with the sub-kings. For example, Anahita, the bountiful goddess of water, whose temples demonstrated the salient miracle of refreshing pools in the middle of the scorched earth, and Mithra, the judge and 'Lord of the Pastures' to inform the king's wisdom. In his combat with Ahriman, Ahuramazda needed all the help that these subsidiary powers could give. And Ahriman's work, quite clearly, was the desert, barren rock, always threatening to encroach fertile land, or the deadly salt deserts in which nothing could live. The Zoroastrian faithful did not want for signs of evil. They were all around.

Holding the balance between good and evil was a credible role for Ahuramazda as long as he remained a celestial force. But when he descended to embrace the temporal powers he could too easily be compromised. This became the problem as Zoroastrianism was drawn into an alliance with the Sasanian state. If Ahuramazda and the king were interdependent, there was always the danger that one could take the other down with him. And when the Good Lord somehow failed to mitigate famine, heresy could suddenly flourish, as it did through Mazdak and Mani. When the final flux of Sasanian kingship brought disaster to Persia, Zoroastrianism was fatally implicated. It had lost touch with its simple roots and was gradually superseded by Islam which was, as Zoroastrianism had once been, accessible and relevant.

But before Zoroastrianism went into decline, it had exercised an influence on three other faiths of the ancient east: Judaism, Christianity and Islam. All of them absorbed, in their separate ways, the ethical content of Zoroaster's teaching, particularly the doctrine of the final judgement of each soul at death. As a companion development of civilization, Zoroastrianism offered a political as well as a theological moral: the greatly expanded and increasingly variegated units of society, whether city-states or empires, were held together by the concept of good order. Practical men as well as pious ones, whether Constantine or Chosroes *anoshak-ruvan*, could see the value of their respective religions in ordaining the justice and stability which empires needed ... 'Because of justice, God has created the kings, in order that justice should realize itself and that injustice should be abolished.' A Roman emperor might speak in similar terms to the Sasanian king, but a Greek never.

At its nadir, Christianity was kept alive in Byzantium and in the Benedictine monasteries like a bacillus in hibernation; Zoroastrianism found similar refuge in India and in some other enclaves, but had no recuperative power. Islam left it a fascinating remnant, a faith that can be acquired only by birth.

The Nomadic Impetus

Our map without names, seen in relation to Central Asia, makes a striking point: where the Alborz mountains end in the east, there is the yawning gap in the north of Khorasan. The Central Asian migrations were driven west because there was a massive lateral barrier running for two thousand miles north of the Indian sub-continent: the Himalayas. West of the Himalayas and their spur, the Hindu Kush, there was a sudden, irresistible passage, leading first through the pastures of Turkestan, across the rich valley of the Oxus and then, virtually free of impediment except for the climate, into the plateau. Under the migration pressures the tribes had to spill out where there was space to admit them; frequently this meant into Iran.

Three distinct types of migration came through this gap: the 'seeding' migrations of the Indo-Europeans, of whom the Medes and the Persians were a part; the 'subversive' migrations in which tribal groups filtered into the plateau without actually invading it (they could, nevertheless, achieve dominance, like the Turks bought by the Abbasids); and the warrior migrations like the Mongols. The most lasting mark was made by the various Turkish migrants, including the Ghaznavids, the Seljuks, the Safavids and the Qajars. Before they migrated from the steppes, not all of the Turks had been pastoral nomads. In Central Asia there were some compact oasis cultures where intensive farming flourished and where a highly cultured city life developed, but they were vulnerable to the herdsmen who overran them. Ideas and skills developed in these remote settled outposts no doubt became part of the cultural spore carried into the plateau with the Turks.

Gradually many of the Turkish migrants were absorbed and dispersed. But some were not. For example, the Qash'qai tribe who settled in Fars. Today, as the Qash'qai move their herds across the plain by Persepolis on their spring and autumn migrations it is easy to imagine them as the identical descendants of the ancient Persians who appear in the friezes on the palace walls; they seem the same. In fact, the Qash'qai did not leave Central Asia until the tenth century when they moved, with the Ghalzais, into Afghanistan and, like the Ghalzais, forgot their Turkish ancestry before they moved on into Persia. Today the Qash'qai personify the enduring qualities of nomadism in Iran – and the problem of its future as a way of life. They were once a powerful independent force in Fars, headed by their *Khan* who lived in a palace in Shiraz (which now serves as an occasional residence for the Shah). Of the one hundred and fifty thousand or so surviving Qash'qai, a third have given up the nomadic life in favour of the towns. Ironically, the wealthier urban Qash'qai, like affluent westerners, leave the towns in summer for country homes in lands which are still grazed by their nomadic kin.

Comparatively little of the plateau is habitable. What little habitable land there is can support three basic kinds of society: urban, settled rural and nomadic pastoral. Much of the harder land is viable *only* for nomadic grazing; if it were abandoned because of the dying out of nomadism it would be a wasted resource. Once there was a paradox in some regions of the nomads appearing to be more prosperous than the villagers who watched them pass by. Now, with agricultural changes, many of the villagers are looking sufficiently affluent for the nomads to be drawn away into urban work. Young Iranians with rude urban manners sometimes echo the sentiment of Reza Shah that the nomads are no better than 'predatory animals'. Such a prejudice is, perhaps, inevitable, but it is crass. The problem is not that nomadism is obsolete, which it is not, but to arrange its successful participation in the revolution of rising expectations *without* destroying its character and qualities.

And the country's history clearly shows the value of the nomadic impetus. Many of the qualities developed in the struggle to control the elements of plateau life have given Persian history a particular ethos, from the nomads. The three great pre-Islamic empires all gained from the nomadic impetus and two of them came from the same place, Fars. All of them, the Achaemenians, the Parthians and the Sasanians, fell when their leaders abandoned the heartland, with its elemental tensions, for the easier life of the Fertile Crescent. But appealing though this may be as a theory of cause and effect, it is too chauvinistic an explanation of dynastic decadence. Dynasties which never left Persia also sank into torpor and depravity. The Safavids rotted in the harem and pleasure palaces of Isfahan (although Abbas himself had the nomad's hatred of lassitude and love of life in the saddle); the Qajars grew obese and absurd in their Tehran palaces.

No, what sapped the virtues of elemental life was not a choice of any one region, on the plateau or in Mesopotamia, but *city life*. Once a monarch preferred it to the life of movement and action the rot set in. The pronounced cyclical fortunes of Persian dynastics are shaped precisely by the habitat of the kings. The life of the saddle, or of action is not, *per se*, philistine. Men who behaved like monsters in the saddle – Timur, Ismail, Abbas – were also the patrons of high artistic achievement. Persian art often seems cyclonic, thriving on turbulence.

The quality of patronage matters. This was not art made by *diktat*. The loot of conquest was useful to attract artists and craftsmen, and in the sense that they came from as far as Egypt, Anatolia, Afghanistan and India (and ideas from China), it may *seem* to have been hybrid art, but that is not the same as bastard art. The catalyst in this process came from somewhere, through the patron. Perhaps it is best to say, with Whistler, simply that 'art happens'. But the nomadic impetus was always present: nomadism has been one of the most invigorating taproots of the plateau's history. To cut it off would be to sever the people from the land in a very real sense.

On a mountain ridge high in remote Luristan, miles from the nearest track and much farther from a road or a power line, a circle of black tents indicates one tribal family moving across the Zagros. Farther south, the regular migration of the Bakhtiari takes them over a ridge at twelve thousand feet in snow, hacking through the ice. Some fall back, never to continue. The migrations can be the harshest form of population control. Farther south still, alongside the shell of Ardashir's three-domed palace at Firuzabad, Qash'qai children proudly clutch their textbooks in the tent of a tribal school, where they are taught by people from their own tribe who have been to college and come back. 'These children are so pure and their mind is so clear that they are really like a white canvas for a painter to paint whatever they want on it,' says the Empress Farah. The oral tradition gives tribal children the great resource of memory; when they come to literacy they have the retention power of a computer.

As they gain what others have, can the tribes keep what others have lost? The tribal nomads are in a laboratory where ancient values and modern devices are delicately poised. Education, medicine and the carbolic arts are tangible advances in their lives. Other things remain beyond their control, or anyone else's. The climate is unreliable: rain varies greatly in both the amount and when it falls. One bad year can cost a family half of its livestock. Their main wealth is in the sheep and goats, subsidized by carpets made at times when the agricultural work is light. Their treks continue, to the highlands in the spring and back to the warm lowlands in the autumn. Historically their journey is timeless, like the land.

Principal Historical Consultants

Achaemenian Period

559–530 BC: David Stronach, Director, British Institute of Persian Studies.

559–336 BC: Professor Richard N. Frye; Aga Khan, Professor of Iranian Studies, Harvard; Dr Shapur Shahbazi, Director of the Institute of Achaemian Studies, Persepolis.

Alexander, The Seleucids, The Parthians
Robin Lane Fox, Worcester College, Oxford; Dr Malcolm A. R. Colledge, University of London; Dr Georgina Herrmann, editor of *Iran*, journal of the British Institute of Persian studies.

The Sasanians
Professor Peter Brown, University of London.

The Arab Conquest
Dr Robert Hillenbrand, University of Edinburgh; Professor Jerome Clinton, Princeton; Dr Patricia Crone, Oxford University; Professor Richard N. Frye.

The Mongols and The Timurids
Dr Robert Hillenbrand, University of Edinburgh; Dr David Morgan, University of London.

Isfahan and The Safavid Dynasty
Dr John Gurney, the Oriental Institute, Oxford.

The Qajar Period
Shaul Bakhash, Tehran.

Valuable additional assistance was also given by Professor Oleg Grabar, Harvard; Professor Dr Walther Hinz, Gottingen University; Professor Friedrich Krefter, Bonn; Mr R. W. Ferrier, Group Historian and Archivist, the British Petroleum Co. Ltd; Alison White, Somerville College, Oxford; Shaul Bakhash, Tehran; and Vesta Sarkhosh.

Bibliography

Rather than give a comprehensive bibliography, which would include many works which call for considerable qualifications in the light of modern studies, this list is confined to two kinds of sources: those which are reliable general introductions to the subject, or those whose interest as primary sources is paramount. A. T. Olmstead's *History of the Persian Empire* (Cambridge University Press 1948; Chicago University Press 1948) covers pre-Islamic Persia. Although since overtaken in many details, this remains impressive for its range and coherence. Professor Richard Frye's *The Golden Age of Persia* (Weidenfeld & Nicolson, London 1975; Praeger, New York 1975), covering much the same period, gives extraordinary insights into the cultural traditions of Persia. *Persia and the Greeks* (Edward Arnold 1962; St Martin's Press, New York 1962) by A. R. Burn is a masterly and lucid study of the two inimical powers, and *Xerxes' Invasion of Greece* (Oxford University Press, Oxford and New York 1963) by C. Hignett though overly sceptical of Persian behaviour, is excellent on military detail. *Herodotus, The Histories* (Penguin Classics Series, London and New York 1971) is an impeccable translation by Aubrey de Selincourt of this eternally compulsive masterwork, and George Cawkwell's introduction to Xenophon's *The Persian Expedition* (Penguin Classics Series, London and New York 1949) makes a refreshingly impartial assessment of this very partial work. Arrian remains the best single source on *The Campaigns of Alexander* (Penguin Classics Series, London and New York 1976). The opaque origins of Zoroaster and his religion are highly disputed, but the most impressive work of modern scholarship is Dr Mary Boyce's study, *A Study of Zoroastrianism* (E. J. Brill, Leiden 1975) and Dr Boyce's analysis of *The Letter of Tansar* (trans. Dr Mary Boyce, Rome Oriental Series Vol. 38, Literary and Historical Texts from Iran, 1, Rome 1968) illuminates the roots of Persian kingship. The de-coding of ancient scripts is historical detection of an irresistible kind; *Babylonian Historical Texts* (Methuen, London 1924) by Sidney Smith is a goldmine, Henry Rawlinson's original analysis of *The Bisitun Inscriptions* (Parker, London 1850) is worth pestering a library for; the full grisly Text from Bisitun (from *Ancient near Eastern Texts relating to the Old Testament*, ed. James Pritchard, Oxford University Press 1955; Harvard University Press 1955) and all the Persepolis inscriptions are the true voice of Darius. The underrated Parthians are rehabilitated by Dr Malcom Colledge in *The Parthians* (Thames & Hudson, London 1968; Praeger, New York 1967). The doyen of modern Iranian studies, Professor V. Minorsky, published twenty essays in *Iranica* (Publications of the University of Tehran, Vol. 775, 1964) which underpin much of the new scholarship. *Studies in Frontier History* (Oxford University Press, Oxford and New York 1963) by Owen Lattimore explains the background of Mongol life and culture from remarkable first-hand studies, and is rich in anecdotes, while Professor Bertold Spuler's *History of the Mongols* (Routledge & Kegan Paul, London 1971; California University Press 1971) is drawn directly from contemporary sources, east and west, and brings the period alive. Laurence Lockhart's two works, *Nadir Shah* (Luzac, London 1938) and *The Fall of the Safavid Dynasty* (Cambridge University Press, London and New York 1958) are highly readable basic sources. Of the many books on the subject, *The Art of Iran* (Allen & Unwin, London 1965; Praeger, New York 1965) by André Godard is exemplary. Arguably the best travel book written about Persia, *The Road to Oxiana* (Jonathan Cape, London 1966) by Robert Byron pre-dates colour photography and filmed histories, and instead makes brilliant pictures in words which survive detailed comparison with their subjects. *The Persians* (Elek, London 1971; St Martin's Press, New York 1971) by Alessandro Bausani is one of the few compact over-view histories, with an economic and cultural slant. Finally, a book that seldom failed the test of being taken to every site researched for this story, Sylvia Matheson's *Persia: an Archaeological Guide* (Faber & Faber, London 1973; Noyes Press, New Jersey 1973) newly revised, and truly indispensable.

Index

Page numbers in *italic* refer to the illustrations and their captions

Index

Index